One by One
from the Inside Out

One by One from the Inside Out

*Essays and Reviews on
Race and Responsibility in America*

Glenn C. Loury

THE FREE PRESS

New York   London   Toronto   Sydney   Tokyo   Singapore

Copyright © 1995 by Glenn C. Loury

The Free Press
A Division of Simon & Schuster Inc.
1230 Avenue of the Americas, New York, N.Y. 10020

Printed in the United States of America

printing number

1 2 3 4 5 6 7 8 9 10

Library of Congress Cataloging–in–Publication Data

Loury, Glenn C.
    One by one from the inside out : essays and reviews on race and responsibility in America / Glenn C. Loury.
        p.   cm.
    Includes bibliographical references and index.
    ISBN 0–02–919441–5
    1. United States—Race relations.   2. United States—Race relations—Book reviews.   3. Racism—United States.   4. Racism —United States—Book reviews.   I. Title.
    E185.615.L68   1995
    305.8'00973—dc20   94–46593
                                                    CIP

For Linda, Glenn II, and Nehemiah

Author and publisher wish to thank the following publications for allowing us to reproduce articles by Glenn C. Loury which appeared previously in these publications, sometimes in a slightly different form:

"Free at Last? A Personal Perspective on Race and Identity in America," reprinted (in somewhat altered form) from *Commentary*, October 1992, by permission, all rights reserved

"Black Dignity and the Common Good," in *First Things*, a monthly journal published in New York City by the Institute on Religion and Public Life, June/July 1990

"The Moral Quandary of the Black Community," reprinted with permission of *The Public Interest*, number 79, Spring 1985, pp. 9–22. Copyright © 1985 by National Affairs, Inc.

"A New American Dilemma," in *The New Republic*, December 31, 1984

"Two Paths to Black Progress," in *First Things*, a monthly journal published in New York City by the Institute on Religion and Public Life, October 1992

"The End of an Illusion: Black–Jewish Relations in the Nineties," from *Moment*, June 1994, reprinted with permission of the author

"Economic Discrimination: Getting to the Core of the Problem," in *Harvard Journal of African American Public Policy*, vol. 1, Fall 1992

"The Effect of Affirmative Action on the Incentive to Acquire Skills: Some Negative Unintended Consequences," in *The Annals of the American Academy of Political and Social Sciences*, vol. 523, pp. 19–29. Copyright © 1992 by Sage Publications, Inc.

"Second Thoughts and First Principles," originally called "The Saliency of Race," chapter 10 in *Second Thoughts about Race in America*, Peter Collier and David Horowitz, eds. Copyright © 1991 by Peter Collier and David Horowitz. Reprinted by permission of the publisher, Madison Books, Inc.

"Professors and the Poor," a portion of which appeared as "God and the Ghetto," Op-Ed, *The Wall Street Journal*, February 25, 1993

"Preaching to the Converted," a review of *Race Matters* by Cornel West, from *The Wilson Quarterly*, Summer 1993. Copyright © 1993 by the Woodrow Wilson International Center for Scholars

Contents

Part III: A Critical Look at the Field (Selected Reviews)

It's a Spiritual Thing, You Wouldn't Understand 303
   The Bell Curve by Richard J. Herrnstein and
   Charles Murray

Epilogue: New Life: A Professor and *Veritas* 311

Prologue

Free at Last? A Personal Perspective on Race and Identity in America

Then Peter opened his mouth and said, Of a truth I perceive that God is no respecter of persons: But in every nation he that feareth him, and worketh righteousness, is accepted with him.

—Acts 10:34–35

A formative experience of my growing up on the South Side of Chicago in the 1960s occurred during one of those heated, earnest political rallies so typical of the period. I was about eighteen at the time; Woody, who had been my best friend since Little League, suggested that we attend. Being political neophytes, neither of us knew many of the participants. The rally was called to galvanize our community's response to some pending infringement by the white power structure, the exact nature of which I no longer remember. But I can still vividly recall how very agitated about it we all were, determined to fight the good fight, even to the point of being arrested if it came to that. Judging by his demeanor, Woody was among the most zealous of those present.

Despite this zeal, it took courage for Woody to attend that meeting. Though he often proclaimed his blackness, and though he had

1

a Negro grandparent on each side of his family, he nevertheless looked to all the world like your typical white boy. Everyone, on first meeting him, assumed as much. I did, too, when we began to play stickball together nearly a decade earlier, just after I had moved into the middle-class neighborhood (called Park Manor) where Woody's family had been living for some time.

There were a number of white families on our block when we first arrived; within a couple of years they had all been replaced by aspiring black families like our own. I often wondered why Woody's parents never moved. Then I overheard his mother declare to one of her new neighbors, "We just wouldn't run from our own kind," a comment that befuddled me at the time. Somewhat later, while we were watching the movie "Imitation of Life" on television, my mother explained how someone could be black, though they looked white. She told me about people like that in our own family—second cousins living in a fashionable suburb on whom we would never dare simply to drop in, because they were "passing for white." This was my earliest glimpse of the truth that racial identity in America is inherently a social and cultural construct, not simply a biological one—that it necessarily involves an irreducible element of choice.

From the moment I learned of it, I was at once intrigued and troubled by this idea of "passing." I enjoyed imagining my racial brethren surreptitiously infiltrating the citadels of white exclusivity. It allowed me to believe that, despite appearances and the white man's best efforts to the contrary, we blacks were nevertheless present, if unannounced, *everywhere* in American society. But I was disturbed by an evident implication of the practice of passing—that denial of one's genuine self is a necessary concomitant of a black person making it in this society. What passing seemed to say about the world was that if one were both black and ambitious, it was necessary to choose between racial authenticity and personal success. Also, it seemed grossly unfair to my adolescent mind that however problematic it might be, this passing option was, because of my relatively dark complexion, not available to me!

It dawned on me after the conversation with my mother that Woody's parents must have been passing for white in preintegration Park Manor. The neighborhood's changing racial composition had confronted them with a moment of truth. They had elected to stay and to raise their children among "their own kind." This was a fateful decision for Woody, who, as he matured, became determined not simply to live among blacks but, perhaps in atonement for his parents' sins, unambiguously to become one. The young men in the neighborhood did not make this easy. Many delighted in picking fights with him, teasing him about being a "white boy" and refusing to credit his insistent, often-repeated claim: "I'm a brother, too!"

The fact that some of his relatives were passing made Woody's racial identity claims more urgent for him, but less compelling to others. He desperately wanted to be black, but his peers in the neighborhood would not let him. Because he had the option to be white—an option he radically rejected at the time—those without the option could not accept his claim to a shared racial experience. I knew Woody well. We became good friends, and I wanted to accept him on his own terms. But even I found myself doubting that he fully grasped the pain, frustration, anger, and self-doubt many of us felt upon encountering the intractability of American racism. However much he sympathized with our plight, he seemed to experience it only vicariously.

So there we were, at this boisterous, angry political rally. A critical moment came when the leaders interrupted their speech making to solicit input from "the people." Woody had an idea, and enthusiastically raised his voice above the murmur to be heard. He was cut short before finishing his first sentence by one of the dashiki-clad brothers-in-charge, who demanded to know how a "white boy" got the authority to have an opinion about what black people should be doing. That was one of our problems, the brother said; we were always letting white people "peep our hole card," while we were never privy to their deliberations in the same way.

A silence then fell over the room. The indignant brother asked if anyone could "vouch for this white boy." More excruciating silence ensued. Now was *my* moment of truth; Woody turned plaintively toward me, but I would not meet his eyes. To my eternal disgrace, I refused to speak up for him. He was asked to leave the meeting, and he did so without uttering a word in his own defense. Subsequently, neither of us could bear to discuss the incident. I offered no apology or explanation, and he asked for none. Though we continued to be friendly, however, our relationship was forever changed. I was never again to hear Woody exclaim, "I'm a brother, too."

————————

I recall this story about Woody because his dilemma, and mine, tell us something important about race and personal identity in American society. His situation was made so difficult by the fact that he embraced a self-definition dramatically inconsistent with the identity reflexively and stubbornly imputed to him by others. This lack of social confirmation for his subjective sense of self left him uncertain, at a deep level, about who he really was. Ultimately there seemed to be no way for him to avoid living fraudulently— either as a black passing for white, or a white trying too hard to be black. As his close friend and frequent companion, I had become familiar with, and occasionally shared in, the pitfalls of this situation. People would assume when they saw us together both that he was white, and that I was "the kind of Negro who hangs out with white boys." I resented that assumption.

Since then, as a black intellectual making my living in the academic establishment during a period of growing racial conflict in our society, I have often experienced this dissonance between my self-concept and the socially imputed definition of who I am supposed to be. I have had to confront the problem of balancing my desire not to disappoint the expectations of others—both whites and blacks, but more especially blacks—with my conviction that one should strive to live life with integrity. This does not make me a heroic figure; I eschew the libertarian ideologue's rhetoric about the glorious individual who, though put upon by society, blazes his own path. I acknowledge that this opposition between individual and society is ambiguous, in view of the fact that the self is inevitably shaped by the objective world, and by other selves. I know that what one is being faithful to when resisting the temptation to conform to others' expectations by "living life with integrity" is always a socially determined, if subjectively experienced, vision of the self.

Still, I see this incident of a quarter century ago as a kind of private metaphor for the ongoing problem of living in good faith, particularly as it relates to my personal identity as a black American. I have since lost contact with Woody. I suspect that, having tired of his struggle against society's presumptions about him, he is now passing. But that moment of truth in that South Side church basement, and my failure in the face of it, have helped me understand the depth of my own need to be seen by others as "black enough."

Upon reflection, my refusal to stand up for Woody exposed the tenuous quality of my personal sense of racial authenticity. The fact is, I willingly betrayed someone I had known for a decade, a person whom I loved and who loved me, in order to avoid the risk of being rejected by strangers. In a way, at that moment and often again later in my life, I was "passing" too—hoping to be mistaken for something I was not. I had feared that to proclaim before the black radicals in the audience that this "white boy" at my side was in fact our "brother" would have compromised my own chance of being received among them as a genuine colleague. Who, after all, was there to vouch for me if I had been dismissed as an "Uncle Tom"?

This was not an unfounded concern, for at that meeting, as at so many others of the period, people with insufficiently militant views were berated as self-hating, shuffle-along, "house nigger" types, complicit with whites in the perpetuation of racial oppression. Then, as now, blacks who befriended (or, heaven forbid, married) whites, who dressed or talked or wrote or wore their hair a certain way, who listened to certain kinds of music, read certain books, or expressed certain opinions, were laughed at, ostracized, and generally demeaned as inauthentic by other, more (self-)righteous blacks. The indignant brother who challenged Woody's right to speak at that rally was not merely imposing a racial test ("Only blacks are welcome here"), he was applying a loyalty test ("Are you truly with us or against us?"), and this was a test that anyone present could fail through a lack of conformity to the collective definition of what it meant to be genuinely black. I feared that speaking up for Woody would have marked me as a disloyal "Tom" among the blacker-than-thou crowd. In those years, this was a fate the thought of which I could not bear.

I now understand how this desire to be regarded as genuinely black, to be seen as a "regular brother," has dramatically altered my life. It narrowed the range of my earliest intellectual pursuits, distorted my relationships with other people, censored my political thought and expression, informed the way I dressed and spoke, and shaped my cultural interests. Some of this was inevitable, and not all of it was bad, but in my experience the need to be affirmed by one's racial peers can take on a pathological dimension. Growing into intellectual maturity has been, for me, largely a process of becoming free of the need to have my choices validated by "the brothers." After many years I have come to understand that until I became willing to risk the derision of the crowd, I had no chance to discover the most important truths about myself or about life— to know and accept my calling, to perceive what I really value and what goals are most worth striving toward. In a perverse extension of the lesson from "Imitation of Life," I have learned that one does not have to live surreptitiously as a Negro among whites in order to be engaged in a denial of one's genuine self for the sake of gaining social acceptance. This is a price that blacks often demand of each other as well.

I used to think about the irony in the idea of some blacks seeking to excommunicate others for crimes against the race, given that the distinctions that so exercised the blacker-than-thou crowd were invisible to most others. I was still a nigger to the working-class toughs waiting to punish—with their fists—my trespass onto their "white" turf, yet I could not be a brother to the middle-class radicals with whom I shared so much history and circumstance. Whatever my political views or cultural interests, I would always be black in white America, yet my standing among other blacks could be made conditional upon my fidelity to the prevailing party line of the moment. I would ponder this paradox, chafing at the restraint of an imposed racial uniformity, bemoaning the unfairness that I should have to face a threat of potential ostracism as punishment for the sin of being truthful to myself. In short, I would wallow in self-pity, which is always a waste of time. These days I am less given to, if not entirely free of, such inclinations.

Underlying my obsession with this paradox was a premise I now believe to be mistaken: that being an authentic black person involves in some elemental way seeing oneself as an object of mistreatment by white people, while participating in a collective consciousness of that mistreatment with other black people. As long as I believed that my personal identity as a black American was necessarily connected to our country's history of racial violation, and derived much of its content from my sharing with other blacks in a recollection of and struggle against this violation, I was destined to be in a bind. For as my evolving understanding of our history began to clash with the black consensus, and as my definition of the struggle took on a more conservative form than that popular among other black intellectuals, I found myself cut off from the group, my racial bona fides in question. I was therefore forced to choose between my intellectual integrity and my access to that collective consciousness of racial violation and shared struggle that I saw as essential to my black identity. Like Woody, lacking social confirmation of my subjective sense of self, I was left uncertain about who I really was.

I no longer believe that the camaraderie engendered among blacks by our collective experience of racism constitutes an adequate basis for any person's self-definition. Even if I restrict attention to the question "Who am I as a black American at the end of the twentieth century?" these considerations of historical victimization and struggle against injustice do not take me very far toward finding an answer. I am made "black" only in the most superficial way by being the object of a white racist's hate. The empathetic exchange of survivors' tales among "brothers," even the collective struggle against the clear wrong of racism, does not provide a tableau sufficiently rich to give meaning and definition to the totality of my life. I am so much more than the one wronged, misunderstood, underestimated, derided, or ignored by whites. I am more than the one who has struggled against this oppression and indifference; more than a descendant of slaves now claiming freedom; more, that is, than either a "colored person" (as seen by the racist) or a "person of color" (as seen by the anti-racist.)

Who am I, then? Foremost, I am a child of God, created in his image, imbued with his spirit, endowed with his gifts, set free by his grace. The most important challenges and opportunities that confront me derive not from my racial condition, but rather from my human condition. I am a husband, a father, a son, a teacher, an intellectual, a Christian, a citizen. In none of these roles is my race irrelevant, but neither can racial identity alone provide much guidance for my quest to discharge these responsibilities adequately. The particular features of my social condition, the external givens, merely set the stage of my life; they do not provide a script. That script must be internally generated. It must be a product of a reflective deliberation about the meaning of this existence for which no political or ethnic program could ever substitute.

Or, to shift the metaphor slightly, the socially contingent features of my situation—my racial heritage and family background, the prevailing attitudes about race and class of those with whom I share this society—are the building blocks, the raw materials, out of which I must construct the edifice of my life. The expression of my individual personality is to be found in the blueprint that I employ to guide this project of construction. The problem of devising such a plan for one's life is a universal problem that confronts all people, whatever their race, class, or ethnicity. By facing and solving this problem we grow as human beings, and we give meaning and substance to our lives. In my view, a personal identity wholly dependent on racial contingency falls tragically short of its potential because it embraces too parochial a conception of what is possible and what is desirable.

Thus, ironically, to the extent that we individual blacks see ourselves primarily through a racial lens, we sacrifice possibilities for the kind of personal development that would ultimately further our collective racial interests. We cannot be truly free men and women while laboring under a definition of self derived from the perceptual view of our oppressor, confined to the contingent facts of our oppression. In *A Portrait of the Artist as a Young Man* James Joyce says of Irish nationalism: "When the soul of a man is born in this country there are nets flung at it to hold it back from flight. You talk to me of nationality, language, religion. I shall try to fly by these nets. . . . Do you know what Ireland is? . . . Ireland is the old sow that eats her farrow." It seems to me that a search for some mythic authentic blackness too often works similarly to hold back young black souls from flight into the open skies of American society. Of course there is the constraint of racism also holding us back. But the trick, as Joyce knew, is to turn such "nets" into wings, and thus to fly by them. One cannot do that if one refuses to see that ultimately it is neither external constraint nor expanded opportunity, but rather an in-dwelling spirit, that makes this flight possible.

———————

In the winter of 1992, on a clear, cold Sunday afternoon, my three-year-old son and I were walking in the woods near our New England home. We happened upon a small pond, which, having frozen solid, made an ideal skating rink. Dozens of men, ranging in age from late teens to early thirties, were distributed across the ice in clusters of ten or so, either playing or preparing to play hockey. They glided over the pond's surface effortlessly, skillfully passing and defending, stopping and turning on a dime, moving with such power, speed, and grace that we were spellbound as we watched them. Little Glenn would occasionally squeal with delight as he marveled at one astounding feat after another, straining against my grip, which alone prevented him from running out on the ice to join in the fun.

All of these men were white—every last one of them. Few took notice of us at the pond's edge, and those who did were not particularly generous with their smiles, or so it seemed to me. I sensed that we were interlopers, that if we had come with sticks and skates we would not necessarily have been welcome. But no words were exchanged; I do not really know what they thought of our presence. I do know that my son very much enjoyed watching the game, and I thought to myself at the time that he would, someday too soon, come asking for a pair of skates, and for his dad to teach him how to use them. I found myself consciously dreading that day.

The thought of my son playing hockey on that frozen pond did not sit well with me. I much preferred to think of him on a basketball court. Hockey, we all know, is a white man's game: who was the last brother to play in the NHL? Of course, I immediately sensed that this thought was silly and illegitimate, and I attempted to banish it from my mind. But it kept coming back. I could not avoid the feeling that something important was at stake here.

I decided to discuss it with my wife. Linda and I had carefully considered the implications for our children of our decision to buy a house in a predominantly white suburb. We joined and became active in a church with many black families like our own, in part so that our boys would be provided with suitable racial peers. We are committed to ensuring that their proper education about black history and culture, including their family history, is not left to chance. We are ever vigilant concerning the effect on their developing psyches of racial messages that come across on television, in their books, at their nursery school, and so forth. On all of this Linda and I are in full accord. But she thought my concerns about hockey were taking things a bit too far.

I now believe that she was right, and I think I have learned something important from our conversations about this issue. My aversion to the idea of my son's involvement in that Sunday afternoon ritual we witnessed was rooted in my own sense of identity as a black American man who grew up when and where I did, who has had the experiences I have had. Because *I* would not have felt comfortable there, I began to think that *he* should not want to be a part of that scene either. I was inclined to impose upon my son, in the name of preserving his authentic blackness, a limitation of his pursuits deriving from my life but not really relevant to his. It is as if I were to insist that he study Swahili instead of Swedish because I could not imagine myself being interested in speaking Swedish!

The fact is that, given the class background of our children and the community in which we have chosen to make our lives, it is inevitable that their racial sensibilities will be quite different from ours. Moreover, it is impossible to predict just what self-definition they will settle upon. This can be disquieting to contemplate for those of our generation concerned about retaining a "genuinely black" identity in the face of the social mobility we have experienced within our lifetimes. But it is not, I think, to be feared.

The alternative seems much more frightening to me—stifling the development of our children's personalities by imposing upon them an invented ethnicity. I have no doubt that my sons will be black men of the twenty-first century, but not by their singing of racial anthems peculiar to our time. Theirs will be a blackness constructed yet again, out of the external givens of their lives, not mine; shaped by a cultural inheritance that I am responsible to transmit, but expressed in their own voices and animated by a divine spirit whose dwelling place lies deeper than the color of any man's skin, and whose source is "no respecter of persons."

I

Race and Responsibility in the Post–Civil Rights Era

1
Black Dignity and the Common Good

Therefore, since we are surrounded by such a great cloud
of witnesses, let us throw off everything that hinders, and
the sin that so easily entangles, and let us run with
perserverance the race marked out for us.

—Hebrews 12:1, NIV

A "great cloud of witnesses" surrounds us—the spirits of our forebears, whose courage, sacrifices, and faith have made possible the
freedoms we enjoy today. These witnesses of course include the
great figures of black American political and cultural history, but
also the Founding Fathers, who conceived this still maturing
democracy of ours, and the humble Americans whose names are
not recorded in history books—the simple people who believed in
the ideals on which our country was founded even when our political practice strayed far from those ideals, those who made the ultimate sacrifice (at Gettysburg, at Normandy, or in Mississippi) so
that we might live as free men and women enjoying equally the
rights and responsibilities of citizenship.

For black Americans, this struggle for freedom and equality is
the central theme in our historical experience. This struggle, in

13

turn, has played a profound role in shaping the contemporary American social and political conscience. The trauma of slavery, the fratricide of the Civil War, the profound legal ramifications of the Reconstruction amendments, the long dark night of post-Reconstruction retreat from the moral and practical implications of black citizenship, the collective redemption of the civil rights movement—these have worked to make us Americans the people we are. Only the massive westward migration and the still continuing flow of immigrants to our shores rival this history of race relations as factors defining the American character.

Beginning in the mid-1950s and culminating a decade later, the civil rights movement wrought a profound change in American race relations. The civil rights revolution largely succeeded in its effort to eliminate legally enforced second-class citizenship for blacks. The legislation and court rulings to which it led effected sweeping changes in the American institutions of education, employment, and electoral politics. This social transformation represents a remarkable, unparalleled experience, graphically illustrating the virtue and vitality of our free institutions. In barely the span of a generation and with comparatively little violence, a despised and largely disenfranchised minority descendant from chattel slaves used the courts, the legislature, the press, and the rights of petition and assembly of our republic to force a redefinition of its citizenship. One can begin to grasp the magnitude of this accomplishment by comparing it with the turmoil that continues to beset those many nations around the world suffering long-standing conflicts among racial or religious groups.

Yet, despite this success, the hope that the Movement would produce true social and economic equality between the races remains unfulfilled. No compendium of social statistics is needed for us to see the vast disparities in economic advantage that separate the inner-city black poor from the rest of the nation. No profound talents of social observation are required to notice the continuing tension, anger, and fear that shroud our public discourse on matters concerning race. When in 1963, Martin Luther King, Jr., declared his "dream"—that we Americans should one day become a society where a citizen's race would be an irrelevancy, where black and white children would walk hand in hand, where persons would be judged not by the color of their skin but by the content of their character—this seemed to many Americans both a noble and an attainable goal. Today, after his birth has been made an occasion for national celebration, this "dream" that race should become an irrelevancy seems naively utopian; indeed, *this* dream is renounced even by those who now claim his mantle of leadership.

Thus, at the first national celebration of Martin Luther King Day, in 1986, Jesse Jackson decried the widespread focus on King's great speech and stressed instead King's opposition to the Vietnam War—an opposition, be it noted, that King came to only after long agonizing with his conscience and that he always carefully distinguished from the position of the extremists within the antiwar movement. Jackson offered his own interpretation of the 1963 speech: "That so-called 'I have a Dream speech' . . . was not a speech about dreamers and dreaming. It was a speech describing nightmare conditions. . . . Dr. King was not assassinated for dreaming." A few days later, Jackson clarified the meaning of this last comment when, to a national television audience, he stated his belief that King had been killed with the assistance of the FBI and/or the CIA.

Now I mention this not to disparage Reverend Jackson, but merely to indicate the bitterness that continues to characterize race relations in our country. But we must not lose sight of the vision King placed before us; we must not allow the universal truths he championed to be lost amid partisan bickering. It is worth considering at greater length what Martin Luther King actually had to say about his American dream. At the 1961 commencement at Lincoln University he described it thusly:

One of the first things we notice in this dream is an amazing universalism. It does not say some men [are created equal], but it says all men. It does not say all white men, but it says all men, which includes black men. It does not say all Gentiles, but it says all men, which includes Jews. It does not say all Protestants, but it says all men, which includes Catholics.

And there is another thing we see in this dream that ultimately distinguishes democracy and our form of government from all of the totalitarian regimes that emerge in history. It says that each individual has

certain basic rights that are neither conferred by nor derived from the
state. To discover where they come from, it is necessary to move back
behind the dim mist of eternity, for they are God-given. Very seldom, if
ever, in the history of the world has a socio-political document
expressed in such profoundly eloquent and unequivocal language the
dignity and the worth of the human personality. The American dream
reminds us that every man is heir to the legacy of worthiness.

The contrast between this eloquently patriotic statement of King
and the partisan carping of many of his successors speaks volumes
about how the tone of racial advocacy has changed over the past
generation.

Nevertheless, black Americans, and the nation, face a challenge
different in character from though perhaps no less severe in degree
than that which occasioned the civil rights revolution. It is the challenge of making real for all of our citizens the American dream that,
as King aptly put it, "every man is heir to the legacy of worthiness."
The bottom stratum of the black community has compelling problems that can no longer be blamed solely on white racism, that will
not yield to protest marches or court orders, and that force us to
confront fundamental failures in lower-class black urban society.
This profound alienation of the ghetto poor from mainstream American life has continued to grow worse in the years since the tri-
umphs of the civil rights movement, even as the success of that
movement has provided the basis for an impressive expansion of
economic and political power for the black middle class.

The plight of the black lower class reveals an extent of deprivation, a degree of misery, a hopelessness and despair, an alienation
that are difficult for most Americans, who do not have direct experience with this social stratum, to comprehend. These conditions
pose an enormous challenge to the leadership of our nation and to
the black leadership. Yet we seem increasingly unable to conduct a
political dialogue out of which a consensus might develop about
how to respond to this reality. Two common, partisan themes dominate the current debate: One is to blame it all on racism, to declare
that this circumstance proves the continued existence of old-style
American racial emnity, only in a more subtle, modernized and
updated form. This is the view of many civil rights activists. From
this perspective the tragedy of the urban underclass is a civil rights

problem, curable by civil rights methods. Black youth unemployment represents the refusal of employers to hire competent and industrious young men because of their race. Black welfare dependency is the inescapable consequence of the absence of opportunity. Black academic underperformance reflects racial bias in the provision of public education. Black incarceration rates are the result of the bias of the police and judiciary.

The other theme, characterized by the posture of many on the right in our politics, is to blame the conditions of the black lower class on the failures of "Great Society liberals," to chalk the problem up to the follies of big government and big spending, to see it as the legacy of a tragically misconceived welfare state. A key feature of this view is the apparent absence of any felt need to articulate a "policy" on this new race problem. It is as though those shaping the domestic agenda of this government do not see the explicitly racial character of this problem, as if they do not understand the historical experiences that link, symbolically and sociologically, the current urban underclass to our long, painful legacy of racial trauma. Their response has been to promulgate a de facto doctrine of "benign neglect" on the issue of continuing racial inequality. They seem to think that it is enough merely to be right about liberals having been wrong on this question.

These responses feed on each other. The civil rights leaders, repelled by the public vision of conservatives, see more social spending as the only solution to the problem. They characterize every question raised about the cost-effectiveness or appropriateness of a welfare program as evidence of a lack of concern about the black poor; they identify every affirmative action effort, whether aimed at attaining skills training for the ghetto poor or at securing a fat municipal procurement contract for a black millionaire, as necessary and just recompense in light of our history of racial oppression. Conservatives in or out of government, repelled by the public vision of civil rights advocates and convinced that the programs of the past have failed, when addressing racial issues at all talk in formalistic terms about the principle of "color-blind state action." Under President Reagan, federal civil rights officials absurdly claimed that *they* were the true heirs of Martin Luther King's moral legacy, by virtue of their having remained loyal to his "color-blind" ideal—as if King's moral leadership consisted of this and nothing else. Conservative spokesmen pointed to the "trickling down" of the benefits of economic growth as the ultimate solution to these problems; at times they even seemed to court the support of and respond to the influence of segregationist elements; they remained without a positive program of action aimed at narrowing the yawning chasm separating the black poor from the rest of the nation.

There is merit, many would now admit, in the conservative criticism of liberal social policy. It is clear that the Great Society approach to the problems of poor blacks has been inadequate. Intellectually honest persons must now concede that it is not nearly as easy to truly help people as the big spenders would suggest. The proper measure of "caring" ought not to be the size of budget expenditures on poverty programs, if the result is that the recipients remain dependent on such programs. Moreover, many Americans have become concerned about the neutrality toward values and behavior that was so characteristic of the Great Society thrust, the aversion to holding persons responsible for those actions that precipitated their own dependence, the feeling that "society" is to blame for all the misfortune in the world. Characterizing the problem of the ghetto poor as due to white racism is one variant of this argument that "society" has caused the problem. It overlooks the extent to which values and behaviors of inner-city black youths are implicated in the difficulty.

Many Americans, black and white, have also been disgusted with the way in which this dangerous circumstance is exploited for political gain by professional civil rights and poverty advocates. They have watched the minority youth unemployment rate be cited in defense of special admissions programs to elite law schools. They have seen public officials, caught in illegal indiscretions, use the charge of racism as a cover for personal failings of character. They have seen themselves pilloried as "racists" by civil rights lobbyists for taking the opposite side of legitimately arguable policy debates.

Yet none of this excuses (though it may help to explain) the fact that our national government has failed to engage this problem with the seriousness and energy it requires. Ideology has been permitted to stand in the way of formulating practical programs that might begin to chip away at this dangerous problem. The ideological debate has permitted the worthy goals of reducing taxes and limiting growth in the size of government to crowd from the domestic policy agenda the creative reflection that obviously will be needed to formulate a new, non–welfare oriented approach to this problem.

Ironically, each party to this debate has helped to make viable the otherwise problematic posture of the other. The lack of a positive, high-priority response from a series of Republican administrations to what is now a long-standing, continuously worsening social problem has allowed politically marginal and intellectually moribund elements to retain a credibility and force in our political life far beyond that which their accomplishments would otherwise support. Many observers are reluctant to criticize the civil rights extremists because they do not wish to be identified with a Republican administration's policy on racial matters. Conversely, the shrill, vitriolic, self-serving, and obviously unfair attacks on administration officials by the civil rights lobby have drained their criticism of much of its legitimacy. The "racist" epithet, like the little boy's cry of "wolf," is a charge so often invoked these days that it has lost its historic moral force.

The result of this symbiosis has been to impede the establishment of a political consensus sufficient to support sustained action on the country's most pressing domestic problem. Many whites, chastened by the apparent failures of 1960s-style social engineering but genuinely concerned about the tragedy unfolding in our inner cities, are reluctant to engage this issue. It seems to them a political quagmire in which one is forced to ally oneself with a civil rights establishment no longer able to command broad respect. Many blacks who have begun to doubt the effectiveness of liberal social policy are hindered in expressing an alternative vision by fear of being too closely linked in the public mind with a policy of indifference to racial concerns. We must find a way to rise above this partisan squabbling. A part of our nation is dying. And if we fail to act, that failure will haunt us for generations.

I can personally attest to the difficulties this environment has created. I am an acknowledged critic of the civil rights leadership.

I have gladly joined the Republican side on some highly partisan policy debates: on federal enterprise zones, on a youth opportunity wage, on educational vouchers for low-income students, on stimulating ownership among responsible public housing tenants, on requiring work from able-bodied welfare recipients, on dealing sternly with those who violently brutalize their neighbors. I am no enemy of right-to-work laws; I do not despise the institution of private property; I distrust the capacity of public bureaucracies to substitute for the fruit of private initiative. I am, to my own continuing surprise, philosophically more conservative than the vast majority of my academic peers. And I love and believe in this democratic republic.

But I am also a black man, a product of Chicago's South Side, a veteran in spirit of the civil rights revolution. I am a partisan on behalf of the inner-city poor. I agonize at the extraordinary waste of human potential that the despair of ghetto America represents. I cannot help but lament, deeply and personally, how little progress we have made in relieving the suffering that goes on there. It is not enough—far from enough—for me to fault liberals for much that has gone wrong. For me this is not a mere contest of ideologies or competition for electoral votes. And it is because I see this problem as so far from solution, yet so central to my own sense of satisfaction with our public life, that I despair over our government's lack of commitment to its resolution. I believe that such a commitment, coming from the highest levels of our government, without prejudice with respect to the specific methods to be employed in addressing the issue but involving a public acknowledgment of the unacceptability of the current state of affairs, is now required. This is not a call for big spending. Rather, it is a plaintive cry for the need to actively engage this problem, for the elevation of concern for racial inequality to a position of priority on our government's domestic affairs agenda.

In much of my past writing on this subject, I have placed great weight on the importance to blacks of "self-help" (see chapter 2). Some readers may see my current posture as at variance with those arguments. It is not. I have also written critically of blacks' continued reliance on civil rights era protest and legal strategies, and of the propagation of affirmative action policies throughout our employment and educational institutions (see chapter 6). I have urged blacks to move beyond civil rights. I have spoken of the difference between the "enemy without"—racism—and the "enemy within" the black community—those dysfunctional behaviors of young blacks that perpetuate poverty and dependency. I have spoken of the need for blacks to face squarely the political reality that we now live in the "post–civil rights era"; that claims based on racial justice now carry much less force in American public life than they once did; that it is no longer acceptable to seek benefits for our people in the name of justice while revealing indifference or hostility to the rights of others (see chapter 4). Nothing I have said here should be construed as a retraction of these views.

But selling these positions within the black community is made infinitely more difficult when my black critics are able to say: "But your argument plays into the hands of those who are looking for an excuse to abandon the black poor"; and I am unable to contradict them credibly. The deteriorating quality of our public debate about civil rights matters has come to impede the internal realignment of black political strivings that is now so crucial to the interest of the inner-city poor and the political health of the nation. There is a great existential challenge facing black America today: the challenge of taking control of our own future by exerting the requisite moral leadership, making the sacrifices of time and resources, and building the needed institutions so that black social and economic development may be advanced. No matter how windy the debate becomes among white liberals and conservatives as to what should be done in the public sphere, meeting this self-creating challenge ultimately depends on black action. It is to make a mockery of the ideal of freedom to hold that, as free men and women, blacks ought nonetheless to wait passively for white Americans, of whatever political persuasion, to come to the rescue. A people who languish in dependency while the means exist through which we might work toward our own advancement have surrendered our claim to dignity and to the respect of our fellow citizens. If we are to be a truly free people, we must accept responsibility for our fate even when it does not lie wholly in our hands.

But to say this—which is crucial for blacks to consider at this late date—is not to say that there is no public responsibility. It is obvious that in the areas of education, employment training, enforcement of antidiscrimination laws, and provision of minimal subsistence to the impoverished, the government must be involved. Some programs—preschool education for one—cost money, but seem to pay even greater dividends. It is a tragic error that those of us who make the self-help argument in internal dialogue concerning alternative development strategies for black Americans are often construed by the political right as making a public argument for a policy of benign neglect. Expanded self-reliance is but one ingredient in the recipe for black progress, distinguished by the fact that it is essential for black dignity, which in turn is a precondition for true equality of the races in this country.

It makes sense to call for greater self-reliance at this time because some of what needs to be done cannot, in the nature of the case, be undertaken by government. Dealing with behavioral problems; with community values; with the attitudes and beliefs of black youngsters about responsibility, work, family, and schooling are not things government is well suited to do. The teaching of "oughts" properly belongs in the hands of private voluntary associations: churches, families, neighborhood groups. It is also reasonable to ask those blacks who have benefited from the special minority programs, such as the set-asides for black businesses, to contribute to alleviating the suffering of poor blacks, for without the visible ghetto poor, such programs would lack political support. Yet, and obviously, such internal efforts cannot be a panacea for the problems of the inner city. This is truly an American problem; we all have a stake in its alleviation; we all have a responsibility to address it forthrightly.

Thus to begin to make progress on this extremely difficult matter will require enhanced private and public commitment. Yet to the extent that blacks place too much focus on the public responsibility, we place in danger the attainment of true equality for black Americans. By "true equality" I mean more than an approximately equal material provision. Also crucial, I maintain, is equal respect in the eyes of one's fellow citizens. Yet much of the current advocacy of blacks' interests seems inconsistent with achieving equal respect for black Americans. Leaders in the civil rights organizations as well as in the halls of Congress remain wedded to a conception of the black condition and a method of appealing to the rest of the polity which undermine the dignity of our people. Theirs is too much the story of discrimination, repression, hopelessness, and frustration and too little the saga of uplift and the march forward to genuine empowerment whether others cooperate or not. They seek to make blacks into the conscience of America, even if the price is the loss of our souls. They require blacks to present ourselves to American society as permanent victims, incapable of advance without the state-enforced philanthropy of possibly resentful whites. By evoking past suffering and current deprivations experienced by the ghetto poor, some black leaders seek to feed the guilt and, worse, the pity of the white establishment. But I hold that we blacks ought not to allow ourselves to become ever-ready doomsayers, always alert for an opportunity to exploit black suffering by offering it up to more or less sympathetic whites as a justification for incremental monetary transfers. Such a posture seems to evidence a fundamental lack of confidence in the ability of blacks to make it in America, as so many millions of immigrants have done and continue to do. Even if this method were to succeed in gaining the money, it is impossible that true equality of status in American society could lie at the end of such a road.

Much of the current, quite heated, debate over affirmative action reveals a similar lack of confidence in the capabilities of blacks to compete in American society. My concern is with the inconsistency between the broad reliance on quotas by blacks and the attainment of true equality. In one sense the demand for quotas, which many see as the only path to equality for blacks, concedes at the outset the impossibility that blacks could ever be truly equal citizens. For aside from those instances in which hiring goals are ordered by a court subsequent to a finding of illegal discrimination, and with the purpose of providing relief for those discriminated against, the use of differential standards for the hiring of blacks and whites acknowledges the inability of blacks to perform up to the white standard.

So widespread has such a practice become that, especially on the elite levels of employment, all blacks must now deal with the perception that without a quota, they would not have their jobs. All blacks, some of our "leaders" seem proud to say, owe their accomplishments to political pressures for diversity. And the effects of such thinking may be seen in our response to almost every instance of racially differential performance. When blacks cannot pass a high school proficiency test as a condition of obtaining a diploma, throw out the test. When black teachers cannot exhibit skills at the same level as whites, the very idea of testing teachers' skills is attacked. If black athletes less frequently achieve the minimal academic standard set for those participating in intercollegiate sport, then let us promulgate for them a separate, lower standard, even as we accuse of racism those suggesting the need for a standard in the first place. If young black men are arrested more frequently than whites for some criminal offense, then let us proclaim the probability that police are disproportionately concerned about the crimes blacks commit. If black suspension rates are higher than whites' in a given school district, well, let's investigate that district for racist administrative practices. When black students are unable to gain admission at the same rate as whites to the elite public exam school in Boston, let's ask a federal judge to mandate black excellence.

The inescapable truth of the matter is that no judge can mandate excellence. No selection committee can create distinction in black scholars. No amount of circuitous legal maneuvering can obviate the social reality of inner-city black crime or of whites' and blacks' fear of that crime. No degree of double-standard setting can make black students competitive or comfortable in the academically exclusive colleges and universities. No amount of political gerrymandering can create genuine sympathy among whites for the interests and strivings of black people. Yet it is to such maneuvering, such double-standard setting, such gerrymandering that many feel compelled to turn.

Signs of the intellectual exhaustion and increasing political ineffectiveness of this style of leadership are now evident. Yet we cling to this method because of the way in which the claims of blacks were most successfully pressed during the civil rights era. These claims were based, above all else, on the status of blacks as America's historical victims. Maintenance of this claiming status requires constant emphasis on the wrongs of the past and exaggeration of present tribulations. He who leads a group of historical victims, as victims, must never let "them" forget what "they" have done; he must renew the indictment and keep alive the supposed moral asymmetry implicit in the respective positions of victim and victimizer. He is the preeminent architect of what British philosopher G. K. Minogue has called "suffering situations." The circumstance of his group as underdog becomes his most valuable political asset. Such a posture, especially in the political realm, militates against an emphasis on personal responsibility within the group and induces those who have been successful to attribute their accomplishments to fortuitous circumstance, not to their own abilities and character.

A graphic illustration of this theme is John Edgar Wideman's poignant and brilliantly written account of two brothers, one who is serving a life sentence for murder in a Pennsylvania penitentiary and the other who is the author. In *Brothers and Keepers*[1] Wideman, a highly acclaimed novelist and college professor, can find only societal and circumstantial explanations for the difference in outcomes between himself and his brother, assiduously avoiding the possibility that distinctions of character and values might somehow be involved. It is not his brother but "society" that has failed. In a central passage, after describing the death of Garth, his brother's close friend who had received inadequate care at a public health clinic, Wideman relates his mother's (and evidently his own) view of the matter:

> Mom expects the worst now. She peeped their [the system's] whole card. She understands they have a master plan that leaves little to accident, that most of the ugliest things happening to black people are not accidental but the predictable results of the workings of the plan. What she learned about authority, about law and order didn't make sense at first. It went against her instincts, what she wanted to believe. . . . Garth's death and [brother] Robby's troubles were at the center of her new vision. Like a prism, they caught the light, transformed it so she could trace the seemingly random inconveniences and impositions coloring her life to their source in a master plan.

Notice the alternatives: Outcomes are either accidents (possibly fortuitous, as in his own case) or the result of a "master plan" against blacks, but never the consequence of individuals' willful acts. Indeed, at one point in the book he seems to be arguing that it was his brother's courage and strength to rebel against the rules laid down by racist whites—rules that he dutifully followed, all the while harboring a resentment and rage barely concealed beneath a veneer of refinement and civility—that account for their different circumstances. He offers, in his brother's voice, the following "explanation" of the behavior of "young black men in the street world life":

> So this hip guy, this gangster or player or whatever label you give these brothers we like to shun because of the poison that they spread, we, black people, still look at them with some sense of pride and admiration, our children openly, us adults somewhere deep inside. We know they represent rebellion—what little is left in us. Well, having lived in the "life," it becomes very hard—almost impossible—to find any contentment in joining the status quo. Too hard to go back to being nobody in a world that hates you.

The work is suffused with the guilt of the survivor—that agonizing dilemma of those who, having escaped catastrophe intact, are forever plagued with the unanswerable question, "Why was I spared, and not the others?" Wideman's answer, which seems to be "I was just lucky," is belied by the very account he provides. He manages to effect this moral sleight of hand without fundamentally undermining the literary integrity of his book only because of his great skill as a writer. His evocation of the humiliating plight of those trapped in the cage of prison, subject to the near-unlimited powers of their keepers, is simply unforgettable. Yet, though there is little to be done now about the tragedy of brother Robby, consider the message sent by Wideman's book, and the many others of this genre that have appeared since, to young black men in similar circumstances throughout the country, who might yet avoid his brother's plight: "Your life is not your own to build as you will; they've got a 'master plan.' You can submit and be a 'nobody in a world that hates you' or have the courage to rebel and die in a cage." This seductive intellectual nihilism, motivated by an understandable agony of grief for those lost to the ravaging legacy of racism, throws away the infinite possibilities of the many who, with sustained effort inspired by their loved ones' highest expectations, might yet overcome that legacy.

It is difficult to overemphasize the self-defeating dynamic at work here. The dictates of political advocacy require that personal inadequacies among blacks be attributed to "the system" and that emphasis by black leaders on self-improvement be denounced as irrelevant, self-serving, dishonest. Individual black men and women simply cannot fail on their own, they must be seen as never having had a chance. But where failure at the personal level is impossible, there can also be no personal success. For a black to embrace the Horatio Alger myth, to assert as a guide to *personal* action that "there is opportunity in America," becomes a *politically* repugnant act. For each would-be black Horatio Alger indicts as inadequate or incomplete the deeply entrenched (and quite useful) notion that individual effort can never overcome the inheritance of race. Yet where there can be no black Horatio Algers to celebrate, sustaining an ethos of responsibility that might serve to extract maximal effort from the individual in the face of hardship becomes impossible as well.

James Baldwin spoke to this problem with great insight long ago. In his essay "Everybody's Protest Novel" Baldwin said of the protagonist of Richard Wright's celebrated novel *Native Son*:

> Bigger Thomas stands on a Chicago street corner watching airplanes flown by white men racing against the sun and "Goddamn" he says, the bitterness bubbling up like blood, remembering a million indignities, the terrible, rat-infested house, the humiliation of home-relief, the intense, aimless, ugly bickering, hating it; hatred smoulders through these pages like sulphur fire. All of Bigger's life is controlled, defined by his hatred and his fear. And later, his fear drives him to murder and his hatred to rape; he dies, having come, through this violence, and we are told, for the first time, to a kind of life, having for the first time redeemed his manhood.

But Baldwin rejected this "redemption through rebellion" thesis as untrue to life and unworthy of art. "Bigger's tragedy," he concluded,

> is not that he is cold or black or hungry, not even that he is American, black; but that *he has accepted a theology that denies him life, that he admits the possibility of his being sub-human and feels constrained, therefore, to battle for his humanity according to those brutal criteria bequeathed him at his birth.* But our humanity is our burden, our life;

we need not battle for it; we need only to do what is infinitely more difficult—that is, accept it. The failure of the protest novel lies in its rejection of life, the human being, the denial of his beauty, dread, power, in
its insistence that it is his categorization alone which is real and which
cannot be transcended.[2]

While Baldwin's interest was essentially literary, mine is political. In either case, however, our struggle is against the deadening
effect that emanates from the belief that, for the black man, "it is
his categorization alone which is real and cannot be transcended."
The spheres of politics and culture intersect in this understanding
of what the existence of systemic constraint implies for the possibilities of individual personality. For too many blacks, dedication to
the cause of reform has been allowed to supplant the demand for
individual accountability. Race, and the historic crimes associated
with it—real crimes!—has become the single lens through which
to view social experience. The infinite potential of real human
beings has been surrendered on the altar of protest. In this way
does the prophecy of failure, evoked by those who take the fact of
racism as barring forever blacks' access to the rich possibilities of
American life, fulfill itself: "Loyalty to the race" in the struggle to
be free of oppression requires the sacrifice of a primary instrument
through which genuine freedom might be attained.

Moreover, the fact that there has been in the United States such
a tenuous commitment to social provision to the indigent, independent of race, reinforces the ideological trap. Blacks think we
must cling to victim status because it provides the only secure
basis upon which to press for attention from the rest of the polity
to the problems of our most disadvantaged fellows. It is important
to distinguish here between the socioeconomic consequences of
the claims that are advanced on the basis of the victim status of
blacks (such as the pressure for racially preferential treatment) and
their symbolic, ideological role. For even though the results of this
claiming often accrue to the advantage of better-off blacks and in
no way constitute a solution to the problems of the poor, the desperate plight of the poorest makes it unthinkable that whites could
ever be let off the hook by blacks relinquishing the historically
based claims—that is, by a broad acceptance within the black com-

munity of the notion that individual blacks bear personal responsibility for their fate.

The dilemmas of the black underclass pose in stark terms the most pressing, unresolved problem of the social and moral sciences: how to reconcile individual and social responsibility. The problem goes back to Kant. The moral and social paradox of society is this: On the one hand, we are determined and constrained by social, cultural, not to mention biological forces. Yet on the other hand, if society is to work we must believe that and behave as if we do indeed determine our actions. Neither of the pat political formulas for dealing with this paradox is adequate by itself. The mother of a homeless family is not simply a victim of forces acting on her; she is in part responsible for her plight and that of her children. But she is also being acted on by forces—social, economic, cultural, political—larger than herself. She is not an island; she is impacted by an environment; she does not have complete freedom to determine her future. It is callous nonsense to insist that she does, just as it is mindlessness to insist that she can do nothing for herself and her children until "society" reforms. In fact, she is responsible for her condition; but we also must help her—that is *our* responsibility.

Now blacks have in fact been constrained by a history of racism and limited opportunity. Some of these effects continue to manifest themselves into the current day. Yet now that greater opportunity exists, taking advantage of it requires that we accept personal responsibility for our own fate, even though the effects of this past remain with us in part. But emphasis on this personal responsibility of blacks takes the political pressure off those outside the black community, who also have a responsibility, as citizens of this republic, to be actively engaged in trying to change the structures that constrain the black poor in such a way that they can more effectively assume responsibility for themselves and exercise their inherent and morally required capacity to choose. That is, an inherent link exists between these two sides of the "responsibility" coin: between acceptance among blacks of personal responsibility for our actions and acceptance among all Americans of their social responsibilities as citizens.

My point to conservatives should be plain. Rather than simply incanting the "personal responsibility" mantra, we must also be engaged in helping those people who so desperately need our help. We are not relieved of our responsibility to do so by the fact that Ted Kennedy and Jesse Jackson are promoting legislation aimed at helping this same population with which we disagree. Remember King's description of the animating idea of the Declaration of Independence: "*Every* man is heir to the legacy of worthiness." "Those people" languishing in the drug-infested, economically depressed, crime-ridden central cities—those people are *our* people. We must be in relationship with them. The point here transcends politics and policy. The necessity of being engaged with the least among us is a moral necessity. We Americans cannot live up to our self-image as a "city on a hill," a beacon of freedom and hope for all the world, if we fail this test.

My point to blacks should also be plain. We must let go of the past and take responsibility for our future. What may seem to be an unacceptable political risk is also an absolute moral necessity. This is a dilemma from which I believe we blacks can escape only by an act of faith: faith in ourselves, faith in our nation, and ultimately, faith in the God of our forefathers. He has not brought us this far only to abandon us now. As suggested by the citation from the Book of Hebrews with which I began, we are indeed "surrounded by a great cloud of witnesses"—the spirits of our forebears who, under much more difficult and hostile conditions, made it possible for us to enjoy the enormous opportunities we have today. It would be a profound desecration of their memory were we to preach despair to our children when we are in fact so much closer than they were to the cherished goal of full equality. We must believe that our fellow citizens are now truly ready to allow us an equal place in this society. We must believe that we have within ourselves the ability to succeed on a level playing field if we give it our all. We must be prepared to put the past to rest; to forgive if not forget; to retire the outmoded and inhibiting role of the victim.

Embracing the role of the victim has unacceptable costs. It is undignified and demeaning. It leads to a situation where celebration among blacks of individual success and of the personal traits associated with it comes to be seen as betrayal of the black poor, because such celebration undermines the legitimacy of what has proved to be their most valuable political asset—their supposed helplessness. There is, hidden in this desperate assertion of victim status by blacks to an increasingly skeptical white polity, an unfolding tragedy of profound proportions. Black leaders, confronting their people's need and their own impotency, believe they must continue to portray blacks as "the conscience of the nation." Yet the price extracted for playing this role, in incompletely fulfilled lives and unrealized personal potential, amounts to a "loss of our own souls." As consummate victims we lay ourselves at the feet of our fellows, exhibiting *our* lack of achievement as evidence of *their* failure, hoping to wring from their sense of conscience what we must assume, by the very logic of our claim, lies beyond our individual capacities to attain, all the while bemoaning how limited that sense of conscience seems to be. This way lies not the "freedom" so long sought by our ancestors but, instead, a continuing serfdom.

2

The Moral Quandary
of the Black Community

The civil rights movement now confronts its greatest challenge—
to redefine an agenda created during the turbulent 1950s and
1960s, so that it may conform with the sociopolitical realities of the
1990s and beyond. My argument here is that this redefinition
should be centered around an effort to expand the range of activities that directly seek to mitigate the worst conditions of lower-
class black life.

A long tradition of philanthropy and internally directed action
aimed at self-improvement exists among black Americans, predat-
ing the emancipation. The Urban League, a major civil rights organization today, was founded early in the twentieth century to help
new black migrants from the rural South adjust to life in northern
cities. Similarly, black fraternal and professional organizations,
through a wide array of programs and activities, have been "giving
something back to the community" for decades. Yet the nature of
problems facing the black community today, the significant recent
expansion of opportunities for blacks in American society, and the
changing political environment in which black leaders now operate all require that greater emphasis be placed upon strategies that
might appropriately be called "self-help."

33

For notwithstanding this noble tradition of mutual concern, and despite the greater emphasis that has been placed on problems internal to the black community in the last decade, it remains the dominant tendency among today's public advocates of black interests to emphasize the responsibility of government to resolve the problems of blacks. To be sure, policies of local, state, and federal government significantly affect the welfare of black Americans. And no one would deny, in turn, that blacks have the right and responsibility to participate in shaping those policies. But it is now beyond dispute that many of the problems of contemporary black American life lie outside the reach of effective government action, and require for their successful resolution actions that can be undertaken only by the black community itself. These problems involve at their core the values, attitudes, and behaviors of individual blacks. They are exemplified by the staggering statistics on pregnancies among young, unwed black women and the arrest and incarceration rates among black men. Such complicated problems, partly a cause and partly an effect of the economic hardship readily observed in the ghettos of America, defy easy explanation. These problems will not go away with the return of economic prosperity, with the election of a more liberal Democrat to the presidency, or with the doubling in size of the congressional black caucus.

The fact is, any effective response to such difficulties will necessarily require the intimate involvement of black institutions, politicians, educators, and other concerned individuals, and far more attention than is now received from these quarters. My concern is that too much of the political energy, talent, and imagination abounding in the emerging black middle class is being channeled into a struggle against an enemy without, while the enemy within goes relatively unchecked.

In short, there is a profound need for moral leadership among blacks. The challenge now facing the movement is to find a way to provide that much-needed leadership.

This is not to say that racism has disappeared; so long as there are distinct races of human beings, there will be racism. Nor is it to say that government cannot or should not pursue policies aimed at helping the poor. I intend only to acknowledge that profound change has occurred since the 1950s, reducing the ability of racist whites to act on their prejudices. Today the most hotly contested civil rights issue—affirmative action—concerns the extent to which past racism warrants special, not simply equal, treatment of blacks. For blacks, the problem has always been not the existence of racism but its management. We now have at our disposal numerous legal means for managing the enemy without.

Meanwhile, the enemy within continues to wreak havoc. The level of violence by blacks against other blacks is of alarming proportions. The academic performance of our young people, even in comparison to recent immigrants for whom English is a foreign language, is dismal. Each year, more black women give birth while still in high school than are graduated from college. The proportion of black children dependent on welfare is much greater now than it was in the 1960s. Young black men can be heard to brag about the children they have fathered but need not support.

Fault Versus Responsibility

Some may object that problems of family instability and crime are themselves manifestations of oppression—the historical and ongoing racism of the enemy without—and that to focus on self-help strategies aimed at the behavior of blacks is to treat the symptoms of oppression, not its causes. If jobs were provided for those seeking work, the argument continues, and if a commitment to civil rights could be restored at top levels of government, these internal problems would surely take care of themselves.

I believe this argument to be seriously mistaken, and under certain circumstances possibly quite dangerous, for it invariably ends by placing the *responsibility* for the maintenance of personal values and social norms among poor blacks on the shoulders of those who do not have an abiding interest in such matters. It is important to emphasize, however, that in rejecting this argument I am not questioning the existence of a link between behavioral difficulties and the effects of racism. To the extent that, say, the percentage of black children raised in single-parent homes is greater because black men are denied employment opportunities, one could correctly conclude that the problem has been caused by the racist denial of opportunity. One might then assign blame or fault to racist whites, to the extent that their racism can be determined in this way to have caused certain difficulties among blacks.

Even so, this argument founders when it assumes a concomitant responsibility to resolve the difficulties that have emerged. As the sociologist Orlando Patterson has brilliantly argued, fault and responsibility must not be presumed to go hand in hand. It is absolutely vital that blacks distinguish between the fault that may be attributed to racism as a cause of the black condition, and the responsibility for relieving that condition. No people can be genuinely free so long as they look to others for their deliverance.

The pride and self-respect valued by aspiring peoples throughout the world cannot be the gift of outsiders; they must derive from the thoughts and deeds of the peoples themselves. Neither the guilt nor the pity of one's oppressor is a sufficient basis upon which to construct a sense of self-worth. When faced with the ravages of black crime against blacks, the depressing nature of social life in many low-income black communities, the alarming incidence of pregnancy among unwed black teenagers, or the growing dependency of blacks on transfers from an increasingly hostile polity, it is simply insufficient to respond by saying, "This is the fault of racist America. These problems will be solved when America finally does right by its black folk." Such a response dodges the issue of responsibility, both at the level of individual behavior (the criminal perpetrator being responsible for his* act), and at the level of the group (the black community being responsible for the values embraced by its people).

Consider, as an illustration of this point, a public statement made in 1984 by thirty prominent black leaders and intellectuals who had been convened to address the problems of the black family:

> No strategy designed to improve the status of black Americans can ignore the central position of the black family as the natural transmitter of the care, *values,* and *opportunities* necessary for black men, women, and children to reach their full potential as individuals.[1]

---

*For the sake of simplicity, I will use the male third-person pronoun throughout this book to refer to individuals who may in fact be of either gender. No offense to females is intended.

Thus there is clear recognition that values and opportunities available only within families, and unavailable to many blacks, play a crucial role in determining individual achievement. This is a welcome observation, too seldom seen in the public pronouncements of black leaders. But in the very next sentence responsibility for this state of affairs is laid at the door of American society:

> The present black family crisis, characterized chiefly by the precipitous growth of poor female-headed households, can be traced almost directly to American racism. . . . As large numbers of blacks migrated to large cities from rural areas, black males have often been unable to find work, and government policies and other social forces further sapped family strength. These trends proceed apace today, aided by the widespread failure even to recognize the pressures on the black family as central to other problems, and by failure to devise both preventive and healing strategies.

It is clear from the context that the "failure" being discussed is that of racist American society, not of the political, intellectual, and religious leadership of the black community itself, which might more appropriately be regarded as responsible for the normative health of the group. Certainly one can trace some of these family difficulties to American racism. But having recognized this, it is crucial that we confront the question of how to change the behavior of the young blacks raised in such families. Whatever *fault* may be placed upon racism in America, the *responsibility* for the behavior of black youngsters lies squarely on the shoulders of the black community itself.

There is potential for great danger in ignoring this responsibility, as those who may be legitimately held at fault for the black condition may nonetheless fail to act to improve that condition. It seems increasingly obvious that the animating spirit of the Great Society era, during which government took seriously the responsibility to help solve the problems of the black poor, is on the wane. It is by no means certain that the leaders of either party will in the years ahead continue to have an expansive sense of government obligation to the black poor. John Jacobs, president of the National Urban League, stated the problem quite clearly in the mid-1980s:

> We see the problems facing black families as being problems facing our nation. But the nation is not addressing those problems. The Adminis-

tration and the Congress have cut lifeline programs that help all poor people and especially poor black families. They have drastically cut programs that help poor children survive—including nutrition and health programs. . . . Given that failure to act, we feel that the network of black institutions must play a greater role both in the advocacy on behalf of the black family, and in concrete programmatic ways that provide aid to black families—assistance to help two-parent families stay intact, resources to help single-parent families survive, and programs that help our children to take their rightful place in our society. We are confident that the black community has the institutional and voluntary resources to be effective in this great task. . . . For every element of our society must deal with that aspect of the problem for which it is best suited. . . . That means government must be supportive, black institutions must marshal volunteer resources, *and individual black people must accept responsibility for themselves and for preserving the family values that helped us to survive.* (*Urban League News,* April 1984; emphasis added)

Jacobs was keenly aware of the dangers of inaction in an indifferent, if not actually hostile, political environment. By stressing his confidence in the ability of blacks to grapple with these profoundly difficult problems, he by no means absolved the larger society of its obligations. He recognized, however, that ultimately it is the leaders of the black community, himself among them, who are responsible for addressing these problems.

A New Frontier

The effort of such organizations as the National Urban League to come to grips with these internal difficulties suggests a new direction for the institutional and intellectual resources of the black community (and, more generally, the civil rights community). It is now three decades since the enactment of the Civil Rights Act of 1964, and some forty years since the landmark Brown decision was rendered by the Supreme Court. These and other monumental achievements of the civil rights movement are, for the current generation of American youth, the stuff of history books. Today's young people have no recollection of the struggles. The crowning achievements of this earlier era dwarf in significance anything likely to issue from the litigation and lobbying efforts of today's advocates. In other words, the civil rights strategy—seeking black advancement through the use of the legal system to force America to live by its espoused creed—has reached the point of diminishing returns. It is no exaggeration to say that we now live in the post–civil rights era.

Yet were one to poll the community of activists, lawyers, politicians, and concerned citizens whose effort made "the movement" a reality, I believe a sizable majority would say that the work they began remains seriously incomplete. They would point to the significant economic inequality that remains between the races in the United States. A growing percentage of black children are living below the poverty line; the prisons of the country are disproportionately populated by black men; black families are more often dependent on public assistance than the population as a whole; and residential segregation by race is a commonplace in our central cities, as is the racial segregation of public schools that so often accompanies it. Moreover, it would be observed that overt expressions of racism have not yet vanished from the American scene. Thus, it would be argued, much on the civil rights front remains to be done.

Nevertheless, it is much easier to assert that something must be done than it is to set out an agenda for action. Many veterans of the movement find themselves in the 1990s in the position of sensing how crucial it is that action be taken, and yet not quite knowing what to do. I suggest that the next frontier for the movement should be a concerted effort to grapple directly with the difficult, internal problems that lower-class blacks now face. In this post–civil rights era, the energy and imagination of the individuals and organizations that achieved prominence in the struggle for civil rights may be most usefully employed in efforts to confront the serious internal difficulties that beset our low-income black communities.

It is important to avoid misunderstanding here. I do not suggest that black advocates abandon their traditional concern with the issues of desegregation, equal employment opportunity, or voting rights. There is important work to be done in these areas, even if it consists mainly in defending past gains. But a realistic assessment of the prospects of the poorest black Americans strongly suggests that their lives will not be profoundly altered by the continued pursuit of historically important civil rights strategies. In central-city ghettos across America, where far too many young black mothers struggle alone to raise the next generation of black youths, it is difficult to see the potential for fundamental change via these traditional methods. Even the election of black candidates to the highest municipal offices has so far failed to effect such change. Yet to the extent that we can foster institutions within the black community that encourage responsible male involvement in parenting, help prevent unplanned pregnancies, and support young unwed mothers in their efforts to return to school and become self-supporting, important changes in the lives of the most vulnerable segment of the black population can be made.

These ought not to be seen, then, as mutually exclusive strategies. Financial and other government support may aid internally directed action of the sort described above, and this action will certainly be more effective as the elimination of historical forms of discrimination takes hold. Moreover, the traditional civil rights organizations are especially well situated to undertake these internally directed efforts: they have a strong network of affiliated local organizations, a reputation for service to the black community, the ability to call upon the most talented and accomplished individuals within the black community for assistance, and the respectful regard of many in the philanthropic institutions.

Political Discourse and Self-Imposed Censorship

The undertaking that I advocate—centered, as it is, on the behavior of individuals—will necessarily involve a discussion of values, social norms, and personal attitudes. Such an undertaking is a difficult matter at best, and especially so in recent years for black Americans. Black leaders and intellectuals have, on the whole, sought to avoid public discussion of the role that such normative influences might play in the perpetuation of poverty within the group. This is understandable but unfortunate, because there really is no other way in which such matters can effectively enter public discussion. For government to attempt in the name of public policy to mandate, or even to discuss, what the values and beliefs of any segment of the society should be is to embark on a course fraught with political, constitutional, and moral pitfalls. Moreover, in the political climate of the 1990s, concerned external observers of the black community are in no position to raise such issues if they desire to maintain their credibility as "liberals." Only blacks can talk about what other blacks "should" do, think, or value and expect to be sympathetically heard. That is, *only blacks can effectively provide moral leadership for their people.* To the extent that such leadership is required, therefore, it must come from within.

Even so, such leadership has been in relatively short supply. While black communities and their residents have been dramatically affected by black-on-black crime (many inner-city merchants now offer their goods from behind bulletproof partitions, and black ghetto-dwelling women face a risk of rape higher by several magnitudes than that faced by whites), black congressmen concerned with criminal justice issues focus instead on police brutality. Although police behavior is obviously an issue of legitimate concern to blacks, the damage done by the criminal element within black communities should be regarded as an even greater concern. As the gap in academic achievement between black and white youngsters persists at intolerably high levels, very little can be heard from black leadership (with a few noteworthy exceptions) regarding the extent to which this performance gap is the result of the behavior and values of black children and their parents. As black women struggle to provide for themselves and their children without appropriate financial support from their men, discussion of male irresponsibility has been largely confined to the writings of black feminists.

This is a curious situation, for individual middle-class blacks have long emphasized and lived by values and norms that are entirely inconsistent with the behavior described above. Such behavior is thus not only inconsistent with success in American society, but also with the ethos of much of the black community itself. Current and future black spokesmen and leaders are drawn almost exclusively from this social stratum. But having achieved professional success, they appear not to recognize that their own accomplishments are rooted in the kind of personal qualities that enable one best to take advantage of the opportunities existing in American society. As a result, the opportunity for their lives to stand as examples for the lower class of the community goes relatively unexploited.

A moment's reflection on the history of black Americans will suggest why the discussion of values and norms has been such a limited part of the group's struggle for social advance. Obviously, the atmosphere of racist ideology within which blacks have had to function is of fundamental importance. Since the early days of slavery, and owing to the justification necessary for its practice in a purportedly democratic, Christian society, blacks have been forced to defend their basic claim to an equal humanity before the general American public. The presumed inferiority of the African was the primary rationalization of his enslavement. The social Darwinists of this century and the last, by finding the explanation of blacks' poverty in their culture or genes, posed basic challenges to the integrity and self-respect of the group. The "retrogressionists," who well into this century argued that the black population was doomed to revert to its natural state of depravity without the civilizing influence of paternalistic masters, created an oppressive environment for thoughtful blacks that has been unique among American ethnic groups.

Among the major consequences of this ideological environment is the stifling effect that it has had on the internal intellectual life and critical discourse of the black community itself. Objective assessment and discussion of the condition of the community has been made difficult for blacks because of the concern that critical discourse within the group (about the problems of young unwed mothers or low academic performance, for example) might be happily appropriated by external critics seeking support for their base hypotheses.

It is hard to overstate the significance of this constraint on discourse among blacks. Its consequences have not gone unnoticed by outside observers. As Daniel P. Moynihan once wrote regarding his earlier study of the Negro family:

It is now about a decade since my policy paper and its analysis. As forecasting goes, it would seem to have held up. . . . This has been accompanied by a psychological reaction which I did not foresee, and for which I may in part be to blame. . . . I did not know I would prove to be so correct. Had I known, I might have said nothing, realizing that the subject would become unbearable and rational discussion close to impossible. I accept that in the social sciences some things are better not said.[2]

Moynihan, if course, had argued that the growth of single-parent families posed an emerging and fundamental problem for blacks that would impede the ability of some to advance in the post–civil rights era. It is by now quite evident that he was right. The problem he identified nearly thirty years ago is today twice as severe, with no solution in sight. Yet when Moynihan released his study, he was savagely attacked for "blaming the victim" and for failing to see the inner strengths of these families, whose form represented a necessary adaptation in the face of American racism.

A similar scenario could be offered to describe the reaction of some black leaders to discussions of racial difference in arrest and incarceration rates for various criminal offenses. For example, the NAACP, in its official publication *The Crisis*, has taken the position that this disparity is further evidence of inequality of opportunity: "The only explanation for this . . . discrepancy is conscious choices of key decision-makers to focus on crimes committed more frequently by blacks." This kind of intellectual perspective clearly precludes any serious discussion by black leaders of the problem of criminal behavior. It is incredible, in light of the obvious consequences for those who must live in the crime-ridden neighborhoods of our central cities, that organizations dedicated to improving the welfare of blacks are so reluctant to oppose this behavior forthrightly. There are worse things than blaming the victim.

One could also mention discussions in the social science community of racial difference in performance on intelligence tests, which elicit a similar reaction from black leaders. All of these problems—family instability, criminal behavior, and academic performance—have these features in common: they are essential if one is to understand accurately the condition of the black population, their resolution is fundamental to the progress of blacks, and they are seized on as evidence by those who subscribe to racist propositions about black inferiority. As a result, many blacks have imposed on themselves a kind of censorship; they agree not to discuss these matters frankly in public and to ostracize those blacks who do.

One can generalize about the source of this difficulty. (For a more complete analysis of this problem see chapter 8.) Political discourse within a somewhat insular and legitimately suspicious community requires trust. The nature of the external threat is such that members of the community must always be on guard. There are those who would welcome proof of the group's inferiority, rationalize its predicament, or roll back its progress. These forces may have supporters, witting or not, within the group itself, and members of the group know that their every public utterance must be calculated with this in mind. One cannot know with certainty, then, where a speaker is "coming from," but this in no way inhibits speculation as to his motives. Someone who speaks on behalf of the "free market," or who intimates that there are deep structural problems within black communities having to do with values and attitudes, courts trouble because enemies of the group have made similar claims. In such an environment it is likely that individuals within the community will tacitly agree not to discuss certain ideas, at least not publicly, thereby impoverishing political discourse.

Tacit censorship of this sort tends to perpetuate itself, and for good reason. Once it exists, suspicion of those who violate the implicit accord becomes justifiable; in a sense, the accord acts like a self-fulfilling prophecy. Only someone who places relatively little weight on social acceptance by the community—someone who, therefore, is objectively less likely to share the group's prevailing conception of its interests—would be willing to breach the implicit contract of silence. Self-imposed limits on the group's discourse, then, might live on after most individuals have recognized that something is wrong.

This suggests that when the barriers to discussion finally break down, as they must, the change will be both rapid and complete. Because of their unimpeachable integrity and commitment to the community, such institutions as the black churches, fraternal organizations, and the nationally based civil rights organizations are particularly well suited to this undertaking. While the behavioral problems described here are by no means unique to blacks, the stifling of critical discourse within the black community has impeded analysis and slowed the development of new approaches to resolve these problems.

The irony is that nothing provides greater support for those believing in black inferiority than the continuation of the pathological behaviors to which I have alluded. Of course, I believe blacks are inherently as capable of accomplishment as anyone else in this society. But the only way to prove this is for black people to actually achieve up to this potential. Thus, suppressing discussion of internal failures for fear that racial stereotypes will be confirmed is self-defeating. Blacks' problems lie not in the heads of white people, but rather in the wasted and incompletely fulfilled lives of too many black people.

Black Political Capital

The fact that values, social norms, and personal behaviors often observed among the poorest members of the black community are quite distinct from those characteristic of the black middle class indicates a growing divergence in the social and economic experiences of black Americans. The extent and importance of this divergence is often the subject of acrimonious debate, but its existence is beyond serious dispute. The simple fact is that the opening of opportunities occasioned by the legal and political successes of the civil rights movement has led in a generation's time to a dramatic increase in the number of blacks attending elite colleges and universities, entering the professions, and engaging in successful business enterprises. Yet the ghetto-dwelling residents of central Harlem, of Watts, of the West Side of Chicago, or of eastern Detroit are not often found among this new cadre of aspiring young blacks. Nor is the prospect that their children will enter this social stratum nearly as great as it is for black children elsewhere. There are thus genuine differences in the social circumstances of blacks, differences that suggest the much abused sociological concept of "class."

These differences in social circumstance, together with the realities of political advocacy on behalf of blacks in contemporary

American life, provide a compelling moral argument for the expansion of internal actions aimed directly at improving the circumstances of the black poor. The point (explained below) is that more fortunate blacks benefit, through the political system, from the conditions under which the poorest blacks must live. This implies a concomitant obligation to help improve those conditions, though there may be little incentive to do so.

The methods by which blacks wield influence on the formulation of public policy in this country are legion. There is, of course, the effect of the ballot. Many southern politicians have learned to "sing a different tune" because of their recognition that election without black support has become impossible. In major urban areas throughout the country, black candidates now successfully compete for the highest offices, significantly affecting the conduct of local governments. It is now a case that Democratic party candidates cannot hope to prevail in presidential elections without the overwhelming support of black voters.

In addition to raw political muscle, however, blacks enjoy the benefit of the widely (though not universally) held perception that their demands on the political system are a test of its justice and fairness. The extent to which an administration is perceived as "sensitive" to the claims of blacks has become a measure of its compassion, or a sign of its callousness. Many Americans accept the notion that the government should, in some way, deal with the problems of blacks because that is the proper and decent thing to do. The existence of "liberal guilt" has been instrumental in sustaining political support for initiatives of substantial benefit to blacks.

There are few things more valuable in the competition for government largess than the clearly perceived status of victim. Blacks "enjoy" that status by dint of many years of systematic exclusion from a just place in American life. A substantial source of influence thus derives from the fact that blacks are perceived as having been unjustly wronged and hence worthy of consideration. *The single most important symbol of this injustice is the large inner-city ghetto, with its population of poor blacks.* These masses and their miserable condition sustain the political capital that all blacks enjoy because of their historical status as victims.

The growing black "underclass" has become a constant reminder to many Americans of a historical debt owed to the black
community. Were it not for the continued presence of the worst-off
of all Americans, blacks' ability to sustain public support for affirmative action, minority business set-asides, and the like would be
vastly reduced. (Even women's groups, by citing in support of their
political objectives the "feminization of poverty"—a phenomenon
substantially influenced by the increasing number of black families
headed by women with low incomes—derive benefit from this
source.) The suffering of the poorest blacks creates, if you will, a
fund of political capital upon which all members of the group can
draw when pressing racially based claims.

Thus it is not surprising to find that whenever any black leader
argues for special assistance to some members of his community,
whether that assistance flows directly to the poorest blacks or not,
one will hear about the black teenage unemployment rate or the
increasing percentage of blacks living below the poverty line. The
fact that the median black family income continues to lag behind
white family income is frequently cited by black spokesmen and
others to support the general claim that "nothing has changed." No
major government purchasing effort at the local, state, or federal
level can proceed now without the question being raised of "What
is in this for minority business?" Inevitably the low economic status of the black poor will be referred to as justification for the
claim.

I am saying nothing here about the motives of black leaders,
businessmen, or professionals. I only observe that their advocacy
for policies that benefit blacks who are not themselves poor is most
effective when couched in terms that remind the American polity
of its historic debt, and that this is most readily accomplished by
referring to the condition of the poorest blacks.

And how have the black poor benefited from the policies
extracted from the system in their name? The evidence suggests
that, for many of the most hotly contested public policies advocated by black spokesmen, not much trickles down to the truly
poor. As far as I know, there is no study to support the claim that
set-asides for minority-owned businesses have led to a significant
increase in the level of employment among lower-class blacks. It is

clear from extensive empirical research on the effect of affirmative action standards for federal contractors that it is mainly those blacks in the higher-class occupations who have gained from this program. If one examines the figures on relative earnings of young black and white men by educational class, by far the greater progress has been made among those blacks with the most education. Looking at relative earnings by occupation, one finds that the most dramatic earnings gains for blacks have taken place in the professional, technical, and managerial occupations, while the least significant gains have come in the lowest occupations, like laborer and service worker. Thus, a broad array of evidence suggests that better-placed blacks have been able to take better advantage of the opportunities created since the early 1960s than have those mired in the underclass.

The Marxian notion of exploitation refers to a circumstance in which workers receive less from the process of production than their labor has contributed. It seems evident that contemporary poor blacks gain less from the political process than their votes and misery contribute to the effectiveness of black advocacy. Sadly, this circumstance may continue for some time.

I am not suggesting any malice or bad faith on the part of middle-class blacks who are able to extract concrete gains from the system. Indeed, these individuals need not realize how their behavior, along with that of many others, leads to a situation in which exploitation occurs. It seems to be a feature of the contemporary American political economy that the kind of benefits most readily generated for blacks accrue more often to those who are not most in need of them. It is a simple matter to see that the prime contractor on a large municipal construction project uses a certain percentage of black subcontractors, and much harder to assure that the fatherless child of a poverty-stricken mother avoids the hazards prevalent in the ghetto. We can demand that a consumer franchise company give dealerships to black entrepreneurs, but not that the high school valedictorian be black.

This, to my mind, is a solid basis for the moral argument that ways must be sought to enlist those blacks who have achieved a modicum of security and success in the decades-long task of eradicating the worst aspects of black poverty. The nature of the problems besetting inner-city communities, the character of political advocacy by blacks in the post-civil-rights era, and the drift of politics in contemporary America seem to require that any morally defensible and realistic program of action for the black community must attend first to the fostering of a sense of self-confidence and hope for the future among members of the black underclass. Certainly the federal government can play a critical role in this process. Yet it is equally clear that the black business, academic, and political elites must press for improvement in their own peoples' lives through the building of constructive internal institutions, whether government participates or not.

3

A New American Dilemma

In 1944 Swedish economist Gunnar Myrdal argued in *An American Dilemma* that the problem of race in the United States cut to the very core of our definition as a people. Myrdal described America as a nation that, although founded on the ideals of individual liberty and personal dignity, could not bring itself—through either law or social practice—to treat the descendants of slaves as the equals of whites. The dilemma for white leaders in particular was that these racial practices were so deeply ingrained that even if they wanted to get rid of them, it seemed politically impossible to do so. At that time Myrdal hardly could have foreseen the extent to which the United States would confront and begin to resolve this great dilemma. As recently as the early 1960s many conservatives denied as a matter of principle that the government should interfere in private decisions in order to assure equal opportunity for black people. (Ronald Reagan, for example, opposed the 1964 Civil Rights Act.) Three decades later that position has been completely discredited, both legally and morally.

The old racism is not gone, but the disparity between American ideals and racial practice has narrowed dramatically. Today the civil rights debate is dominated by the issue of affirmative action, in

51

which the question is whether the history of racism warrants special—not simply equal—treatment for blacks. Whereas blacks were
once excluded from politics by subterfuge and the threat of violence, they now constitute a potent political bloc with often deci-
sive influence on local and national elections. Martin Luther King,
Jr., whose passionate, relentless, and compelling articulation of
black aspirations made him the nemesis of presidents, governors,
and FBI officials alike, is now honored as a national hero. The
moral victory of the civil rights movement is virtually complete.

And yet racial divisions remain. Since the 1980s we have been
faced with a new American dilemma, one that is especially difficult
for black leaders and members of the black middle class. The bottom stratum of the black community has compelling problems that
can no longer be blamed solely on white racism, and that force us to
confront fundamental failures in black society. The social disorganization among poor blacks, the lagging academic performance of
black students, the disturbingly high rate of black-on-black crime,
and the alarming increase in early unwed pregnancies among
blacks now loom as the primary obstacles to progress. To admit
these failures is likely to be personally costly for black leaders, and
it may also play into the hands of lingering racist sentiments. Not to
admit them, however, is to forestall their resolution and to allow the
racial polarization of the country to worsen. If the new American
dilemma is not dealt with soon, we may face the possibility of a permanent split in our political system along racial lines.

It is deeply ironic that this dilemma has arisen in the wake of
the enormous success of the civil rights movement. In little more
than a generation, the United States has changed from a country
callously indifferent to the plight of its black citizens into one for
which that plight is a central feature of our political life. A new
middle class of well-educated and well-placed blacks has emerged,
whose members can be found in technical, managerial, and professional positions throughout the leading institutions of the nation.
Differences in earnings between young, well-educated black and
white workers have diminished dramatically; and something
approximating parity in economic status has been achieved for
young, intact black families.

Yet in general, even this class of blacks does not view itself as being in the American mainstream. There is a keen appreciation among blacks of all social classes that at least one-third of their fellow blacks belong to the underclass. There is no way to downplay the social pathologies that afflict this part of the black community. In the big-city ghettos the youth unemployment rate often exceeds 40 percent. It is not uncommon for young men to leave school at age sixteen and reach their mid-twenties without ever having held a steady job. In these communities, more than half of all black babies are born out of wedlock. (In central Harlem, the most recently reported figure is 79.9 percent.) Black girls between the ages of fifteen and nineteen constitute the most fertile population of that age group in the industrialized world; their birth rate is twice as high as any other group of women in the West.

The undeniable progress of the black middle class has been accompanied by the undeniable spread of these problems. Today over three of every five black children do not live with both of their parents. The level of dependency on public assistance for basic economic survival in the black population has doubled since the heyday of the Great Society. About one-half of all black children are supported in part by transfers from the state and federal governments. More than half of all black children in public primary and secondary schools are concentrated in the nation's twelve largest central city school districts, where the quality of education is notoriously poor, and where whites constitute only about a quarter of total enrollment. Only about one black student in seven scores above the 50th percentile on the standardized college admissions tests. Blacks, though little more than one-tenth of the population, constitute approximately one-half of the imprisoned felons in the nation.

Among those great many blacks who have entered the middle class since the early 1960s there is, understandably, a deeply felt sense of outrage at the injustice of conditions endured by the black poor. Somewhat less understandable is their reluctance to consider their own success as evidence of the profound change that has taken place in American attitudes, institutions, and practices. The position of poor blacks is perceived as being inherently linked to the racist past of the nation, as proving that the historic injustice of which Myrdal spoke still flourishes.

Moreover, middle-class blacks do not generally look to their own lives as examples of what has become possible for those blacks still left behind. Talented black professionals who in decades past would have had scant opportunity for advancement now, in the interest of fairness and racial balance, are avidly sought in corporate boardrooms or on elite university faculties. Nonetheless they find it possible, indeed necessary, to think of themselves as members of an oppressed caste.

The great majority of Americans do not see the situation of blacks in this way. Whereas black politicians and intellectuals consider the ghetto and all that occurs there to be simple proof that the struggle for civil rights has yet to achieve its goals, others are repelled by the nature of social life in poor black communities. Though most are too polite to say so, they see the poverty of these communities as substantially due to the behavior of the people living there. They are unconvinced by the tortured rationalizations offered by some black and liberal white spokesmen. They do not think of themselves or their country as responsible for these dreadful conditions. Most Americans know something of hardship. Most were not born wealthy; many have parents or grandparents who came here with next to nothing, and who worked hard so that their children might have a better life. Most are not hostile or even indifferent to the aspirations of blacks. In fact, they point with pride to the advancement that blacks have made, to the elaborate legal apparatus erected since 1964 to assure racial fairness, and to the private efforts undertaken by a great number of individuals and institutions to increase black participation in their activities.

A Gallup poll conducted in 1984 for the Joint Center for Political Studies, a black think tank in Washington, revealed the dimensions of the gulf between black and white perceptions. More than two out of three whites said they believe that "all in all, compared with five years ago, the situation of black people in this country has improved," compared to only about one in three blacks. Nearly one-half of the whites polled were "satisfied with the way things are going at this time," but only one-seventh of blacks were. One-half of blacks felt that "blacks should receive preference in getting jobs," compared to one in eleven whites. Some 72 percent of blacks but only 31 percent of whites thought of Ronald Reagan as "prejudiced."

The 1984 Presidential election made distressingly clear why this gap is not likely to be bridged. Two-thirds of all whites voted for Reagan, while nine-tenths of all blacks voted against him. And black leaders went beyond merely opposing the president. Roger Wilkins lambasted the administration for engaging in a "concerted effort to constrict the democratic rights" of blacks, an effort that Coretta King said was aimed at "turning back the clock" on black progress. Benjamin Hooks declared that the administration had to be "eliminated from the face of the earth."

It strains credulity to attribute Reagan's broadly based landslide that November to a resurgent racism among whites. Much broader forces are evidently at work, just as there are forces broader than racism sustaining and encouraging the social pathology of the ghetto. But black leaders, like their constituents, cannot seem to bring themselves to admit this. They prefer to portray the problems of the ghetto as stemming from white racism, and to foster racial politics as the primary means of fighting it. Within the Democratic party, racial splits such as the one created by Jesse Jackson's presidential candidacies or the civil war between Chicago mayor Harold Washington and his white opponents in 1983 may well be a sign of things to come. By casting their political battles in starkly racial terms, black leaders help to promote a racial schism in American political life without necessarily addressing the most fundamental problems of their constituents.

Unfortunately, neither Democratic, Republican, nor black leaders have much incentive to prevent this political fracas from exacerbating the general racial division of American society. The Democrats, having just finished a campaign in which a quarter of the votes for their candidate were cast by blacks, appear to have a big stake in the perpetuation of racial schism. Far from viewing the "color gap" with alarm, Democratic strategists have come to depend on it. Yet under electoral pressure the Democrats also have had to keep their distance at times from the black leadership. The Democrats' chief problem is how to maintain the enthusiasm of black supporters without alienating white supporters. Witness one of the central dilemmas of the Mondale, Dukakis, and Clinton candidacies: how to keep Jesse Jackson close enough to win blacks but far enough away to placate whites.

The Republicans, in the short run, do not expect to win much support from blacks, no matter what they do. Moreover, any such overt appeal to blacks by a Republican presidential candidate would risk alienating the extreme conservative end of his constituency. Some right-wing Republican candidates are not above exploiting the vestiges of racism; Jesse Helms, for example, managed to mention Jesse Jackson's name twenty-four times in a fundraising solicitation during his recent reelection campaign. Thus, the benefits of rapprochement will seem slight, and the costs potentially great. Jack Kemp's speeches in which he makes an overt appeal for black support, pledging to include the black poor in his "new opportunity society," are a hopeful exception to the Republicans' indifference.

But of all the actors in this drama, black leaders play the most important role, and the most problematic. The prevailing ideological cast of many prominent black leaders and intellectuals is considerably to the left of the national mainstream and often of the black community itself. Because of the long history of racist exclusion, many blacks place group solidarity above mere philosophical differences when deciding whom to support. A black ideologue of the left (or, for that matter, of the right—Louis Farrakhan, for example) is almost immune from challenge by another black, since it is precisely in ideological terms that whites most often oppose him. By posing a challenge, the black critic seems to ride with whites against his own race. The black challenger may thus forfeit black political support if he expands his appeal to white voters by criticizing incumbent black leadership. The opposition of whites to the black incumbent is taken by other blacks as proof that he is "sticking it to the man" and thus deserves support. The black challenger winds up appearing, in the eyes of his own people, to be an agent of forces inimical to their interests.

As a result, many black leaders act in ways that exacerbate their isolation from the American political mainstream without fear of reproach by more centrist blacks. The way in which the Voting Rights Act has come to be enforced compounds the problem. To avoid redistricting battles in courts, legislatures routinely create overwhelmingly black, electorally "safe" districts for black incumbents. As a result, most nationally prominent black politicians do not require white support to retain their prominence. Those blacks who do require white support—former Los Angeles mayor Tom Bradley, for example—are discernibly closer to the center of the Democratic party.

The results can be bizarre. Jesse Jackson actually campaigned in the deep South urging local politicians to join his Rainbow Coalition so that, working together, they might enact the Equal Rights Amendment, eliminate state right-to-work laws, and secure a nuclear freeze. Most candidates running in the South on such a platform have short political careers. Lasting alliances between poor southern blacks and whites, if they are to emerge at all, will not emerge with this as the substance of the black politician's appeal. Yet southern whites who are repulsed by such "progressive" candidates are written off as racists. And the incentive for the emergence of a centrist black leadership that might someday achieve significant white support is diminished ever further.

Philosopher Robert Nozick once gave a lecture at Harvard entitled "Why Do Intellectuals Hate Capitalism?" and found one intellectual's answer scribbled on a poster announcing the talk: "Because we're smart!" Black leaders might answer the question of why they are so uniform in their expressed philosophic perspective the same way—they are smart enough to understand black interest and to recognize them to be well served by a left-liberal politics.

But this argument, while not implausible, is not necessarily correct. An alternative explanation for the ideological posture of black leaders is this: the outcome of the internal struggles among black elites for leadership is sharply affected by the general perception of the black community on the quality of race relations. When most blacks think that things are going poorly for the group (as they do now), relatively radical forces in the leadership will be strengthened. When the American political establishment, liberal or conservative, reacts negatively to these radical leaders, it becomes all the more difficult for moderate blacks to challenge them.

This is what happened in 1984. During the campaign Jesse Jackson's candidacy came under severe criticism from Democrats and Republicans alike. There was talk of not permitting him to speak at the Democratic Convention unless he repudiated Louis Farrakhan. Conservative commentators were extremely critical of his postprimary junket to Central America and Cuba. At the convention many blacks were disappointed by the limited concessions Mondale offered Jackson supporters. Their discomfort was enhanced by the adoption by the Republicans in Dallas of the most conservative major party platform in the last fifty years. As a result, the black leadership was fiercely critical of both Mondale and Reagan (for different reasons, of course), but virtually silent about some of Jackson's more extreme views. It would have required great courage for any black leader of prominence to criticize publicly, say, Jackson's foreign policy positions, or to acknowledge publicly the serious problem of black anti-Semitism during the campaign— and virtually none did.

This alternative explanation accounts for two central features of black politics in the 1990s that the "Because we're smart" retort cannot. First, it suggests why black political debate, though by no means nonexistent, is so truncated. Consider that between 1965 and 1979 the number of low-income blacks who were victims of robbery rose by 1,266 per 100,000; among middle-income whites the increase was 359. But the residents of inner-city Detroit, who face one of the highest criminal victimization rates anywhere, regularly return to Congress John Conyers, who uses his position as chairman of the House Subcommittee on Criminal Justice to crusade against police brutality and white-collar crime but spends little time publicly addressing the plight of the victims of street crime. No serious challenge to Conyers has ever been waged by a black attacking him for failing to represent the community's interest in reducing crime. Here is a case where, arguably, blacks' interests are not served by Conyers's traditional left-liberal perspective. Blacks in Detroit may need less, not more, uniformity of opinion.

What conceivable justification can black leaders offer for such limited debate among the victims of crime about Conyers's views on the subject? To argue that ordinary black people identify with and excuse the criminals who brutalize them would be to plumb the depths of fatuity and condescension. And yet consider how the NAACP, the largest and oldest civil rights organization in the country, characterized the inner-city crime problem in the April 1983 issue of its magazine, *The Crisis*:

> Blacks make up . . . 12 percent of the nation's total population . . . [and] an incredible 50 percent of the total prison population . . . [but] only 4

percent of the nation's law enforcement personnel. . . . Why are so
many blacks in prison and . . . so few blacks in law enforcement? One
inescapable answer applies to both questions: racism. Superficially, it
would appear that blacks commit more crimes than anyone else . . .
[but the] only explanation for this . . . discrepancy is conscious choices
of key decision makers to focus on crimes committed more frequently
by blacks.

If the common ideology of the black leadership is this reticent to
express principled opposition to the damaging criminal behavior of
a relatively few young black men, it simply does not serve the welfare of blacks.

Second, the "Because we're smart" argument cannot explain the
ubiquitous coolness that nationally prominent black politicians
exhibit toward the defense of American interests abroad. The most
vulnerable segment of the American population to any major set-
back abroad are the black inner-city poor. If vital raw materials
become scarce, who will suffer first and most? If markets abroad
disappear, if trading partners can no longer afford to buy our
goods, who will be unemployed? Of course, factors beyond the
narrow interests of constituents should determine one's foreign
policy positions. Still, the answers to these questions are sufficiently uncertain that those advocating the interests of the inner-
city poor would do well to consider them carefully.

Again, they do not seem to be doing so, which only widens the
schism between blacks and the American mainstream. It is
unhealthy that NBC correspondent Marvin Kalb could feel
obliged in 1984 to ask Jesse Jackson, before a television audience
of millions, whether his loyalties were first to America or first to
black people—especially when the answer was the latter. When
Jackson ended a speech that year at the University of Havana with
"Long live Cuba! Long live the United States! Long live President
Castro! Long live Martin Luther King! Long live Martin Luther
King! Long live Ché Guevara! Long live Patrice Lumumba!" the
clear suggestion was that Martin Luther King's movement and
Ché Guevara's movement are on the same moral and political
plane. Such cavalier use of King's moral legacy will only squander
it. And yet while the rest of the electorate gasps, blacks seem to
slumber.

To be sure, ordinary black people feel a genuine ambivalence about their American nationalism. Blacks find themselves in America only because their ancestors were kidnapped and brought here as slaves. In the century following emancipation, black artists and intellectuals—whose legacy continues to exert a powerful influence on educated young blacks—found they could only gain freedom of action and the recognition for their accomplishments by exiling themselves. The complicity of the federal and state governments in sustaining Jim Crow laws and the de facto system of racial caste, and the ubiquity of racist assumptions and practices throughout American life, have left deep scars. There can be no forgetting that Martin Luther King, Jr., was hounded as a suspected enemy of the state by the FBI even as he was helping to effect the nation's great moral awakening. When the Reagan administration seemed to flinch from condemning the ugly racism of South African apartheid, it made many blacks even more reluctant to embrace fully their American nationalism.

Thus white leaders, too, if they do not seek to understand the nature and sources of black political alienation and respond sensitively to it, are in danger of making our racial dilemma worse. White Democrats and white Republicans who are elected to office without black support will be tempted, as all politicians are, to reward their friends (that is, whites), and punish their enemies (that is, blacks). If they succumb to this temptation, they will make it infinitely harder for black leaders to adopt positions that make mutual compromise and accommodation possible.

This is the great problem confronting the next Republican presidential candidate. Even in the absence of any short-term political gain, he must seek to reach out to blacks and include them in his new majority. He need not pretend to be a liberal Democrat. He should act on the statement Ronald Reagan made in 1982 to the National Black Republican Council:

> No other experience in American history runs quite parallel to the black experience. It has been one of great hardships, but also of great heroism; of great adversity but also great achievement. What our Administration and our party seek is the day when the tragic side of the black legacy in America can be laid to rest once and for all, and the long, perilous voyage toward freedom, dignity, and opportunity can be completed, a day when every child born in America will live free not

only of political injustice, but of fear, ignorance, prejudice, and dependency.

This candidate must recognize the damage that is done to the
country by poor judgment in policy decisions of powerful symbolic
importance. Two examples of this problem from Ronald Reagan's
first term come to mind. The administration appeared to support
segregationist Bob Jones University in its efforts to gain tax exemption; and it failed to give early support to a compromise version of
the bill to extend the Voting Rights Act, thus permitting itself to be
portrayed as opposing the measure. Such mistakes served only to
insult and alienate further a tenth of the population.

The next Republican presidential candidate must also push with
greater vigor and urgency those initiatives many conservatives
already support: enterprise zones, a subminimum wage for the
hard to employ, ownership possibilities for responsible public
housing tenants, and support for the development of a strong black
entrepreneurial class. He has to show he is willing to take some
risks, and make some compromises, to see that these and other initiatives are enacted. Presidents Reagan and Bush seemed reluctant
to appear before black audiences—perhaps because they feared an
ugly reception. Yet by taking blacks seriously enough to directly
seek their support, a conservative candidate can take the lead in
healing the country's racial wounds.

Should a white conservative be prepared to take these steps, a
historic opportunity will present itself to the black leadership. The
black underclass cannot afford another four years of wishful thinking from its leaders about the drift of political ideas in contemporary America. Those leaders must find the courage and wisdom to
heed the growing signs of racial isolation, and to seek accommodation and compromise. They need not become conservative Republicans. What is required is that black leaders, from a mature and
varied set of ideological positions, adopt strategies consonant with
the shifting political realities. Until they do so, the new American
dilemma will be perpetuated by blacks and whites alike.

4

Two Paths to Black Progress

We Americans remain a nation struggling to confront intractable problems of race. Our polity has had to face, on an enormous scale, the difficulty of incorporating into the estate of full and equal citizenship the descendants of African slaves. This process, though well advanced, remains incomplete a century and a quarter after the emancipation. We now face the fundamental problem of determining whether and how further progress shall be made.

This pronoun "we" has an ambiguous antecedent. Discourse on matters of race may be usefully undertaken openly by the nation as a whole as part of our larger political conversation, but also by and among black Americans as part of a communal deliberation. Both conversations have been ongoing for some time. Contemporary national debates over civil rights policy, affirmative action, multicultural education, voting rights, and appointments to the Supreme Court directly raise the question of race. Other issues— crime or welfare policy, for example—indirectly, though powerfully, engage the racial theme.

Among black Americans, public and communal life is dominated by questions of race. Through internal dialogue, sometimes heated, blacks have endeavored to come to terms with our condition, to wrestle a measure of dignity out of the inherited disability of a second-class citizenship, to mount effective protest against a multitude of wrongs, to define ourselves as a people, and to make progress as a race. There have always been different schools of thought among blacks on these matters. And blacks have always been concerned about how public expression of such differences might adversely affect the way in which the larger American public looks upon and reacts to the group.

These two levels of deliberation over racial questions—within the national polity as a whole, and among ourselves as blacks—interact in important and complex ways. What is acceptable and effective to argue in either forum depends on the nature of the discourse taking place in the other. No prudent act of political argument about racial matters can be undertaken without a consideration of the context in which the argument is being made.

For example, I recognize that in this book I am engaged in two related but distinct conversations, a kind of doublespeak—talking, if you will, out of both sides of my mouth (though not, one hopes, with a forked tongue). I write as a social scientist and social critic—a public man, an American—to a national readership offering observations on how we (that is, all Americans) should think about questions of race. But I also write as a black, addressing "my people" about how we (that is, black Americans) should endeavor to make progress. This limits what I can communicate without risk of misunderstanding, or worse, by one or the other of my audiences. Because of race both audiences may extend to me a certain license but, also because of race, demand a certain fealty. I am aware that each reader will search my argument for evidence of disloyalty to cherished values, or confirmation of strongly held convictions. I know also that, inevitably, some must be disappointed. Nevertheless, I must endeavor to state what I see as the truth. Such are the subtleties affecting our national deliberations on racial matters. (For a fuller exploration of such subtle impediments to effective public discourse, see chapter 8.)

The nomination and confirmation of Clarence Thomas to the Supreme Court powerfully illustrated this theme. Thomas, a black of humble origins and conservative political philosophy, met with vehement opposition from much of the national black leadership, as well as from other quarters. The racial aspect of the appointment—that Thomas replaced on the Court Thurgood Marshall, the only other black ever to have served there—was a key factor in explaining the nature of both support for and opposition to the appointment. The character of public deliberation over the nomination showed how the two levels of discourse on racial matters referred to above interact with each other, on both sides of the political divide. For the attack on Thomas would have been crippled from the start without a sufficient measure of black authorization, while his nomination would surely have been defeated without the massive support he received from blacks throughout the South, which authorized key votes cast on his behalf by Senate Democrats.

The communal debate among blacks about the suitability of Clarence Thomas as a replacement for Thurgood Marshall has historic resonance. This argument has pitted liberal civil rights advocates (for decades now the established orthodoxy among respectable exponents of black opinion) against advocates of a conservative philosophy for advancement based on direct empowerment of the poor, relying significantly on self-help and dubious about the ability of government programs to resolve the deepest problems affecting black society.

This conflict between Thomas's black supporters and his black critics recalls to mind the epochal struggle over public ideas among blacks that raged at the turn of the century between the followers, respectively, of Booker T. Washington and of W. E. B. Du Bois. Washington was a conservative advocate of a philosophy of self-help; Du Bois was a radical exponent of a strategy of protest and agitation for reform. While he lived, Washington's view was the orthodoxy. He expended considerable energies to ensure that this was so, using his far-reaching influence among whites to cut off his critics from sources of financial support. Nevertheless, in the end the ideas of the Du Bois camp prevailed, leading to the founding of the National Association for the Advancement of Colored People and providing the impetus for the decades-long legal struggle that culminated in the *Brown* decision, which was successfully argued before the Supreme Court by Thurgood Marshall.

Though no doubt something of an oversimplification, it is possible to see Justices Clarence Thomas and Thurgood Marshall as

direct intellectual descendants of these two great black protago-
nists of nearly a century ago. Of course, the Du Bois–Marshall
view is today's orthodoxy, an orthodoxy defended fiercely by the
civil rights establishment from the criticism of radical dissidents
(like Thomas) just as Washington defended his, and with similar
methods. But there are signs that a new era is dawning, and that in
the contemporary struggle over which ideas will inform efforts to
improve the black condition into the twenty-first century, the principles laid down by Booker T. Washington will be rediscovered and
play an important role. I intend here to urge that this be so.

What are those principles? They are, fundamentally, an understanding about how blacks should respond to the great philosophical and political problems created by our history of degradation
and the fact of our unequal citizenship. The debasements and
severe constraints of slavery left black Americans in an objectively
inferior state of social development at the time of the emancipation. The newly freed slaves were a backward, ignorant, and
impoverished peasantry. But they were also new citizens of the
republic, empowered by amendments to the Constitution to participate equally in the political life of the nation. In the early
decades after the end of slavery these political rights were stripped
away throughout the South. A racial caste system evolved,
enforced by law, that relegated blacks to a second-class citizenship.
At the same time, and in part because of this political retrogres-
sion, blacks continued to suffer from a lack of social and economic
development. Black leaders and intellectuals of this first post-
slavery generation were preoccupied with the problem of con-
structing a response to these conditions.

At the programmatic level Booker T. Washington believed the
response should be to concentrate on the development of blacks'
capacities to exploit such opportunity as already lay at hand. As
such development was seen to proceed, blacks would come into a
stronger position to make a successful claim for the full rights of
citizenship. Washington saw two factors preventing blacks from
enjoying the status in American society that was their due: actual
defects of character, as manifested in patterns of behavior and ways

of living among the black masses; and the racist attitudes of whites. He believed that blacks had both an opportunity and a duty to address the former difficulty, and that in so doing they would go a long way toward overcoming the latter. He preached constantly a litany of self-improvement; he emphasized the Protestant virtues of thrift, industry, cleanliness, chastity, and orderliness; and he urged above all else that blacks must make themselves *useful*—to their families, their neighbors, and their fellow citizens.

All of this sounds quaint today. But this programmatic focus on self-help was actually not very controversial at the time. What stimulated opposition was Washington's rejection of mass political agitation as a strategy. He thought the active pursuit of civil rights to be premature and dangerous for blacks: "Brains, property, and character for the Negro will settle the question of civil rights." "The best course to pursue in regard to the civil rights bill in the South is to let it alone; let it alone and it will settle itself." "It is the duty of the Negro to deport himself modestly in regard to political claims, depending upon the slow but sure influences that proceed from the possession of property, intelligence, and high character for the full recognition of his political rights." Surely, said his opponents, this was madness, nothing less than an unmanly acquiescence by blacks in their own oppression. And it invited the delighted contempt of whites, whose lives were made so much easier for being "let off the hook."

Writing from Boston in 1901, William Monroe Trotter, the first black elected to Phi Beta Kappa at Harvard, denounced Washington as a traitor to the race and called for "a black Patrick Henry" to arise who would "save his people from the stigma of cowardice . . . rouse them from their lethargy . . . and inspire [them] with the spirit of those immortal words: 'Give Me Liberty or Give Me Death.'" Two years later Trotter got his wish as Du Bois, in his famous essay "Of Mr. Booker T. Washington and Others," offered this forceful rebuttal:

> On the whole the distinct impression left by Mr. Washington's propaganda is, first, that the South is justified in its present attitude toward the Negro because of the Negro's degradation; secondly, that the prime cause of the Negro's failure to rise more quickly is his wrong education in the past; and, thirdly, that his future rise depends primarily on his

own efforts. Each of these propositions is a dangerous half-truth. The supplementary truths must never be lost sight of: first, slavery and race-prejudice are potent if not sufficient causes of the Negro's position; second, industrial and common-school training were necessarily slow in planting because they had to await the black teachers trained by higher institutions . . . and, third, while it is a great truth to say that the Negro must strive and strive mightily to help himself, it is equally true that unless his striving be not simply seconded, but rather aroused and encouraged, by the initiative of the richer and wiser environing group, he cannot hope for great success.

In his failure to realize and impress this last point, Mr. Washington is especially to be criticized. His doctrine has tended to make the whites, North and South, shift the burden of the Negro problem to the Negro's shoulders and stand aside as critical and rather pessimistic spectators; when in fact the burden belongs to the nation, and the hands of none of us are clean if we bend not our energies to righting these great wrongs.

It is not difficult to find the contemporary relevance in this classic dispute of black American political thought. To be sure, Washington's was a different time than our own; the quality of black citizenship is now dramatically improved, due largely to the efforts of advocates working in the tradition of the NAACP. Moreover, given the political and economic forces that combined to limit economic development throughout the South in the first half of this century (and ultimately encouraged massive migrations of blacks away from that region), one may doubt that Washington's strategy would have worked even if it had been assiduously followed.

Thus it cannot be said that history has proven Washington right and Du Bois wrong in their debate about what blacks should have done nearly a century ago. Yet given the way in which the history of black Americans has evolved, it can now be seen that the animating *spirit* of Booker T. Washington's philosophy offers a sounder guide to the future for blacks than that reflected in the worldview of his critics. The problem of second-class political status for blacks, which so exercised Du Bois and which he devoted much of his life to fighting against, has been resolved. But the problem of underdevelopment—the "brains, property, and character" problem that Washington spent a lifetime trying to address—remains very much with us. Full equality of social standing in

American society, the goal that blacks now seek, can never be attained until the fact of black underdevelopment is squarely faced and reversed. As Washington grasped intuitively, equality of this sort rests more on the performance of blacks in the economic and social sphere than it does on the continued expansion of legal rights.

In his highly esteemed comparative historical treatise *Slavery and Social Death* sociologist Orlando Patterson defines slavery as the "permanent, violent domination of natally alienated and generally dishonored persons."[1] One aspect of this definition that warrants emphasis is its focus on the systematic dishonoring of enslaved persons. Patterson rejects a property-in-people definition of slavery, arguing that hierarchical symbolic relations of respect and standing between masters and slaves are what really distinguish slavery from other systems of forced labor. He finds the parasitic phenomenon, in which masters derive honor from their power over slaves, while slaves suffer an extreme social marginality by virtue of having no existence in society except that which is mediated by their masters, to be a common feature of slavery wherever it has occurred. Patterson concludes that it is impossible to understand slavery without grasping the importance of the concept of honor.

This insight into the nature of slavery has the implication that emancipation—the legal termination of the masters' property claims—cannot by itself possibly be sufficient to make slaves (or their descendants) into genuinely equal citizens. The historically generated and culturally reinforced "lack of honor" of the freedmen must also be overcome. How is the former slave, who just yesterday was socially dead, without honor or the possibility of honor, to become a citizen—a coequal participant in the national enterprise? This is not a matter that formal legal resolutions alone can dispel. How are the deeply entrenched presumptions of inferiority, of intellectual and moral inadequacy, to be extinguished? How are the doubts of former masters and the self-doubts of former slaves to be transcended?

This problem of honor is a tenacious ideological remnant of our origins as a slave society. Securing the respect of whites and enhancing self-respect has been a central theme in black American history. Du Bois himself wrote eloquently of the "peculiar sensation . . . of measuring one's soul by the tape of a world that looks on in amused contempt and pity." Historian Nathan Huggins put the matter in illuminating terms when he noted that blacks, unlike the various American immigrant groups, are not an alien population in this society but an *alienated* one—an essentially indigenous people who by birthright are entitled to all the privileges and immunities of citizenship. The political history of black Americans may be instructively viewed in terms of the struggle to secure an acknowledgment of this birthright claim.

Thus Huggins argues that the frustrated claim of birthright "explains the power of the desegregation issue. [Though] few blacks would deny the possibility of superior black schools . . . to accept segregation . . . would be to deny a historic claim to being sharing partners in the commonwealth." It is no small irony that, decades after participating in its founding, Du Bois was driven from his editorship of the NAACP's journal and out of the organization in the 1930s when, having lost confidence in the quest for integration, he began to advocate the development of economic cooperatives among rural blacks as an alternative strategy.

Booker T. Washington would surely have supported the elder Du Bois in his emphasis on a proactive strategy of cooperation among black farmers in preference to a legal fight against segregation. He would also have appreciated the subtle implications entailed by Patterson's ideas about honor for the possibility of blacks achieving a true emancipation. Indeed, Washington argued that

> it is a mistake to assume that the Negro, who had been a slave for two hundred and fifty years, gained his freedom by the signing, on a certain date, of a certain paper by the President of the United States. It is a mistake to assume that one man can, in any true sense, give freedom to another. Freedom, in the larger and higher sense every man must gain for himself.[2]

Monroe Trotter's views to the contrary notwithstanding, this is neither a cowardly nor a race-traitorous sentiment. Quite the contrary, this is the candid exhortation of a leader who has understood a hard truth about the condition of his people: to be able to look their former masters squarely in the eye, they must first raise themselves from their current level. Nor is this the rhetoric of an apologist for the crimes of others. Rather, it is the unapologetic embrace of responsibility for one's own freedom. Consider that Washington lived out his entire life in the South, among the poor blacks of his time, building from nothing (and in the midst of white reactionaries) an institution that, a century later, still helps to meet the needs and expand the opportunities of his people.

The philosophy and example of Booker T. Washington speak with a profound relevance to the racial dilemmas of our time. Political philosopher Herbert Storing pointed toward this conclusion when, in the early 1960s, he made this defense of Washington's position:

> Yet when the harsh words have been said, when the blame is assigned, when many rights have been granted and are actually enjoyed, Washington's soft, tough words still speak. Opportunities are limited. How well have we used those that are open? Rights are still curtailed. Have we prepared to exercise those we have? The Negro is blamed for too much of American crime. Are we nevertheless responsible for too much of it? The Negro is less than completely free. Do we know what freedom is? The Negro is a second-class citizen. Are we fit for first-class citizenship? The Negro can find deficiencies, in these respects and countless others, in every phase of American life, but his own deficiencies are not one whit removed by pointing out those of others. The Negro can serve himself, as he can serve his country, only by learning and thereby teaching the lesson that Theodore Roosevelt said was "more essential than any other, for this country to learn, . . . that the enjoyment of rights should be made conditional upon the performance of duty."[3]

These are unpalatable words to the modern political ear, carefully attuned as it is to the possibility of giving offense. Still, without raising the question of the "fitness" of blacks for citizenship, it is fair to ask now about opportunities unexploited, about rights unexercised, about whether blacks are too much responsible for what ails our urban centers, and about duty and obligation. It is fair to inquire, with the many cries for "Freedom Now!" ringing out from angry protesters on behalf of racial justice across the land, whether they have a clear conception of what freedom in the larger and higher sense really is, of what being responsible participants in this democratic polity actually requires. It is necessary to question what it takes to stand truly equal among one's fellows; to explore the limits of a rights-oriented approach to the problem of racial inequality in our contemporary national life; to deal with issues of dignity, shame, personal responsibility, character and values, and deservingness.

It is time to recognize that further progress toward the attainment of equality for black Americans, correctly understood, depends most crucially at this juncture on the acknowledgment and rectification of the dysfunctional behaviors that plague black communities, and that so offend and threaten others. Recognize this, and much else will follow. It is more important to address this matter effectively than it is to agitate for additional rights. Indeed, success in such agitation has become contingent upon effective reform efforts mounted from within the black community.

The necessity of engaging such matters is clear from the tenor of contemporary national discussions, explicit and tacit, of racial issues. There is a tremendous cultural struggle ongoing in national politics, manifest in disputes over abortion, capital punishment, gun control, crime, welfare, affirmative action, gay rights, school prayer, and other kindred things, many of which have a subtle racial dimension. This cultural tension works to the political disadvantage of blacks. It is believed by many observers to exert a profound influence on presidential politics, to account for the disadvantage of liberal candidates in national elections (especially in the South and West and among white voters), and to be implicated in the reaction of ethnic working-class voters in the cities against racially progressive policies.

As Washington would have said, black Americans should not focus in the first instance on the passage of civil rights bills. Such bills may or may not be needed, but it is beyond doubt that their passage will not significantly alter the quality of life, or equality of standing, of those blacks whose condition bespeaks the fundamental and age-old crisis for the American polity, namely, the incompleteness of the process of incorporating many descendants of African slaves into the estate of full and equal American citizenship. (See chapter 7 for a more complete discussion of this point.)

The progress which must now be sought is that of achieving honor, respect, equal standing in the eyes of one's political peers, and worthiness as subjects of national concern.

Such progress, of course, requires public action as well as self-help. Medical care for the poor, education in the inner city, job training for welfare mothers, discipline for criminally offending youths, funding for housing, nutrition for infants, drug treatment for addicts seeking help—all of these things and more require the provision of public funds and are essential to black progress. But these things can only be achieved by persuading one's fellow citizens to tax themselves so as to provide the needed services. Success in that task of persuasion depends on how "deserving" the beneficiaries are perceived to be. This in turn depends on how they comport themselves. And such comportment is not a matter that public policy alone can or should address.

The point on which Booker T. Washington was clear, and his critics seemed not to be, is that progress such as this must be earned, not simply demanded. He understood that when the effect of past oppression is to leave a people diminished, the attainment of true equality with the former oppressor cannot depend overly much on his generosity; it must ultimately derive from an elevation of their selves above the state of diminishment. It is of no moment that historic wrongs may have caused current deprivation, for justice is not the issue here. The issues are honor, dignity, respect, and self-respect, all of which are preconditions for true equality between any peoples. The classic interplay between the aggrieved black and the guilty white, in which the former demands (and the latter conveys) a recognition of the historical injustice is, quite simply, not an exchange among equals. Neither, one suspects, is it a stable exchange. Eventually it may shade into something else, something less noble—into patronage, into a situation where the guilty one comes to have contempt for the claimant, and the claimant comes to feel shame and its natural accompaniment, rage, at his impotence.

Nevertheless, the basic thrust of today's civil rights advocacy looks to the "signing, on a certain date, of a certain paper by the President," or by a federal judge, to deliver freedom to blacks. In so doing, rights advocates avoid the necessary hard work of facilitating internal reforms for their people, reforms which would help to reverse the diminishing effect of past violations of rights. Instead, they seek to lay responsibility for the hard realities of contemporary ghetto life on the shoulders of whites, citing the fact that whites have not treated blacks as justice would require. They argue as Du Bois once did: "If they accuse Negro women of lewdness and Negro men of monstrous crime, what are they doing but advertising to the world the shameless lewdness of those Southern men who brought millions of mulattos into the world? . . . Suppose today Negroes do steal; who was it that for centuries made stealing a virtue by stealing their labor?"

But this argument concedes far too much black dignity for the sake of being able to demand white sympathy. Can we really expect whites to agree that black "lewdness" or criminality are no more than the consequences of white's depravity—that is, conditions for which whites, not blacks, are ultimately responsible? Do we really believe it ourselves?

———

Today's civil rights orthodoxy is to denounce as "racist" the revulsion of ordinary people at ways of life among blacks that offend and threaten them, as well as policies (such as quotas) that strike them as basically unfair. If whites express fear of crime in central cities, which is committed disproportionately by blacks, and if politicians exploit these fears, the problem is defined as the racist exploitation of baseless stereotypes. If whites reject racial preferences as unfair to them, and if politicians campaign on the issue, the problem is construed as a lack of restraint by unscrupulous candidates who are willing to use divisive tactics to achieve their ends. Today's orthodoxy holds in contempt the need to express concern for and acknowledge the legitimacy of the sensibilities of whites when they run up against the presumed interests of blacks. What Washington understood—something as true today as it is difficult to say out loud—is that *attending to the sensibilities of whites is directly in the interest of blacks*. Because we live in a democracy, we bear the burden of persuading our fellows of the worth of our claims upon them.

This practice of crying racism in the face of every form of opposition to, say, busing or affirmative action has brought on the current crisis in the politics of both blacks and white liberals. To take the expression of such policy preferences as evidence that whites subconsciously harbor unacceptable ethical values is a dangerous denial of political reality. Let us stipulate that the infamous Willie Horton ad from the 1988 presidential campaign should not have been run. What then do we say about the fact that it worked so well? Let us assume that the widely denounced "white hands" anti-quota ad used by Jesse Helms against his black opponent in the 1990 North Carolina senatorial race was inappropriate. What are we to make of the fact that it had such an impact?

The orthodox answer, as we know, is that these phenomena give further evidence of the fundamentally racist character of the American polity. Rights advocates hope to banish such tactics from the political arena through moral suasion. They set out to achieve unilateral conservative disarmament, as if conservatives' restraint in appealing to whites' concerns will somehow cause those concerns to disappear. This is the ambition of people who simply do not take American voters seriously. It is not useful to assume that all of the voters responding to Jesse Helms, Pat Buchanan, or even David Duke, are simply racists. No doubt some of them are, but that is besides the point. These voters have legitimate, vital concerns to which an effective politics must give answers, not lectures on racial etiquette.

Washington readily accepted the constraint that progress for blacks depended upon their being sensitive to the concerns of whites. Indeed, every black leader who has managed to wield any influence has had to work within such a constraint. Only in our time has the notion been advanced that "authentic" black leadership should be unencumbered by the need to assuage white opinion. Only in our time do we draw electoral district lines so that black representatives may be assured of election without the inconvenience of having to solicit white votes. Not that such redistricting is always wrong, but a fundamental trade-off is involved here. Majority black districts raise the likelihood of the black candidate's success while lowering the probability that the candidate's election will bring along white support for his or her program.

A central feature of the old civil rights activism was its aim to persuade. Martin Luther King, Jr., and his followers engaged in open protest on behalf of clear principles of social justice.* They clearly did not share Booker T. Washington's aversion to civil rights agitation. But they sought through nonviolent civil disobedience to compel the affirmation of common principles by their fellow citizens, relying on the humanity and decency of the vast majority of Americans, and thereby showing respect for the moral integrity of their fellows. They always appealed to *someone's* moral sensibilities—if not those of their immediate foes, then to those of white onlookers who tacitly accepted segregation, and also to blacks whose complicity had made the system easier to sustain.

Dr. King was a leader of both black and white Americans. His stature in each community depended upon his influence in the other. The dramatic public confrontations he and others in the movement engineered were viewed by multiple audiences— white and black—with each being aware that the others were watching. By the morally persuasive nature of his appeal, King mobilized the conscience of the white majority. In doing so, he also convinced many blacks that there was a realistic hope that their essential interests would at long last be accommodated. King thus confronted the most critical task any leader faces when seeking to promote racial harmony: assuring the "good people" on each side of the racial divide that their counterparts on the other side do in fact exist. He sought to create a dynamic within which growing numbers of Americans could embrace a strategy of reconciliation among decent people of both races.

It is a telling commentary on the moral confusion of today's orthodoxy that so many young blacks see in Malcolm X and Martin Luther King a legitimate polarity of philosophic alternatives. On the point that the interests of blacks, properly understood, are inescapably intertwined with the concerns and sensibilities of whites, Malcolm provides very poor guidance. But it is to the radicalism of Malcolm X that Afrocentrist, rejectionist rabble-rousers like Al Sharpton look for inspiration. And it is precisely because the civil rights establishment has lost sight of the need to take

---

*The analysis in this and the next several paragraphs draws heavily on my conversations with Harold A. Pollack.

whites' fears and revulsions seriously that they are willing and able to remain speechless in the wake of the excesses of Sharpton, Leonard Jeffries, Louis Farrakhan, and others.

What, for example, did we see in response to the Central Park jogger episode? Incredible public displays of contempt for white opinion, in defense of the indefensible and all with the tacit, if not explicit, support of much of mainstream black opinion. What did we see in Crown Heights? Murderously rampaging mobs of black youths, openly incited by Sharpton and others, who through this rampage gain status and prestige for themselves as brokers of the peace. Leaders like Sharpton are the natural consequence of the abandonment by more respectable black advocates of the cardinal principle that Washington understood so well. The message sent out is that blacks are openly contemptuous of white opinion, seeking not to persuade but to frighten. Although Sharpton leads marches through white neighborhoods as King did, the Italians and Jews of Brooklyn are mere supernumeraries in a political drama within the black community itself. Sharpton wants blacks to see whites at their most primitive and racist, and if he creates occasions for whites to see blacks at their most atavistic and violent, this suits his purposes as well. The apparently intended effect of such "leadership" is to ensure that the people of bad will in both races will find each other, the better to keep conflict alive.

The truth is that whites do not need to be shown how to fear black youths in the cities; instead, they must be taught how to respect them. This means that effective, persuasive black leadership must project to these whites the image of a disciplined, respectable black demeanor. That such comportment is not inconsistent with protest for redress of grievance is a great legacy of the civil rights movement. But it is not just disciplined protest that is required. Discipline, orderliness, and virtue in every aspect of life contribute to the goal of creating an aura of respectability and deservingness. Such an aura is a valuable political asset.

Because racial oppression tangibly diminishes its victims, both in their own eyes and in the eyes of others, the construction of new public identities and the simultaneous promotion of self-respect are crucial tasks facing those burdened with a history of oppression. Without this there can be no genuine recovery from past victimization. A leading civil rights advocate teaches the exhortation,

"I *am* somebody." True enough. But the crucial question is, so what? The answer is that because I am somebody, I will not accept unequal rights. Because I am somebody, I will waste no opportunity to better myself. Because I am somebody, I will respect my body by not polluting it with drugs or promiscuous sex. Because I am somebody—in my home, in my community, and in my nation— I will comport myself responsibly, I will be accountable, and I will be available to serve others as well as myself. It is the doing of these fine things, not the saying of any fine words, which teaches oneself and others that one *is* somebody.

————

But how is this to be done? One must operate at two levels, playing the "inside game" and the "outside game." The outside game aims to secure one rights by petitioning for redress of grievance. Booker T. Washington thought this could wait; he may have been tragically wrong, but we have since made up for his omission. Even so we must proceed carefully, wary not to move in violation of clear public norms. Nonviolence was the key factor in securing the ultimate success of the revolt against Jim Crow that eventually came to the south. Perhaps paradoxically, nonviolence was the more manly course, as well as the more publicly acceptable one. This is where Malcolm X and his followers in the urban centers of the 1990s have gotten it so badly wrong. Some black spokespersons seem not to appreciate the danger of using public threats of violence to "persuade" whites to be more responsive to their demands for expanded social programs and the like. To make such threats is to throw away what may be blacks' most powerful tool of persuasion—the compelling morality of our claims.

Immanuel Kant once wrote that enlightenment is "man's release from his self-incurred tutelage." Obviously blacks' tutelage has not been entirely self-incurred. Still, the link between liberation and enlightenment is just as real for us: the black nonviolent protester realizes his own freedom by accepting the constraints of universal moral laws, by maintaining civility under strong provocation even when others do not. For the discipline nonviolence demands provides irrefutable evidence of the humanity of the protester, despite the oppressor's best efforts to perpetuate the myth of racial inferiority. It establishes that the protester is somebody, in a way that violent protest never can.

The philosophy of self-help, of good old-fashioned "uplift," applies this principle to the inside game: the striving for moral reform within the black community. Working diligently to overcome the profound pathology to be found in some quarters of contemporary black life establishes what too often is only asserted—that blacks are indeed a great people struggling under terrible odds to overcome the effects of profound historic wrongs. The doing of such work is the means by which blacks can gain freedom in the larger and higher sense. As are free human agents, blacks are obligated to strive to reverse the debilitating patterns of social life that limit our progress, and they are rightly judged by the extent to which this responsibility is met. The liberal transaction, in which victimized blacks insist upon relief from guilt-ridden whites, too often points away from this necessity to be engaged in our own improvement. It leads to a perverse exhibitionism of nonachievement by blacks (for example, the remorseful recitation of statistics showing that more black men are in prisons than in colleges). It is as if the fact of our failure to meet a certain standard or surmount a certain obstacle must of necessity constitute evidence of a social or political failing by the larger society. Yet even (or perhaps especially) when whites accept this exchange, one cannot help suspecting that they do not really believe what they say, that for them black nonachievement has another, less respectable explanation.

The inside game is critical, because much of what needs doing cannot be done by outsiders. Only an overly simplistic socioeconomic determinism insists on finding the explanation for all manner of self-destructive and dysfunctional behavior now rampant in some black populations in the fact of our historical victimization or, on the other side of the aisle, in the incentive provisions of certain government transfer programs. How, then, could it be that other disadvantaged communities have a way of overcoming such assaults and temptations? It is to take the black poor less seriously than they deserve to assume that unless white people somewhere change what they are doing, poor blacks must live as many are now living.

It would be hard to overestimate the difficulty of the task, but one must nevertheless believe that the levels of gang violence, drug abuse, family instability, sexual promiscuity, sloth, indifference to responsibility, and so forth can be changed through concerted effort at the propagation of alternative values. In any case we must try, through religious, civic, and voluntary efforts of all sorts. It is not a matter to be seen exclusively along racial lines, but race is an important factor. Nor can the effort to overcome these problems be guided by a single program or strategy; literally a thousand points of light, "of salt and of light" as the Christians say, shall be needed.

Any internal effort to reform the ways in which people live is not a task for the state in our liberal society. Rather, it is one for what Peter Berger and Richard Neuhaus have called the "mediating institutions." Mutually concerned persons who trust one another enough to be able to exchange criticism constructively, establish codes of personal conduct, and enforce social sanctions against what they judge to be undesirable behavior can create and enforce communal norms that lie beyond the capacity of the state to promulgate effectively. The coercive resources of the state, though great, are not subtle, to put it mildly, and their application is rightly limited by constitutional protections of an individual's rights. But no one has a right to good standing among his fellows. We must strive through the inside game to create conditions in the communities of greatest concern where such status rewards may be denied those whose behavior violates reasonable norms of right conduct.

Finally, self-help is critical to securing the sympathetic support of the rest of the political community. It is essential to establishing in the minds of whites what is true, which is that the bulk of poor blacks are deserving of the help they so desperately need. Making the effort to help yourself clearly conveys this message. This is why the movement toward welfare reform that focuses on placing some onus of responsibility on recipients does not threaten blacks. On the contrary, such developments are a godsend, for they help to diffuse a potentially damaging stigma associated with the disproportionate dependency of blacks on state-funded transfers. Moreover, by according them the expectation that they are capable of meeting commonly held norms about how people should conduct their lives, welfare reform shows respect for the beneficiaries. Thus self-help is not a substitute for government provision but rather an essential complement to it, ensuring that the state-funded assistance is more effective, and that it is seen as legitimate by the political majorities that must approve of it.

This argument cannot be proven beyond a doubt. Besides being woefully politically incorrect, it is not based on scientific data. Some among the multiple audiences reading this book will object that it gives aid and comfort to the political right. They will question my motives for having presented it publicly, and they will doubt my commitment to the cause of racial progress. I know that a public man can, figuratively speaking, get himself lynched for such loose talk as this.

Nevertheless, it is crucially important to our nation that there be no more one-note politics from the African American community. America is a great nation. Together we form a great people, and our national ideals, to which blacks are every bit as much heir as anyone, are literally the envy of the world. The opportunities of this land, which continue to beckon to peoples the world over, are the birthright of black Americans. Yet too many blacks lag behind others in exploiting these opportunities. We blacks must empower ourselves to seize the resources at hand more aggressively, so that we can fulfill what I believe God has ordained for us to do.

Can it really be seriously maintained that no legitimate black spokesman may enunciate views such as these without fatally violating some norm of political loyalty? The sophisticated and well-advanced effort to defend a bankrupt civil rights orthodoxy by discrediting the expression of these views is sheer, self-destructive folly. Are blacks truly better off with this kind of thinking barred from American politics? Do the ideas of Booker T. Washington, as I have tried to elaborate them here, really have no place in the deliberations of the Supreme Court? Are such ideas, whether labeled conservative or not, obviously unauthentic or not genuinely "black"? Must we conclude that blacks espousing such ideas are a discredit to their race? That clearly was the message of the nearly successful campaign to destroy Clarence Thomas's aspirations for higher office. Some black politicians and intellectuals still seek to discredit him, to deny his voice the weight that it deserves to command among our people and in the national dialogue.

Should these defensive and essentially conservative reactions of the civil rights advocates prevail, it will not be only a few outspoken individuals, or even only the black American political community, who will be the losers. This is not about Clarence Thomas, or myself, or any other black critic of today's orthodoxy. What ultimately is at stake in our halting efforts to widen the national dialogue on racial matters is the determination of whether we Americans are going to fall apart, fighting with and picking at each other for the next two generations, or whether we are going to find some way to pull ourselves together and go forward into the twenty-first century as a strong, world-competitive, multiethnic nation. This is about whether we can develop and sustain sufficient ties across the many boundaries that separate us to enable us to cooperate in our mutual interest.

This is not a message to be directed to blacks alone, of course. Neither Democrats nor Republicans have distinguished themselves with national leadership on this issue. But because of the relationship between permissible expression in national discourse and the subnational discourse that takes place among blacks, a broadening of debate among the latter may encourage white politicians and intellectuals to speak with candor on this issue.

Advocates of a new public philosophy for black Americans, like Clarence Thomas, are drawing on an old wisdom that is well suited for our times. To advocate self-help; to argue that affirmative action cannot be a long-run solution to the racial inequality problem; to suggest that some of what is transpiring in black communities reflects a spiritual malaise; to note that fundamental change will require that individual lives be transformed in ways that governments are ill suited to do; to urge that we must look to how black men and women are relating to each other, how parents are bringing up their children, and what values inform the behavior of our youth—to do these things is not to take a partisan position or to vent some neoconservative ideological screed. Rather, to take this line of departure from the orthodoxy of the day is to speak what, for many blacks, is a truth inherited from our ancestors: a truth we know as a result of our awareness of our history coming out of slavery, and a truth reflected in the ambiguous but great legacy of Booker T. Washington.

5

The End of an Illusion

Black–Jewish Relations in the Nineties

Relations between American blacks and Jews are clearly in deep trouble. The controversy over anti-Semitic remarks in a speech given by Nation of Islam Minister Khalid Muhammad at Kean College in New Jersey in the fall of 1993 was only one of what seems to be an endless sequence of public spats. Bitter words and hurt feelings have been displayed all around. People of goodwill in both groups long for restoration of the kind of intergroup cooperation in pursuit of social justice so well exemplified by the civil rights movement. There are well-meaning blacks and Jews, particularly among political liberals who seek to quiet the angry voices. They encourage moderation and compromise. They hope to mend a tear in the fabric of progressive politics which, they think, if unmended will only benefit conservative forces that are the common enemy of black and Jewish political aspirations.

These black and Jewish moderates are laboring in vain. I predict that there will be no restoration of the golden age of black–Jewish cooperation—no return to a "special relationship" between the groups. During the civil rights movement the political objectives of blacks and Jews were very much in line. Each group sought to put the force of law behind the idea that no person should be denied an equal opportunity to participate in our public life because of race, sex, or religious belief. The struggle to achieve this objective was successful, and our nation is much the better for it.

Yet in the decades since the enactment of the great civil rights laws, the goals that blacks and Jews have sought to attain through political activity diverged. More importantly, the principled commitments—the ideals and beliefs that animate and inform public action by members of the groups—have also grown far apart. Ultimately it is this conflict of public visions between the black and Jewish political elites that lies behind the current difficulties. The conflict of visions, about the nature of American society and the role of its governing structures in promoting the welfare of its citizens, is now so severe as to preclude a restoration of the historic cooperative relationship between the groups.

I must emphasize that this conflict of which I speak is not among the extremists in the two groups, but rather among their respective mainstreams. It is too easy to attribute these problems to the excesses of a few thousand Black Muslim zealots or an even smaller number of angry members of the Jewish Defense League. Minister Louis Farrakhan is not the reason that black–Jewish relations are now so deeply troubled. He is merely an opportunist who promotes himself by exploiting the structural tensions that exist between the groups; he did not create these tensions.

These tensions arise from three sources: First, whether Jews recognize it or not, they have a great investment in the idea of America as a meritocratic, open society in which rewards are ultimately available to those who prepare and apply themselves. Blacks now have an equally great investment in the idea of America as a closed society in which "people of color," regardless of their individual merit, suffer systematic disadvantages in the competition for economic and social benefits. These distinct visions about the American social order are fundamentally and irreconcilably in conflict. The many well-intended words of black and Jewish moderates spoken over the last two decades have done little to mitigate the tension between these respective visions.

Second, both blacks and Jews see themselves as historical victims, and indeed both groups have been victimized. As a consequence of their historical experiences, blacks and Jews demand, both from other Americans and from each other, recognition of their past travails and sensitivity to their concerns that historic crimes not be repeated. Yet a conflict inevitably arises when each group demands the respect of the other for its status as victims. Such "comparative victimology"—as I call this destructive public contest to establish that "*our* suffering has been the greater"—can never be resolved to the satisfaction of both parties.

Third, blacks and Jews vie for and exercise power in American society. But they do so in different ways and with unequal effects. This is a source of much resentment within both groups. Jews are richer than blacks; they have advanced farther in the professions and in academia; they are better organized and on the whole quite successful when pressuring the government in protection of what they consider to be their vital collective interests, especially with regard to Israel. Blacks' impact on the public realm is rather different. They rely more heavily on bloc voting at the local level and are more dependent on political patronage and special dispensations associated with redress of their historic grievances. (For example, a good deal more was at stake for blacks than for Jews in the 1993 New York mayoral election. There was no widespread Jewish alarm at the defeat of Ed Koch by David Dinkins in 1989; Jewish influence wasn't much weakened. But because so much black influence is dependent on the exercise of political power, Dinkins's defeat in November 1993 by a white Republican symbolized for blacks a return to the hostility and, at best, indifference of the Koch years.) Moreover, some blacks exert a powerful impact on life in the urban centers of America. If Jews wield more power "in the suites," then these blacks exert more power "in the streets." Many whites, including Jews, are frightened of the young black men whose demeanor, style of self-presentation, and occasional violent behavior can dominate the urban milieu. In a perverse way, these blacks exercise and relish a kind of power that many Jews resent.

What is really at stake with affirmative action, and what causes blacks and Jews such stress in the public debates over the issue, is that arguments about quotas serve to highlight the weaknesses as well as the strengths of the black and Jewish positions in American society. Jews fought against quotas because the quotas impose a ceiling limiting Jewish achievement. Blacks cling to quotas because they sustain a floor supporting black achievement. The demand for preferential treatment by blacks is therefore a confession of weakness. When Jews resist that demand they are accused by blacks of insensitivity. When they acquiesce in that demand, from their own position of strength, they are accused by many blacks of condescension. There really is no entirely satisfactory Jewish response to blacks' demands on this issue, given the successes of Jews and the vulnerabilities of blacks.

Conversely, the ability of blacks to sustain support for quotas, in the face of general public displeasure with a policy so frequently in conflict with basic notions of fairness and race neutrality, underscores blacks' political strength in a way that makes many Jews uncomfortable. The idea that the unregulated competitive arena of American society is biased against blacks, who must therefore be guaranteed their share of rewards, conflicts with the idea held by many Jews that *they* will manage just fine in the competition as long as the state does not actively oppose them. When black political muscle is used to push through a policy of quotas or to foist on the public some aggressive multiculturalist vision, it serves to remind many Jews that the terms of their own existence in this society are not entirely secure.

The noted black scholar Cornel West has written that "visible Jewish resistance to affirmative action and government spending on social programs [are] assaults on black livelihood."[1] Yet West fails to see that, by denying the relationship between success in this society and the meritorious achievements of individuals (whether blacks, Jews, or others), he is engaged in what amounts to an assault on Jewish livelihood and security. As an identifiable and somewhat insular minority enjoying disproportionate economic success, Jews are critically dependent on the quintessential American ideological proposition that, given fair rules, unequal results reflect unequal talents and/or efforts. Otherwise the Jews' own relatively privileged position cannot be justified before hostile political majorities. History has proved the importance of this point with tragic consequences. Black claims for special treatment call this entire ideological edifice into question. Yet if those claims are not honored, then blacks' weak position in the social competition will be exposed. Either way, conflict is unavoidable.

Moreover, the arguments used to justify preferential treatment force blacks and Jews to confront publicly their very different understandings of the American experience. The primary rationale offered by blacks for racial preferences is a historical one: that blacks have been so wronged by American society in the past that justice now requires they receive special consideration. This is, at bottom, a reparations argument. It cannot be made without the question arising, Why do the wrongs of this particular group and not those of others deserve recompense? A mere recitation of the unique sufferings attendant on the slave experience does not make the question go away. Many millions of white Americans descend from forebears who suffered mistreatment at the hands of hostile majorities, both here and in their native lands. Yet they make no claim to the public acknowledgment and ratification of their past suffering, as do blacks through affirmative action. The reparations-based justification for special treatment of blacks in employment and education therefore confers special public status on the historic injustices that befell its beneficiaries and hence implicitly devalues the injustices endured by others.

The *public* character of this process is quite important. The issue of quotas arises constantly in electoral politics, in corporate boardrooms, and in university faculty meetings. The public consensus required for the broad use of such preferences leads, de facto, to the complicity of every American in a symbolic recognition of extraordinary societal guilt and culpability regarding the plight of blacks. Many whites, Asians, Hispanics, and Jews simply do not feel culpable, though. Many note that Asian Americans seem not to need special treatment, although they too were discriminated against in the past. Was the anti-Asian sentiment in the Western states, culminating in the Japanese internments during World War II, "worse" than the discrimination against blacks? Were the restrictions and the poverty faced by Irish immigrants to Northeastern cities a century ago "worse" than those confronting black migrants to those same cities some decades later?

The granddaddy of all such exercises asks whether the Holocaust was a more profound evil than chattel slavery. Such a question is unanswerable. We cannot assess degrees of suffering and extents of moral outrage by different peoples. There is no neutral vantage point from which to take up such a comparison. Yet many critics of racial preference can be heard to say, "Our suffering has been as great"; and many defenders of racial quotas for blacks have become "tired of hearing about the Holocaust." These are enormously sensitive matters, going to the heart of how each group defines its collective identity.

We must not underestimate what is at stake here. The status as America's preeminent victims is vital to the economic position of millions of blacks. And the sacred remembrance of the historical travails of the Jewish people is a fundamental element of the Jewish identity. It is therefore a measure of the diabolical intelligence of those behind Farrakhan's tract, *The Secret Relationship between Blacks and Jews*, that so much is made in that book of the purported "overrepresentation" of Jews among slave owners in the antebellum South. (Farrakhan claims that 75 percent of those owning slaves were Jewish; the true figure is closer to .3 percent.) What that outrageous and unsupported claim is really saying is this: "Jews have no special claim to moral sympathy with blacks as fellow sufferers of a racial outrage. Indeed, Jews were (are) primary perpetrators of the outrage against blacks." Coupled with the anti-Semite's ritual denial of the severity (or even the existence) of the Holocaust, this ploy aims to reserve the sacred ground of historical victimhood for blacks alone. This is problematic for many Jews.

We can see these problems most sharply on college campuses. Due in part to preferential admissions in higher education, large numbers of middle-class, well-educated, upwardly mobile, and racially conscious blacks have been thrust into highly competitive academic and professional environments in which Jews are well represented and have flourished for decades. In such head-to-head competition blacks often fare poorly. In many colleges and professional schools, black students on the whole perform well below the average of their classes and Jewish students perform well above the average. This generalization is not without exceptions, and certainly need not reflect any inherent differences in individuals' innate capacities, but it is nonetheless broadly true. Also, Jews are better represented among the alumni and the faculties of these schools. The asymmetries of power, status, and security inherent in this situation invite attitudes of condescension and contempt by some Jews and of resentment and envy by some blacks—a poisonous mix.

Khalid Muhammad, whose speech shocked so many with its vitriolic anti-Semitic and anti-white rhetoric, was no stranger to college campuses. Indeed, Farrakhan and his disciples are frequently
invited to speak on major college campuses up and down the East
Coast and across the nation. The tape of Muhammad's speech at
Kean College records the audience, which consisted primarily of
black students and faculty, laughing approvingly at some of his
more outrageous statements. That, to my mind, is the single most
chilling fact to come out of the whole affair. Later, when reporters
converged on the campus to interview students and faculty about
the event, many blacks were willing to defend Minister Muhammad's speech and their reaction to it. This, to put it mildly, bodes
ill for the future of black–Jewish cooperation.

What we see, when we look at this situation unflinchingly, is that
far from reflecting a mass anti-Semitic sentiment among poor
blacks in the urban core, Farrakhan and company are marketing
their hateful products to a select audience of relatively elite blacks,
the ones who come most frequently into contact with Jews and
find that they come up short in the competition for status and
resources in academe. Outside New York City there is very little
urban friction between blacks and Jews. It was not Jews but Koreans who were objects of attack in the Los Angeles riots. I doubt
that your typical poor or working-class black urban resident
spends much time reflecting on the "crimes of Jews against
blacks." I am less confident about your typical black sociology
major on a state university campus. The latter is the real audience
for those copies of *The Protocols of the Elders of Zion* that are
being sold at a nominal fee by Minister Farrakhan's organization.

We can also gain insight into the diminished possibilities for
black–Jewish reconciliation by examining the events that followed
Khalid Muhammad's speech. Jewish organizations publicized its
contents, demanding that "legitimate" black leaders denounce the
speech and the speaker. This reaction culminated in the demand
that Minister Farrakhan disassociate himself from his disciple's
comments. After much suspense and with some fanfare, Farrakhan
called a news conference in which he refused to repudiate the contents of Muhammad's remarks, but he expressed disapproval of the
manner in which this "truth" had been delivered. Meanwhile, after
some protest at being put on the spot and some equivocation, most

black members of Congress and leaders of major civil rights groups expressed dismay at the Black Muslim's anti-Semitism and distanced themselves from Farrakhan's organization.

There is something curious, indeed pathetic, about this whole charade. Farrakhan has not been marginalized by these ritual denunciations more or less grudgingly issued by black leaders. (For example, the NAACP did not exclude Farrakhan from a leadership conference on the problems of the inner cities.) Moreover, it is far from clear what satisfaction Jewish advocates could have hoped to achieve by appealing for public statements from people like Rev. Benjamin Chavis of the NAACP, Rev. Jesse Jackson, or Rev. Al Sharpton, who are not themselves exactly paragons of virtue. Minister Farrakhan has been around for a long time. His "Judaism is a gutter religion" statement is nearly a decade old. There should have been no need for black leaders to issue *new* denunciations of Farrakhan; they should have been able to cite old ones issued last month, last year, and last decade as proof of where they stood. But there were no such historical statements to cite.

Indeed, weeks before Farrakhan's disciple made his famous speech, Representative Kweisi Mfume, leader of the Congressional Black Caucus, along with the Reverend Jackson and the Reverend Chavis, Congresswoman Maxine Waters, and others, announced a cooperative undertaking with the Nation of Islam aimed at solving the problems of the inner-city black poor. These are the leaders who advocate group entitlements, not individual rights. These are the black leaders who, in the quarter century since the death of Martin Luther King, Jr., have managed to turn the civil rights movement from a moral crusade with universal appeal into a parody of its former self, mired in special pleading. These black leaders are the ones who convene "gang summits," where black "youths" who lead interstate criminal conspiracies that mainly prey upon their own people are gathered, purportedly to solve their community problems. These black leaders, whose denunciation of Farrakhan's disciple's speech was so prized by Jewish liberals, are the same people who rationalized the murderous rampage against Korean businessmen in Los Angeles two years ago as a form of political protest. They have not stood on principle in over twenty years; their denunciations are virtually meaningless.

It is an illusion to think that a "special relationship" between blacks and Jews can be built on such a foundation. It is a profound error, in my judgment, to infer from the fact that most blacks and most Jews still vote Democratic in presidential elections, that some special intimacy and cooperation between the groups can be achieved. The roots of the conflicting public visions held by elites within the two groups are too deep—deeper than any single personality or issue. The sensitivities and insecurities of the groups grate against each other in subtle and multiple ways. This situation will not soon dissipate; indeed, it will likely get worse before it gets better: Rumors circulate among blacks about Jewish doctors infecting blacks with the HIV virus. Jews talk of blacks conducting a pogrom against Jewish residents of a New York City neighborhood. The demagogues like Farrakhan, whose real aim is to gain greater influence among blacks at the expense of more conventional leaders, lie waiting to exploit every opportunity to exacerbate the conflict.

The one prospect of reconciliation that I can see is rooted in the common spiritual heritage of these two peoples. Many blacks, like many Jews, are deeply religious. Blacks practice a brand of Christianity that takes the Old Testament witness of God's chosen people quite seriously. What blacks and Jews share that is most relevant to healing the current breach is not membership in the Democratic party, but rather a knowledge of the prophet Isaiah, a respect for the builder Nehemiah, an appreciation of the poetry of David. But contemporary public discourse has little tolerance for explicitly religious dialogue. Our focus is on elections, policy debates, power plays. We bring lawsuits, call news conferences, mount publicity campaigns. Where blacks and Jews are praying together, to the same God if in different tongues, is where our rifts are closest to being healed. I find it quite interesting that a comparatively tiny number of Black Muslims, an explicitly religious cult, dominate public discussion of black–Jewish relations without being challenged on theological grounds by a mainstream black leadership drawn heavily from the Christian Church. I am reminded of the account, in Hillel Levine and Lawrence Harmon's book *The Death of an American Jewish Community*,[2] of the rapid transformation from predominantly Jewish to predominantly black of a series of neighborhoods in Boston during the late 1960s and early 1970s. It is not a pretty tale. (See the review in chapter 18 for more details.)

The bitterness, anger, and fear experienced by Boston's Jewish residents, who perceived their community to be under siege, are palpable. The tremendous sense of loss felt by Jews who, like Harmon, had grown up in these neighborhoods is clear. Yet as the transition was occurring, many decent people fought to maintain an integrated neighborhood. Of course, they failed. Today one drives south through the city along Blue Hill Avenue, once the busy center of a rich Jewish community life, to see not a thriving and prosperous black community, but instead one that is in a state of advanced decay. There is in the book a photograph of the former site of the Temple Mishkan Tefila, a beautiful structure overlooking Boston's Franklin Park Zoo. Built in the 1920s, this proud edifice exudes the confidence of a prosperous people who were putting down roots. By 1968, with its members fleeing to the suburbs, the site of the temple was moved to Newton, Massachusetts. After much public wrangling, and amid angry demands from local blacks, the structure was turned over to an African American arts group for the sum of one dollar. Today it stands boarded and unkempt, as it has for over a decade, overgrown with weeds, decaying like a ruin from some long-lost civilization. The fate of Temple Mishkan Tefila is a tragic metaphor of lost possibility.

The story of Boston's Dorchester, Roxbury, and Mattapan can be repeated for city after city all over the country. That blacks and Jews have shared the same urban space, if often at different periods of time, points to similarity in the social experiences of these two groups of Americans. That both have been outcasts, and that both have struggled against the injustice of that estate, also suggests the possibility of cooperation and empathy. Yet blacks and Jews have learned different lessons from their histories. They occupy very different positions, with quite distinct opportunities, within the contemporary American social order. Despite my deep regret at the matter, I cannot be optimistic about the prospects that a special relationship between blacks and Jews will ever be restored. Perhaps it is best to recognize this situation, rather than to incur the anguish and disappointment that inevitably accompanies attempts to sustain a marriage from which the love has long since departed.

6

Economic Discrimination

Getting to the Core of the Problem

One important measure of the health of an economy is the degree of inequality in its distribution of income. While there is no consensus among economists, philosophers, or politicians as to what constitutes an ideal distribution, there is broad agreement that too much inequality is unjust, inefficient (since the potential productivity of the disadvantaged is impaired by their lack of resources), and threatening to the political stability on which everyone's prosperity depends. Understanding the extent and causes of inequality is among the most important tasks of economic science.

The subject is one of great depth. Two centuries ago, classical political economists were observing the rise of industrial capitalism. The attendant conflicts among agrarian, industrial, and working-class interests led them to be concerned primarily with understanding how the aggregate social surplus comes to be divided among the factors of production—land, labor, and capital—that collaborate in its creation. Pursuit of this question by thinkers like Adam Smith, David Ricardo, and Karl Marx has inspired fundamental contributions to economic thought.

In our time, given the dramatic political and technological changes of the twentieth century, new questions have arisen. We have witnessed the breakup of colonial empires, the globalization of commercial and industrial activities, and recently a turn toward markets in formerly planned economies. In the wake of these events it has become more urgent to identify the factors that explain differences across nations in rates of economic growth and development, and differences across classes within a nation in the extent to which the benefits of growth are shared. This is currently a very active area of economic research.

Ethnic and racial inequality is one of the issues that have now become especially significant. Substantial social segmentation has developed within societies in eastern and western Europe, in Africa, in South and Southeast Asia, and in North America. Ethnic tension threatens political stability in many of these nations. Disparities of power and status between population subgroups challenge governments, which sometimes have enacted far-reaching policies intended to ameliorate these group inequalities. This likely will be an even more important issue in years to come. Formal economic theory has had too little to say about inequality of this sort; here I will discuss racial inequality in the United States.

———————

Because of the peculiarities of American history, racial inequality between blacks and whites has a particular significance. That history involved chattel slavery, and after that the adoption of a thorough-going caste system that for centuries kept blacks at the bottom of the nation's economic life. In 1944 the Swedish economist Gunnar Myrdal surveyed the status of blacks in his classic study *An American Dilemma*. It is sobering to reread that work today.

Myrdal graphically revealed in this study the material consequences of racial caste exclusion as they played themselves out in the lives of black Americans. Poverty was the state of the vast majority of black families; the primary occupations were farm laborer for men and domestic servant for women; malnourishment was commonplace; participation in the professions was very limited; and political influence was virtually nonexistent. Myrdal chronicles the widespread practice of racial discrimination in employment, education, housing, politics, the military, social intercourse, the provision of health care, public services and amenities, and other areas. He concluded that these conditions stood in stark contrast to the professed values and beliefs of most Americans, constituting a profound dilemma for the nation.

As we all know, things began to change in the decades following this dire review. The civil rights movement remade the moral, legal, and political landscape. The Great Society ushered in sweeping programs of social and economic activism. The federal courts revolutionized constitutional jurisprudence by reinterpreting the meaning of the Reconstruction amendments so as to move black Americans closer to an estate of genuinely equal citizenship. And among blacks there was an awakening of political and social action, as well as a change in long-standing notions of identity. There was a stirring of racial pride, of interest in Africa, of urgency for the attainment of freedom at home and abroad. Without doubt, blacks have made historically unprecedented progress toward social and economic equality in the years since World War II.

Assessing the precise extent of this progress, especially in economic terms, and ascribing the change to its alternative possible sources has become an academic industry. Social scientists have produced hundreds of books and thousands of articles on this subject. A committee on the status of black Americans was empaneled to review the evidence several years ago under the auspices of the prestigious National Academy of Sciences. Government reports, newspaper articles, and studies undertaken by various advocacy organizations continue to pour forth, pronouncing on the extent of progress (or, more often lately, the lack of it). I will not attempt a summary of this literature here. Suffice it to say that two things are true: there has been enormous improvement, and there remain enormous problems. On this, and probably on this alone, all fair-minded observers can agree.

I came of age during a period when the issues of race and inequality were quite literally of burning concern to the country. Cities were in flames as civil disturbances spread across the land. There was a great determination on the part of many whites and blacks to tackle our "dilemma." The Kerner Commission had issued its famous report declaring that we were becoming two nations, separate and unequal. Dr. King was preaching, teaching, and ultimately dying before our eyes. In my home and community there was a mixture of hope, rage, excitement, and fear—alternately a sense that new things were possible, and that nothing would ever really change. It was a confusing, stimulating time to be in college, deciding on my future and coming into my own intellectual consciousness.

I ultimately chose to study economics because I wanted to understand better the sources of disparity in material conditions between individuals and various groups of people, and because I hoped that I could contribute to the creation of a better world by gaining such understanding. This idealism was not the only reason, though. As a math major, and someone who loved doing abstract problem solving, I found in economics a field that allowed and even encouraged this mode of reasoning, yet also aimed to address issues of substance about society, politics, and public policy.

I discussed these motivations with my teacher and friend, Bob Solow, when I came to study at MIT in the early 1970s. There I learned that my motivation for coming into economics was not uncommon. He, and many others of his generation, had gravitated toward economics for similar reasons, spurred on by the Great Depression and seeking to find answers to the great problem of unemployment and the business cycle. Several Nobel Prizes later we still have not solved the unemployment problem, nor does it appear that we are about to solve the racial inequality problem. Nevertheless, economic science has made contributions to both areas of social concern. I certainly do not regret my decision.

When I began to study economics, because of the attention that was being focused then on urban problems and racial inequality, a number of the best minds in the field were working on something called "the economics of discrimination." The problem was defined as giving an account, with the use of conventional concepts from modern economics, of how there could be differences in remuneration for the labor of similarly productive workers depending on the workers' racial identities. This fact created a puzzle for economics because of the presumption that the operation of competitive markets would lead to any such differences being competed away by employers who sought to profit from disparity in the wages of equally productive workers. I became interested in this literature and wrote a dissertation contributing to the study of this problem. I remain interested in theoretical problems of this sort, but as time has gone by and as evidence has accumulated, I have become increasingly convinced that this kind of straightforward price discrimination has little to do with the racial inequality problem—that the core of the problem lies elsewhere. Let me explain briefly my reasons for this conclusion.

––––––––––

Put in very simple terms, conventional economic analysis explains racial earnings inequality by applying the concepts of supply and demand in the context of the labor market. Discrimination refers to differences in demand for black and white workers who offer essentially the same quality of labor. Supply difference between the groups may arise as the result of poorer quality and quantity of education and work experience for some workers. Most empirical analysis in effect decomposes group earnings differences into these two sources, attributing to the residual category of discrimination any inequality that cannot be accounted for by reference to measured differences in the supply of skills. Looking over time, these studies suggest (though not without some exceptions) that demand-side factors have declined significantly in importance relative to supply-side factors. Economic discrimination, while it still exists, seems less important in the 1990s than it was in the 1970s, and certainly far less so than in the 1950s, in accounting for the gap between black and white wage earners.

Some analysts attribute this trend to the influence of equal opportunity laws, as well as to the structural, demographic, and attitudinal changes that have been occurring in American society over the last half century. But there have been other trends that are much less encouraging. The unemployment problem among black workers is twice as great as it is among whites. This difference has remained stable, or worsened, since the 1960s. Moreover, the labor force participation rates of black men have declined much more rapidly than those of white men in the last quarter century. Thus in 1985, among men between 25 and 34 years old with a high school education, three in ten blacks were not working, as compared to one in seven whites. Nobody knows why these employment differences are so large and so persistent.

What is clear is that blacks are more sensitive to cyclical swings in the macroeconomy. The income difference between black and white households tends to grow during an economic downturn. Equal opportunity laws have had no effect here, and neither have they affected the growing gap between black and white men in labor force participation.

Another area of concern is the stability of families and the living conditions of children. More than 60 percent of black children did not live in households with both parents present in 1988, as compared with just over 20 percent of white children. These numbers for both races have approximately doubled since 1960, though the scale of the phenomenon is vastly greater among blacks. Indeed, in some central cities as many as one in ten black children are now living with neither parent. About two-thirds of the black children living in single-parent households are poor.

The institution of marriage has been in rapid decline among blacks for more than three decades now. Among black women aged 15 to 44 fewer than three in ten were married with a spouse present in 1988, and nearly 60 percent of black men in the same age range reported that they had never been married. Family life has changed dramatically among blacks since 1960. Of course this is true for the society as a whole, but the scope of these developments among blacks is much greater. The reasons for this are hotly disputed; nobody really knows why. But the implications for the poverty and impaired development of children are clearly substantial and negative. Also clear is the fact that market discrimination is largely irrelevant to this issue.

I note one further development—the growth of the so-called urban underclass. I use this term because everyone understands what I mean when I say it. I recognize that many believe it inappropriately stigmatizes a diverse population of people experiencing problems not of their own making; that is certainly not my intent. In any case, most experts agree that there has been an increase in the extent of extreme, concentrated poverty in the urban centers of the country since the early 1970s. Numerous journalistic accounts of the travails of the urban poor have appeared in recent years. These accounts, along with casual observation of what is going on around us, confirm that this problem is real, and that it is one disproportionately involving black Americans. Violent crime, drug trafficking and addiction, deeply troubled schools, tremendous problems of public health, severely limited opportunity for social mobility—all of these and more are symptoms of the crisis. The growing involvement of young black men with the criminal justice system, especially in large and medium-sized cities, is one indication of this problem. A survey in 1990 reported that more than a quarter of young black men aged 16 to 24 were either incarcerated, on parole, or free pending trial. In 1991 the president of the Detroit school board indicated that over 70 percent of the district's male high school students, the vast majority of whom are black, had some criminal justice involvement, often for major offenses.

If one wants to address the racial inequality problem of our time, one must take seriously the trends that I have been discussing here. While they do not involve discrimination as conventionally understood and conveniently analyzed by economic theorists, they nevertheless engage fundamentally our concerns about economic fairness and efficiency. Unabated continuation of these trends offers the prospect that millions of Americans will be unable to participate fully in our economy and society. It is imperative, as a matter of justice and of national economic competitiveness, that these matters be addressed.

Yet what should be done to reverse these trends is by no means apparent. It does seem clear, though, that in our public debates abut racial inequality we have been distracted from focusing on the core inequality problem of today by our historical and political memory of the problems of yesteryear. For forty years now, racial inequality has been conceived primarily as a matter of civil rights. Legal remedies have been sought, aimed at assuring that formal economic transactions will not take place in a way that disadvantages blacks. The emphasis on civil rights, desegregation, and affirmative action comes out of a concern about classical racial discrimination in employment, credit, housing, and education—the sort that Myrdal chronicled a half century ago. Yet what we confront today is in my view a very different animal, combining in the worst way the joint effects of racial and social class isolation of the very poor. Today's problem is not nearly so much a demand-side discrimination matter as it is a supply-side concern. It is not the result of a "no blacks need apply" mentality, or a "lower black pay for the same work" attitude. Rather, it is more a matter of kids being poorly educated and having little work experience, few work skills, damaging peer influences, unstable family lives, and so forth.

———

The problem is that in our public discourses about racial inequality we seem unable to fix attention on this problem, or to marshal a consensus on what to do about it. Instead, as recent history shows, we are distracted by symbolic struggles over policies that are now peripheral to the main concern. Nowhere is that distraction more clearly revealed than in the debate over affirmative action. Both sides in this debate, which has been raging for twenty years, have missed the core problem. Proponents regard the continuation of affirmative action as a litmus test of our nation's commitment to racial justice. Opponents see it as an unacceptable violation of the ideal of equality of opportunity, and the principle that government should treat its citizens in a color-blind fashion. Each of these views is mistaken.

Our political institutions encourage (sometimes irresponsible) exploitation of the issue, as white resentments and black aspirations are brought into direct conflict. (For example, it is likely that the black senatorial candidate Harvey Gantt lost his race in North Carolina in 1990 against Jesse Helms because of an ad exploiting the fact that he had profited handsomely from a business deal involving racial preferences.) There is an abiding belief in some quarters that any preferential policy is basically unfair. At the same time, many advocates of preferences talk as if a Supreme Court decision limiting a local government's ability to direct contracts to minority businesses will usher in a return to Jim Crow.

This opposition of values—either we show a commitment to right the wrong of racial inequality through the practice of affirmative action, or we adhere to the higher ideal of race neutrality in our public life—is mired in confusion. It is a false and misleading characterization of the problem. I maintain that affirmative action is by and large a poor tool for dealing with racial inequality problems, though it has a limited place. At the same time, given our history, race neutrality is not a compelling public ideal, though we might hope to evolve in this direction in years to come. Much of my own research and writing on the topic of affirmative action has aimed to clarify these apparently contradictory themes.

Let me first discuss the notion that race neutrality should be an ideal of public policy. It derives much of its force from the protracted battle waged in our courts to overturn the doctrine that "separate but equal" public facilities sufficed to meet the equal protection requirements of the Fourteenth Amendment. It is also related to a basic tenet of liberalism, which holds that all citizens should have equal standing as subjects of public concern. Indeed, the individualistic emphasis of liberal political theory leads one to question why there should ever be a particular concern for group inequality at all. Should it not be just as great a violation of our sense of justice that a given disparity of income among citizens exists, regardless of the ethnic identities of the people occupying various positions in the economic hierarchy? In other words, given that we are concerned to reduce economic inequality among individual citizens, why should we care about racial inequality in particular? Such a concern raises a subtle logical problem: to focus on group differences in the presence of continuing overall inequality is, in effect, to demand equality *between* groups of a fixed degree of inequality *within* groups. But why should within-group inequality be less of a problem than between-group inequality? In fact, whenever there is inequality among individuals there is inequality between groups, if one takes those at the bottom to constitute a group. Thus a concern for group inequality presupposes an account of which groups are the salient ones.

Such an account cannot be based simply on economics—it must engage social and historical issues as well. My argument for the importance of racial inequality as an independent public concern is based upon a combined recognition of historical conditions, and of certain structural features of social life in our country. The historical point is that due to slavery and racial caste, there has come into existence a distinct, insular subgroup of our society that began with severe disadvantages (in comparison to others) in the endowments of wealth, experience, and reputation so crucial to economic success. The social structural point is that for as long as one can foresee, and without regard to legal prohibitions against discrimination in formal contract, we may confidently predict the practice of informal social discrimination—that is, discrimination in choice of social affiliation, which occurs partly along these racial group lines. This practice of discrimination in the social sphere implies continuing inequality of opportunity in the economic sphere.

Because this racial inequality is the product of an unjust history, propagated across the generations in part by the segmented social structure of our race-conscious society, it is appropriate that our government should be especially concerned when economic disparity takes a concentrated racial form. Put differently, to view the income distribution without regard to the racial identity of persons occupying particular positions in it is to ignore information critical to assessing the extent of the inequality problem, especially when viewed in an intergenerational context. The reason is that the full economic opportunity of any individual does not just depend on his own income; it is also determined by the incomes of those with whom he is socially affiliated. The patterns of such social affiliation in our society are not arbitrary but derive in part from ethnic and social class identity.

These affiliational behaviors are to be found everywhere in social life. As noted earlier, people make choices about whom to befriend, whom to marry, where to live, with whom to enter into joint business ventures and professional associations, to which schools to send their children, and often (to the extent they can exert influence on this decision) who the prospective mates of their children will be. Factors of race, ethnicity, social class, and religion enter into the making of these discriminating judgments. One of the challenges facing economic analysis is to make use of the fact that societies are not simply amalgamations of individuals pursuing exogenously given goals, nor are they simply the coalitions of agents that form strategically in order to advance their individual interests. Rather, all societies, and therefore all economies, exhibit significant social segmentation. Various groups of individuals and

families are tied together in various ways as a result of their historically derived commonalities of language, ethnicity, religion, culture, class, geography, and the like. *These networks of social
affiliation among families and individuals, while most often not the
consequence of calculated economic decisions, nevertheless exert a
profound influence upon resource allocation, especially those
resources important to the development of the productive capacities
of human beings.*

Think of the development of a skilled adult worker in analogy
with a production process where the output, a skilled worker, is
produced by inputs of education, parenting skills, acculturation,
nutrition, and so on. Some of these inputs are readily acquired
through markets to which all agents at least have access (though
they may lack the requisite financial resources). But many of the
relevant inputs cannot be obtained via such formal economic transactions at all. Instead, they become available to the developing
person only as the byproduct of noneconomic activities. Parenting
services, for example, are not available for purchase on the market
by a developing person but accrue as the consequence of the social
relations between mother and father. So the allocation of parenting
service among the prospective workers in any generation is the
indirect consequence of the social activities of members of the preceding generation.

I recognize that this is an odd way to think about human development, but it is very natural and useful for an economist. Thinking in this way underscores the critical roles played by inalienable,
nonmarketed social and cultural resources in the process of human
development, and therefore in the creation of economic inequality.
The relevance of such factors is beyond doubt. *Whom* you know
affects *what* you come to know and what you can *do* with what you
know. The evidence for this maxim is incontrovertible; the importance of networks, contacts, social background, family connections,
and informal associations of all kinds has been amply documented
by students of social stratification.

Through such network ties flow important information about
economic opportunities. They form the basis for nepotism, which
in large ways and small plays a role advancing for some and hin-
dering for others the attainment of economic success. The status of

sons varies systematically with the occupation and education of fathers; the peer associations of youngsters have been shown to affect subsequent success in school and at work. Attitudes, values, and beliefs of central import for the development of economically relevant skills are shaped by the cultural milieu in which a person develops. Parents' time and effort, a family's traditions and reputation, ethnic identity and loyalty, adolescent peer groups and friendship networks, and religious affiliations all influence the process of individual growth and help determine what becomes of a person's God-given talents. The scholarship of a great many economists and sociologists working on the problem of social mobility provide ample verification that one's position in the network of social affiliation has a substantial impact on one's lifetime economic prospects.

Now consider all of these processes, associated with naturally occurring social relationships among persons, that promote the acquisition of skills and traits valued in the marketplace. They constitute an economic resource that I have called *social capital*, an asset that may be as significant as financial bequests in accounting for the maintenance of inequality in our society, especially inequality between ethnic groups. Beginning with my 1976 doctoral dissertation at MIT, I have tried to address the question of whether race neutrality can be defended as a reasonable ideal of social justice in a world where social capital is unequally distributed between blacks and whites because of past racial discrimination. While I cannot go into the technical details of this work, let me summarize briefly the thrust of it.

A principle of public action can hardly claim general validity if, by adhering to it, it becomes impossible to correct the consequences of its violation. Such a principle would be inconsistent in an essential way, for then a transitory departure from the principle would have permanent deleterious effects. I have shown that the principle of race neutrality is generally inconsistent in just this way. Historical departure from equal opportunity in economic transactions, together with ongoing social segmentation along racial lines, generally means that in the absence of further departures from race neutrality, the implications of the initial violation will be permanent inequality between racial groups.

Because the creation of a skilled work force is a social process, the meritocratic ideal—that in a free society individuals should be allowed to rise to the level justified by their competence—is in conflict with the simple observation that no one travels that road alone. Moreover, in a socially segmented society, those with whom one travels are most probably drawn from one's own ethnic or racial group. Thus, even if transfers of monetary wealth within families were severely limited (through inheritance and gift taxation, for example), and if nondiscrimination in formal economic transactions were assured (through the extensive enforcement of civil rights laws), it would still be true that the economic achievements of an individual only partly reflects his or her individual capabilities. Because generations overlap, because much of social life lies outside the reach of public intervention and regulation, and because prevailing social affiliations influence the development of the intellectual and personal skills of the young, the present pattern of inequality among individuals and ethnic groups will shape the extent of inequality existing in the future.

Inequality in the endowments of social capital in their communities of origin generally implies inequality in the outcomes that otherwise equally competent persons can achieve. Therefore, absent a radical and draconian intervention in the private lives of individuals to neutralize the effects of unequal endowments of social capital, absolute equality of opportunity (where an individual's life chances depend only on his or her innate abilities) cannot be achieved. But it is also true that if government restricts itself to race-neutral action in the face of a racially discriminatory history, then the current members of the disadvantaged racial group may face significantly less auspicious prospects than those whose social capital resources have not been diminished by the unfair treatment of previous generations.

It should be emphasized that social segregation in residential communities, religious affiliations, friendship networks, fraternal organizations, marital relations, and the host of other important associations to which people are attracted has implications not just for the extent of inequality but also for the *efficiency* with which resources are allocated. There is a strong presumption that the outcome will generally not be efficient and can be improved upon by government intervention. Membership in the various networks that form the structure of our social life is not allocated according to market principles. The fact that the benefits to a given individual joining a certain group may exceed the costs does not assure that the inclusion will take place, since there may be no mechanism for expressing the "willingness to pay" or for carrying out the requisite monetary transfers. For example, a very able child born to very poor parents might benefit greatly from the social capital associated with living in a middle-class community and receiving the parenting resources of a better-educated, wealthier couple. Yet there is no way that this child, or the child's parents, could command these resources by promising to compensate those providing them with the gains (in terms of the child's increased future income) that the provision of those resources would make possible. Similarly, an adolescent with interest and aptitude in academic matters, but with peers who have disdain for intellectual pursuits, may not be able to gain access at any price to association with another group of peers whose values would be more complementary with his interests and aptitudes.

As these examples show, efforts to exchange the benefits of social endowments among individuals run into conflict with principles of personal liberty and freedom of association. The asset of being well connected is not readily alienable; only with great difficulty and violence to liberal values can one redistribute these social contacts that contribute to the maintenance of economic inequality. Most democratic societies have constructed a sphere of personal autonomy that leaves considerable scope for the exercise of prejudices and discriminations in the choice of intimate associates, even though these choices have the consequence of creating unequal opportunities for individuals to develop their natural talents.

Of course, a variety of means have been attempted to break down barriers to social participation, integration of education and housing primary among them. But these efforts, by their quite limited success, only underscore how deeply ingrained the practice of discrimination in social affiliation is. For this reason I have come to believe that government intervention aimed specifically at counteracting the effects of historical disadvantage, and taking as given existing patterns of affiliation, will be required. This may mean, for example, less of an emphasis on desegregation, and more stress on targeted efforts to improve the schools, neighborhoods, and families where poor black children are concentrated. Dealing with our current problem of racial inequality may require preferentially greater expenditures (not merely equalization of spending) by public institutions that serve large numbers of poor black people. The general point is that such color-conscious disbursement of public funds should be permitted, where deemed prudent, because we cannot expect laissez-faire policies to produce equality of opportunity between social groups when these groups have experienced differential treatment in the past, and when among the channels through which parents pass on status to their children are included social networks that form partly along group and class-exclusive lines. To do anything about this, the government may well need to take racial group identities into account when formulating its policy.

On the basis of this reasoning I conclude that racial inequality should constitute an independent concern, over and above any concern about inequality in general. Similarly I conclude that the race-neutrality ideal, while worthy in principle, ought not preclude targeted public action intended to reverse specific effects of past racial discrimination in our society. To be blind to color, given our history and our social structure, may well mean that one must be blind to justice as well.

Having made this argument, I might be expected to conclude that affirmative action is the logical remedy for the problem of racial inequality. But I do not reach this conclusion. It is important to distinguish between a concern with racial disparity and an endorsement of racially preferential hiring and admissions policies as the remedy for it. Such preferences have a rather limited role to play in rectifying the problem. I am convinced that direct and large-scale intervention aimed at breaking the cycle of deprivation and the limited development of human potential among the black poor is the only serious method of addressing the racial inequality problem in the long run. And while such intervention definitely constitutes a departure from a color-blind stance, it is not what people usually mean when they call for "affirmative action."

Ironically, our obsession with employment and admissions preferences makes it more difficult to focus on this goal of targeted intervention to help genuinely disadvantaged blacks, and more difficult to marshal the political consensus needed to pursue it. I mentioned the 1990 U.S. Senate race in North Carolina earlier. Most observers at the time castigated Jesse Helms for running an ad that played on white resentment of racial quotas. But if Gantt had not enriched himself by using a program of racial preference, Helms would have had a harder time raising the issue. Then, quite possibly, Gantt would have won that race and become a presence in the Senate working for the enactment of programs to aid the poor black people of our society.

It is hard to see how advocates of racial equality could argue that this trade-off was worthwhile. Yet many seem to argue in just this way. They denounce as racist the political use of white resentment, in effect calling for unilateral Republican disarmament— not a likely occurrence. The view seems to be that blacks of considerable means have a right to benefit from special government consideration, even at the political expense of the black poor, because of the generalized indebtedness that American society incurred as a result of slavery. This is naive in the extreme. Whites have a right to belong to racially exclusive golf clubs, too, but most people running for high office recognize the lack of wisdom in that course.

Certain features of our public discourse over the legitimacy of racial preferences are quite disturbing. The entitlement-oriented rhetoric used to defend the policy (for example, if the Supreme Court finds contrary to affirmative action, it has "turned back the clock") refuses to acknowledge the legitimacy of the competing white interests, and it basically abandons the effort to persuade whites that what is undertaken on behalf of blacks is reasonable and just. Some social psychology literature even purports to measure latent racism by reference to the extent that whites who have affirmed a commitment to principles of nondiscrimination nevertheless continue to oppose busing, quotas, and the like.

Because we live in a democracy, those of us who want badly to deal with the racial inequality problem bear the responsibility to persuade our fellow citizens of the worth of our claims. But how can we hope to solicit the engagement and concern of whites for this problem while calling them racist for taking what are, after all, not unreasonable positions? Moreover, how do we expect to deal with the problem if much of our political influence is expended on a policy that primarily benefits blacks who are fairly well off, while missing the vast numbers of the very poor?

Let me be clear that I am not dismissing affirmative action as such, merely arguing that its role in remedying the racial inequality problem of our time is limited. It certainly does have a place. Efforts to open previously foreclosed opportunities to women and minorities through advertising, outreach, special training programs, and like efforts have become institutionalized in employment and higher education and should be continued. These efforts have been valuable and necessary for overcoming some of the effects of social segmentation discussed earlier. They have led institutions to look in nontraditional places and ways for prospective candidates; as a result, awareness of recruiting practices that inadvertently excluded women and minorities has increased. Affirmative action should be truly affirmative, lifting blacks up to standards rather than pulling standards down to meet them.

Yet as an empirical matter, the contribution of affirmative action to the reduction of racial inequality appears to be quite modest. Though the existence of profound racial disparities, higher poverty and unemployment rates, greater welfare dependency, inner-city problems, and the like provides a primary justification for its use, the evidence suggests that preferences have played a marginal role in alleviating these problems. A study of the impact of minority participation quotas undertaken for the U.S. Department of Transportation in the 1980s found negligible trickle-down employment benefits to black workers. Analyses of the impact of federal contractor regulations show employment effects too small to influence meaningfully the racial difference in unemployment rates. Moreover, these effects cannot be interpreted as net increases in the demand for minority labor, since some reshuffling between covered and uncovered sectors seems likely.

More broadly, looking over the long run at black economic progress since 1940, the consensus view is that much of the gain occurred prior to the onset of affirmative action in the 1970s. Improvements in the quantity and quality of black education, and a decline of overt discrimination and occupational exclusion, seem to be more important than affirmative action in explaining this progress. Moreover, the data show that narrowing of the black–white earnings gap has been relatively greater for blacks with more education and those working in the more prestigious occupations.

The reason for this is straightforward: affirmative action cannot get at the deep effects of past discrimination, namely, poor skills, disrupted family life, communities in decline (in part because of opportunities for mobility for better-off blacks, which desegregation has provided), and the poor quality of inner-city public education. That is, *racial hiring preferences are a poorly targeted method of intervention for the task of reducing racial inequality*, since their benefits are appropriable most readily by those who are least disadvantaged. It is one thing to say that the past demands redress, but another to prescribe employment preferences useful mainly to those persons not suffering the worst consequences of that past.

The goal of securing greater representation of all groups among those wielding power and influence in the society is often advanced as a justification for affirmative action. Here I think there is merit to the argument, but there are also pitfalls and dangers. Most people agree that it is a good thing to have a black American sitting on the Supreme Court, though they may disagree about the judicial philosophy they would like to see espoused by this justice. At the same time, most of us would recognize the danger of having it be widely presumed that an appointment of this sort is made primarily because of race. It seems more acceptable that race be one of many factors used in making the decision, and that other criteria can be cited to show that the individual appointed is distinguished by something more than just his or her color. In general, the exercise of influence by someone in an appointed position may require that their elevation not be perceived as too closely dependent upon their race.

Reliance on preferences to achieve minority representation in highly prestigious positions risks damaging the esteem of the group by encouraging the general presumption that the beneficiaries would not be able to qualify for such positions without the help of affirmative action. Using race as a criterion of selection by the employer creates objective incentives for customers, coworkers, and others to take race into account *after* the employment decision has been made. Selection by race thus encourages further race-conscious thinking. This is a classic example of what an economist might call a "reputational externality."

One of the fundamental characteristics of racial difference is that it provides a salient, easily identifiable physical basis for social perception and statistical discrimination. The classic example is the cab driver who avoids young black men at night out of a fear of crime. Sociologist Elijah Anderson has documented the subtlety and depth of the human tendency to see individuals whom one does not know personally through the filtering lens of racial stereotype. Anderson has spent years observing closely the social life of an urban, integrated community, paying particular attention to how blacks and whites relate to each other in public places. While I cannot review his work in detail, one of his primary conclusions is that stereotypic racial generalizations play an important role in determining the nature of race relations in contemporary American life.

The use of preferences encourages this process of racial generalization, and it does so in a manner likely to generate negative reputational externalities. It is not uncommon to hear from black college students the complaint that some whites presume them to be less competent, since they were admitted according to lower standards. This is grossly unfair and very unpleasant for these students, but it is an obvious consequence of the informational conditions created by preferential policies. One wants to say that all people should be seen as individuals; but the social fact is that in the late twentieth-century United States, we are most often seen first in terms of our racial identities. Only later is it possible for us to know each other as individual persons. The key point here is that the development of relations between persons will be influenced in important ways by initial interactions in which racial generalization is critical.

These observations are intended to point out an aspect of the use of affirmative action that is insufficiently studied and discussed. I do not maintain that racial stereotyping would disappear if preferences were abolished. Nor do I hold that the reputational-externalities effect identified here is always of such significance as to make the use of preferences unwise, but I do suggest that it will sometimes be so. If, for example, a scientific or literary prize is awarded with the idea in mind that each race should be represented proportionately, it could come to be suspected that a black winner of the prize had not really achieved the same degree of distinction as a white. This suspicion would have some rational basis, assuming that previous underrepresentation had not been due to a refusal to credit black achievement. If law review appointments are made to ensure appropriate group balance, as is now the case at many law schools, it could become impossible for students belonging to preferred groups to earn the same degree of honor and esteem available to others, no matter how great their individual talents. External observers will inevitably discount the black student's achievement to some degree because of the possibility that it was influenced by considerations of race and not solely determined by objective performance. That is, the use of racial preferences can change the social meaning of black achievement by altering the inference that an external observer could logically make on the basis of observing it.

Sociologist Charles Moskos illustrates this point in his interviews with black officers in the U.S. Army. He has surveyed the attitudes of soldiers at various levels of the command structure in the wake of the liberalization that has occurred in the armed forces over the past generation. In the 1990s nearly 7 percent of all army generals are black, as is nearly 10 percent of the officer corps. Early in the decade the highest-ranking military officer was Chairman of the Joint Chiefs of Staff Colin Powell, a black. Moskos reports that among the black officers he interviewed, the view was widely held that blacks in the army "still have to be better qualified than whites in order to advance." One senior black officer was "worried about some of the younger guys. They don't understand that a black still has to do more than a white to get promoted. If they think equal effort will get equal reward, they've got a big surprise coming."

Yet despite this awareness that discrimination exists in the army, these officers were dubious about the value of racial preference in the military, for reasons similar to those discussed above. Black commanders were found to be tougher in their fitness evaluations of black subordinates than were white commanders. Even those officers who thought affirmative action necessary in civilian life disapproved of its use in the military. An officer's ability to lead his subordinates effectively, and thus to advance his career, depends critically upon his ability to command their respect, which he cannot do if encumbered with the suspicion that his rise was due to the benefits of preferential treatment. According to Moskos, "They draw manifest self-esteem from the fact that they themselves have not been beneficiaries of such preferential treatment, rather the reverse. Black officers distrust black leaders in civilian life who would seek advancement through racial politics or as supplicants of benevolent whites."[1]

Another problem with preferential treatment, which I have been studying with the aid of formal economic modeling techniques,* is that it can encourage the patronization of black workers or students by those who make hiring and admissions decisions. By "patronization" I mean something quite specific: behavior that does not hold blacks to the same standard of expected accomplishment as whites, because of the belief that blacks are not as capable. What interests me is the possibility that such behavior can become a self-fulfilling prophecy. Observed performance of blacks may be lower in a certain situation precisely because they are being patronized, while the patronization is undertaken because the employer or admissions officer sees the performance difference

---

*An example of this form of analysis is provided as an appendix to this chapter.

but, due to the need to meet affirmative action guidelines, decides to overlook it.

Before giving some examples of this potential problem, I want to emphasize that *this discussion is theoretical*. I cannot be sure of the practical significance of the issues being raised here, but I think it is important to consider them in principle. It is my hope that arguments such as this will inspire a closer empirical assessment of the consequences of affirmative action than has been undertaken to date.

Consider an employment situation in which a supervisor must decide on the promotion of a subordinate worker. The supervisor wants to adhere to the company's policy of affirmative action, and so he is keen to promote blacks where possible. He monitors his subordinates and makes his recommendations on the basis of these observations. The pressure to promote blacks may lead him to overlook or de-emphasize certain deficiencies in the performance of black subordinates, recommending them for promotion when he would not have done so for whites. But this behavior on his part changes the incentives that the blacks have for identifying and correcting their deficiencies. They are denied honest feedback from their supervisor on their performance, and they are encouraged to think that they can get ahead without attaining the same degree of proficiency as whites. (A similar situation would occur if a white supervisor withheld criticism or sanction for the inappropriate conduct of a black subordinate out of concern that such an intervention would be taken as evidence of racism.)

Alternatively, consider a population of students who are applying to some professional schools for admission. The schools, due to affirmative action concerns, are eager to admit a certain percentage of blacks. They believe that in order to do so, they must accept black applicants whose grades and test scores are not as good as some whites whom they reject. Since most schools have this policy, the message sent out to black students is that the degree of performance necessary to attain admission is lower than that which white students must attain. To the extent that the students are responsive to these incentive differences, one would expect to observe a difference between black and white students in the actual level of grades and test scores obtained. In this way, the schools' belief that different admissions standards are necessary becomes self-fulfilling.

The common theme in these two situations is that the desire to see greater black representation is pursued by using different criteria in the selection of black and white candidates. The use of different criteria, in turn, feeds back to undermine the incentives for blacks to develop needed skills. This, of course, does not presume that blacks are innately less capable, merely that an individual's need to make use of a given ability is undermined when that individual is patronized by the employer or the admissions committee.

This problem could be avoided if, instead of using different criteria of selection, the employers and schools in question had determined to meet their needed level of black participation through a concerted effort to enhance performance while maintaining common standards of evaluation. Note that such a targeted effort at performance enhancement among black employees or students is definitely not color-blind behavior. It presumes a direct concern about racial inequality, and it involves allocating benefits to people on the basis of race. What distinguishes it from numerical quotas or targets, though, is that it takes seriously the fact of differential performance and seeks to reverse it directly, rather than trying to hide from that fact by setting a different threshold of expectation for the performance of blacks.

———————

I can briefly summarize my arguments in this chapter as follows. Inequality is a critical question for economic science. Our discipline offers some useful modes of analysis for exploring this problem. Group inequality, especially racial inequality in the United States, has not been adequately represented as an object of study in economic theory. To address this subject properly, we economists must modify our models to take account of the basic fact of social segmentation along ethnic and racial lines. This fact has profound implications for how as economists we approach the issue of the allocation of resources to human development in society, and thus for how we analyze the determination and propagation of group disparities.

Classic analysis of the discrimination problem in economics

looks only at market transactions, and so misses the larger issue of informal discrimination in social affiliation. Yet given our history and the nature of American society, it is arguable that this social discrimination is by far the more significant phenomenon as far as understanding contemporary racial inequality is concerned. Taking account of disparities in social capital causes one to place more emphasis on remedial government policies aimed at building capacity among the communities of disadvantaged persons than on those intended to ensure their fair treatment in formal market transactions. The latter are necessary and important, of course, but they are not generally sufficient to overcome the consequences of a history of oppression.

Special efforts, tailored where necessary to channel benefits to persons belonging to a group that has been discriminated against in the past, are required if the core of the group inequality problem is to be addressed. It is generally not desirable that public actions be constrained to satisfy an ideal of race neutrality, or color blindness, when seeking to deal with this problem. But it is important to be clear about which specific departures from race neutrality are likely to be most productive. Unfortunately, in contemporary American policy debate, affirmative action has become the primary race-conscious policy instrument. It is controversial, of limited power, and attended by deleterious side effects. Therefore affirmative action should probably not be as widely used as it is, and it should certainly not be the principal instrument through which a reduction in racial inequality is to be effected.

I stress that my point here is not to question the legitimacy of affirmative action, but rather its efficacy. Using simple ideas from information economics, I have tried to illustrate how preferential treatment can have counterproductive effects by producing negative reputational externalities, and by encouraging the patronization of its beneficiaries. I have argued that in employment or educational settings where the performance of blacks is less than would be desired, it is generally better to respond with interventions that direct attention to improving black performance, rather than with preferential programs that in effect establish a lower standard for judging black performance.

APPENDIX

The Effect of Affirmative Action on the Incentive to Acquire Skills: Some Negative Unintended Consequences

I have a dream that my four little children will one day
live in a nation where they will not be judged by the color
of their skin, but by the content of their character.
        —Martin Luther King, Jr.
        Washington, D.C., August 1963

Introduction

One often encounters the following argument against affirmative action: Ultimately racial justice requires that people behave toward each other in their economic dealings without regard to skin color—that they obey the "color-blind" ideal so eloquently expounded by Martin Luther King, Jr. Affirmative action, by encouraging the use of color as a basis for allocating positions, directly violates this color-blind ideal and is thus inconsistent with the attainment of racial justice in the long run. How can we hope to achieve a discrimination-free society while engaging, through public policy, in racial discrimination?

Proponents of affirmative action dismiss this concern as naive and ahistorical, arguing as follows: To remedy the effects of past discrimination one must direct benefits to those who, because of color, have had their opportunities reduced. Moreover, the ongoing use of color by employers in ways deleterious to minorities requires offsetting by color-conscious government action to ensure equal opportunity today, regardless of the effects of past discrimination. Granted that affirmative action represents a departure from the color-blind ideal, this is a necessary, temporary concession to the realities of race in our society which will be abandoned in the future, once opportunities have become truly equal.

This appendix first appeared in *The Annals of the American Academy of Political and Social Science*, September 1992. It draws on ideas generated in collaboration with Stephen Coate of the Department of Economics, University of Pennsylvania. Our joint paper "Will Affirmative Action Eliminate Negative Stereotypes?" (*American Economic Review*, December 1993) develops a more thorough analysis of the issues considered here.

While this rebuttal makes several valid points,* I believe the concern that affirmative action may be inconsistent with the ultimate achievement of a color-blind society deserves more serious consideration than it currently receives. The reason is that *a policy of affirmative action may alter the terms on which employers and workers interact with each other so as to perpetuate, rather than eliminate, existing disparities in productivity between minority and majority populations*. In particular, the use of color as a basis for distributing opportunities may have the unintended effect of dulling the incentive to acquire skills for those whom the policy is intended to benefit. The presence of such a counterproductive effect gives greater force to the seemingly naive objection to racial preferences stated above. This is true even when affirmative action has been introduced to counteract the effects of ongoing discrimination by employers.

To illustrate, suppose employers believe minority workers are on average less skillful than majority workers. As a result employers are less willing to assign minority workers to high-level positions. Such discriminatory beliefs can be self-confirming because, knowing it is more difficult for them to get the higher positions, minority workers may rationally choose not to invest in the requisite skills, thereby confirming the employers' initial views. Now suppose an affirmative action policy is adopted, requiring employers to assign minority workers to the higher positions at the same rate as the majority. Believing minority workers are on average less skillful, employers may calculate that to comply with this policy, they must now make it easier for them to get high-level positions. But seeing that they need not be as skilled as their majority counterparts to achieve the same success, minority workers may have

---

*For an extended discussion of problems with a "pure color-blind" approach to public policy in the face of racial inequality, see chapter 6 above and my article "Why Should We Care About Group Inequality?" in *Social Philosophy and Policy*, vol. 5, issue 1 (Autumn 1987), 249–271. I also provide there an informal discussion of some negative unintended effects of affirmative action other than the one analyzed in this chapter. An important conclusion of this article is that, having answered in the affirmative the question, Should "color" ever be taken into account?, preferential treatment will often not be the best method of doing so. I make the case that targeting social service benefits to disadvantaged minorities may be a superior means of taking into account the history of racial discrimination.

less incentive to invest in performance-enhancing skills. If minorities choose to invest less than the majority, employers' beliefs that they are less skillful will once again be confirmed.

When discriminated against, minorities may invest less in skills than majority workers because it is more difficult for them to achieve high-level positions. When favored by affirmative action, they may invest less because, given employers' response to the policy, it has become easier for them to get high-level positions. The point is that the incentive to acquire a skill can be lowered by either (1) reducing the likelihood that a skilled worker will succeed or (2) increasing the likelihood that an unskilled worker will succeed. Behavior by employers that is not color blind can produce the first effect; behavior by the government that is color conscious (affirmative action) can produce the second effect. In both cases, because minorities have lower incentives to invest in skill development than do majority workers, there is a systematic difference in the acquisition of skills by workers in the two racial groups.

Under affirmative action, employers may think they have to "patronize" minorities (i.e., not hold them to as high a standard) to meet government hiring requirements. Yet because this patronization can lower incentives for the acquisition of skills by minorities, it can perpetuate the racial skill differential which made the affirmative action policy necessary in the first place. In this sense the government's departure from the color-blind ideal, by generating the unintended consequence of reduced incentives for the acquisition of skills by minority workers, makes the ultimate attainment of a color-blind outcome impossible. In this appendix I illustrate, with the aid of formal economic reasoning, just how and why such an outcome might come about.

A Formal Model of Discrimination

I want to consider an idealized model of an employer interacting with a racially diverse population of workers. My basic concern is with the standards employers use to decide which workers get desirable positions, the effort workers expend to acquire skills useful in those positions, and the ways in which decisions about these two variables change in the presence of racial hiring standards.

(1) There is an employer and a population of workers divided into two racial groups, blacks and whites. The employer can distinguish between workers by their color and thus has the option to treat black and white workers differently. The sole action of the employer is to assign each worker to one of two tasks, task zero and task one. Think of task one as the more demanding and more desirable of these two positions.

(2) All workers can perform task zero satisfactorily. Workers decide, before the employer assigns them to one of the tasks and without the employer's knowledge, whether to invest in acquisition of a skill essential for effective performance of task one. Such an investment is costly for a worker, the size of this cost varying from worker to worker, but the range being the same for each racial group.* (For example, more able workers find it easier to acquire the skill needed for task one, and the distribution of ability is the same within each group.) The employer cannot observe a particular worker's cost. What he can observe is the group identity of each worker and the outcome of a skills test to be described momentarily. Although the two groups are characterized by the same distribution of ability, they need not exhibit the same pattern of investment. Workers with the same investment cost but belonging to different groups might make different investment decisions, as explained further below.

(3) Since task one is more desirable, a worker is assumed to obtain a premium whenever he gains that assignment, whether or not he has acquired the needed skill. But because an unskilled worker performs inadequately, the employer wants a worker in task one only if he has acquired the requisite skill. Otherwise the employer wants that worker to go to task zero. The employer maximizes profits when skilled workers are assigned to task one and unskilled workers to task zero. The size of the gain from a correct assignment need not be the same in these two cases; the employer may care more about avoiding the error of putting an unskilled

---

*Let c denote a worker's cost. Then I assume that each worker's cost is a random draw from a uniform distribution on the interval $[0,1]$ regardless of his group.

worker in task one than about avoiding the mistake of putting an overqualified skilled worker in task zero, or vice versa.*

(4) The employer wants to match workers to their most productive tasks. Lacking prior information, the employer tests a worker's qualifications for doing task one by gathering information from an interview, analysis of previous work history, written exam, and so forth. I assume that this test has three possible outcomes: (a) it shows clearly that the worker can do task one, (b) it shows clearly that he cannot perform task one, or (c) its outcome is ambiguous, so the employer remains uncertain of the worker's skill. The worker passes the test in case (a); in case (b) he fails it; and in case (c) his result is unclear. Only investors can pass the test and only noninvestors can fail it, but each has some chance of getting an unclear result. Investment guarantees not failing (that is, either passing or getting an unclear result); noninvestment guarantees not passing (that is, either failing or getting an unclear result). I assume the test is better at revealing noninvestors than investors in this sense: An investor has a lower chance of passing the test than does a noninvestor of failing it.†

(5) The behavior of workers and the employer in this model may be described as follows. Each worker, knowing his color and his investment cost, decides whether to acquire the skill needed for task one. The employer then encounters the worker, gives him the test, and on the basis of the test result and a worker's color, assigns the worker to a task. I assume that all these decisions are made in a way that maximizes the decision maker's anticipated net reward given the available information. An "equilibrium" for this model is defined as a joint specification of behavior for the employer and the workers in each racial group that is optimal for all parties given the behavior specified for the others. I will show that, despite the absence of any racially invidious motive on the part of the employer, discrimination against blacks can arise in an equilibrium of this model.

---

*To introduce some notation let ω be a worker's reward if he gains assignment to task one, let x_1 be the employer's net reward if he assigns an investing worker to task one, and let x_0 be his net reward if he assigns a noninvesting worker to task zero. Denote by $r=x_1/x_0$ the relative employer reward from properly placing a skilled, as compared to an unskilled, worker.

†Specifically, let p_1 (p_0) be the probability that an investing (noninvesting) worker gets an unclear test result. Then $1-p_1$ is the probability that an investing worker passes the test, and $1-p_0$ is the probability that a noninvesting worker fails it. I assume $p_0 < p_1$.

(6) To find the equilibria I begin by considering the employer's decision in each contingency. Clearly he assigns anyone passing the test to task one and anyone failing it to task zero, regardless of color. However, if the test result is unclear he needs to estimate the likelihood that the worker has invested in developing skills, to determine which assignment is best. If that likelihood is great enough, he puts the worker in task one; otherwise he puts the worker in task zero.* Given an unclear test result, the odds that the worker producing it is has invested depend on the relative number of investors in the population from which the worker comes and the respective probabilities that investors and noninvestors get unclear results.† For a given worker population, if the employer believes the fraction of investors is large, he will think that anyone with an unclear result is probably an investor. Conversely, if he thinks the fraction of investors is small, he will take an unclear result as a probable indicator of a noninvestor. So his assignment decision for a worker whose test is unclear ultimately rests on his belief about the fraction of investors in the population from which that worker has been drawn. If he thinks the fraction of investors is large enough he will give the benefit of the doubt to a worker with an unclear test, and assign him to task one; otherwise he will assign that worker to task zero.‡

(7) I call the employer "optimistic" about a group of workers if he believes enough of them to have invested that when he sees one with an unclear result he nevertheless assigns him to task one.

---

*Let ξ be the employer's estimate of the likelihood that a worker with an unclear test result is in possession of the skill needed for task one. The employer would rather put him in task one than task zero if $\xi x_1 \geq (1-\xi)x_0$, or equivalently, if $\xi \geq 1/(1+r)$.

†Let π be the fraction of workers in some population whom the employer believes have invested. Let ξ be his estimate of the chance that one of these workers, whose test is observed to be unclear, has invested. A simple application of Bayes's rule implies:

$$\xi = \frac{\pi p_1}{\pi p_1 + (1-\pi)p_0} \tag{1}$$

‡An earlier note established that the employer puts a worker with an unclear test into task one if $\xi \geq 1/(1+r)$. Using Eq. (1) we see this is the same as the requirement that

$$\left(\frac{1-\pi}{\pi}\right) \cdot \left(\frac{p_0}{p_1}\right) \leq r, \text{ or equivalently, } \pi \geq \frac{p_0}{p_0 + rp_1} \equiv \pi^* \tag{2}$$

Think of π^* as the threshold belief above which the employer is willing to place a worker in task one when the test is unclear, and below which he is not.

Otherwise I say he is "pessimistic." I can express this by using the symbol π to denote the employer's belief about the fraction of investors in a group, and by saying there is a critical belief π^* such that if $\pi \geq \pi^*$ then he is optimistic about the group, while if $\pi < \pi^*$ then he is pessimistic. I call the employer "liberal" toward a group if he acts so as to give them the benefit of the doubt and "conservative" if he does not. So the employer is liberal toward groups about which he is optimistic and conservative toward groups about which he is pessimistic. Because the employer observes a worker's color, he can distinguish between workers drawn from the subpopulations of blacks and whites. Therefore if his beliefs about the fractions of investors in these groups are not the same, it is possible that he treats black and white workers with unclear tests differently based on this difference of belief. I say the employer "discriminates" against blacks (and in favor of whites) if he is pessimistic about and conservative toward blacks while being optimistic about and liberal toward whites. To see how the employer might end up discriminating in an equilibrium of this model, we must consider the workers' behavior.

(8) A worker decides to invest only if he expects to gain more by doing so than it costs him. His gain from investing is the difference between the reward he expects if he invests and the reward he expects if he does not. Investing is beneficial because it raises the chance that a worker will be assigned to task one and thus enjoy the reward associated with that assignment. But the amount by which investing raises a worker's chance of getting this reward depends on whether he expects the employer to be liberal or conservative toward members of his group. If the employer is liberal, an investor is guaranteed to get task one while a noninvestor gets it if he does not fail the test. Thus investing raises the chance of getting the reward by an amount just equal to the probability that a noninvestor fails. On the other hand, if the employer is conservative, an investor gets task one only if he passes the test and a noninvestor has no chance to get it. So in this case investing raises the chance of getting the reward by an amount just equal to the probability that an investor passes. Since I assumed the test is better at revealing noninvestors than investors, it follows that the gain from investing is greater if the employer is liberal than if he is conservative. Hence the fraction of a group of workers who would choose to

invest is greater if they expect the employer to be liberal than if they think he will be conservative.*

(9) I now identify the equilibria in this model. Denote by π_l (π_c) the fraction of workers in a group who would invest if they expected the employer to be liberal (conservative). If $\pi_l \geq \pi^*$, then when a group of workers expect the employer to be liberal, sufficiently many invest as to make him optimistic. If $\pi_c < \pi^*$, then when a group of workers expect the employer to be conservative, sufficiently few invest as to make him pessimistic. But an optimistic employer wants to be liberal and a pessimistic one wants to be conservative. So when $\pi_l \geq \pi^*$, it can be an equilibrium for the employer to be optimistic about and liberal toward any group and for that group to invest at rate π_l. And if $\pi_c < \pi^*$, it can be an equilibrium for the employer to be pessimistic about and conservative toward any group and for that group to invest at rate π_c. At least one of these conditions always holds. I will assume the parameters of the model to be such that they both hold, i.e., $\pi_c < \pi^* \leq \pi_l$. Then there can be equilibria in which the employer is either optimistic or pessimistic about any group of workers and in each case his belief turns out to be self-confirming.[†]

(10) When the parameters of this model are such that $\pi_c < \pi^* \leq \pi_l$ it

---

*If the employer is liberal, an investing worker gets to task one with certainty; a noninvesting worker gets there with probability p_0; so the expected gain from investing is $\omega(1-p_0)$. If the employer is conservative, by similar reasoning one calculates this expected gain to be $\omega(1-p_1)$. A worker invests if he expects the gain to exceed his cost, and costs are distributed uniformly on [0,1]. Hence the fraction $\pi_l = \omega(1-p_0)$ of any group invest if they think the employer liberal; and the fraction $\pi_c \equiv \omega(1-p_1)$ invest if they think him conservative. Since $p_0 < p_1$ we know that $\pi_c < \pi_l$. (I am taking ω to be small enough that $\pi_l < 1$.)

[†]To formally characterize the equilibria of the model, notice that when $\pi_c < \pi_l$ there are only three possibilities: (1) $\pi_c \geq \pi^*$. In this case the only equilibrium involves the employer being liberal toward all workers, with the fraction π_l of both groups investing. (2) $\pi_l < \pi^*$. In this case the only equilibrium involves the employer being conservative toward all workers, and the fraction π_c of both groups invests. (3) $\pi_c < \pi^* \leq \pi_l$. Now, in addition to both the outcomes described in (1) and (2) there also exist equilibria in which the employer is liberal toward one group and conservative toward the other, with the former investing at rate π_l and the latter investing at rate π_c. Which of these three cases obtains depends on the values of the parameters (ω, p_0, p_1, and r). For given values of (ω, p_0, p_1) we get case (1) when r is "large" and case (2) when r is "small." Specifically, the discriminatory equilibrium discussed in the text [case (3)] exists only if the parameters are such that

$$\left(\frac{p_0}{p_1}\right)\left[\frac{1}{\omega(1-p_0)} - 1\right] \leq r < \left(\frac{p_0}{p_1}\right)\left[\frac{1}{\omega(1-p_1)} - 1\right] \tag{3}$$

The employer is always liberal (conservative) in equilibrium if r is larger (smaller) than indicated above.

is possible for a *discriminatory equilibrium* to exist. In such an equilibrium the employer is, at the same time, pessimistic about one group (blacks, say) and optimistic about the other. Being pessimistic about blacks, he is conservative toward them when their test result is unclear. Being optimistic about whites, he is liberal toward them in the same situation. By behaving in this discriminatory way, he creates different incentives for workers in the two groups to become skilled at doing task one. But this difference in incentives is precisely what induces black and white workers to invest at different rates in the first place. That is, in a discriminatory equilibrium the belief that blacks are on average less skillful than whites is a self-fulfilling prophecy. Given such beliefs blacks do not enjoy equality of opportunity.

The Problem with Affirmative Action as a Remedy in This Situation

Of course the foregoing model is highly stylized. It does not reflect many important considerations in real-world employment relationships. Nevertheless it captures the essence of the problem I alluded to in the introduction. It shows how an employer can come to rely on color as an indicator of the character of a worker, when other means of assessing the worker's merit (the test) fail. Moveover, it illustrates that the racial generalizations on which the employer relies need have nothing to do with the intrinsic qualities of the groups, but may instead result from the fact that discrimination reduces the incentives for workers in the disadvantaged group to acquire skills.

In this discriminatory equilibrium the employer is obviously not color blind. A natural way for a policy maker to try to correct this discrimination would be to force the employer to assign workers from each group to each task at the same rate.* This policy, which I refer

---

*A more direct way to eliminate discrimination would be to forbid the employer to treat whites and blacks with unclear tests any differently. That is, the government could merely insist on color-blind behavior from the employer without regard to results. This would be difficult to enforce in practice. The government would have to observe all information upon which an employer might base his assignment (interviews, work history, etc.), to determine if he is really treating blacks and whites the same. In most employment situations this sort of government oversight is not possible. The analysis offered here applies to those situations where affirmative action takes mainly a results oriented rather than a process oriented form, with the government's focus being on the numbers hired, not the hiring procedures.

to as "affirmative action," is itself a departure from color-blind practice. It involves the government in monitoring the racial composition of the employer's workforce in each task, insisting on equally proportional representation. I will now use my model to examine whether this intervention eliminates the black-white difference in investment incentives that prevails in the discriminatory equilibrium.

Imagine that the employer, when faced with a worker whose test result is unclear, assigns that worker to task one if he is white and to task zero if he is black. So the fractions π_l of whites and π_c of blacks acquire the skill needed to do task one ($\pi_c < \pi^* \leq \pi_l$). Let the government enact a policy requiring that the same proportion of each racial group be assigned to each task. Initially the employer is violating this policy. All whites who invest, plus those who do not but whose test result in unclear, end up in task one, while only those blacks who invest and pass the test do so. Since proportionately more whites than blacks are investing in this initial situation, a larger fraction of whites are being assigned to task one.*

Therefore, to comply with the affirmative action mandate the employer must assign more blacks or fewer whites to task one. Since he is maximizing his profits in the initial equilibrium, both alternatives lower his net payoff. Which course is least undesirable to him, however, depends on the relative numbers of black and white workers in the population. In general the employer will try to minimize the number of instances where in order to comply with the affirmative action policy, he has to make an assignment he believes will not be most profitable. If blacks are comparatively few, then by assigning more of them than he might desire to task one, he could meet the affirmative action mandate with a relatively small number of unprofitable assignments. On the other hand, if blacks are numerous in comparison to whites, then by reassigning a relatively small number of whites to task zero instead of task one, he could meet the government's hiring requirement at least cost to himself.

I will assume here that blacks are a relatively small proportion of the total workforce. If whites are sufficiently numerous relative to blacks, then the employer's best response to the government's mandate is to increase the number of blacks assigned to task one,

---

*Let ρ_w (ρ_b) denote the fraction of whites (blacks) whom the employer assigns to task one. Then $\rho_w = \pi_l + (1-\pi_l)p_0$, while $\rho_b = \pi_c(1-p_1)$. So $\rho_w > \pi_l > \pi_c > \rho_b$.

while continuing to be liberal toward whites.* Notice, however, that initially he will not think it adequate simply to engage in equal treatment of black and white workers in order to achieve this goal. Because a smaller fraction of blacks than of whites are investing initially, the employer anticipates that even if he becomes liberal toward blacks he will still be assigning them to task one less frequently than whites. To achieve equal racial representation in the face of unequal racial investment rates, the employer will need to assign to task one some of the blacks who fail the test, and who he therefore knows have not invested. When he does this I say he is "patronizing" these black workers. The probability that an arbitrary black worker who fails the test will nevertheless be assigned to task one is what I call the employer's "degree of patronization." The precise degree of patronization the employer thinks he will need depends on his beliefs about the rates of investment in the two racial groups. The less skilled he thinks blacks are relative to whites, the more he sees a need to patronize them to comply with the government's mandate. He engages in no patronization only if he thinks blacks and whites are investing at the same rate.[†]

---

*To calculate how small a minority blacks need to be for this assumption to be justified, let λ be the fraction of the population that is white and $1-\lambda$ be the fraction that is black. Consider putting either ΔB more blacks in task one, or alternatively ΔW more whites in task zero, where the object in each case is to reduce the difference in the proportions of black and white workers going into task one by the same amount. Then it must be that

$$\frac{\Delta B}{1-\lambda} = \frac{\Delta W}{\lambda}, \text{ or equivalently, } \Delta W = \left(\frac{\lambda}{1-\lambda}\right)\Delta B$$

Being liberal toward whites leads the fraction π_l of them to invest. So the employer expects to lose $\xi_l x_1 - (1-\xi_l)x_0$ on each white worker with an unclear result put in task zero instead of task one, where [see Eq. (1)] $\xi_l = \pi_l p_1/[\pi_l p_1 + (1-\pi_l)p_0]$. Conversely, if he puts a black who fails the test in task one instead of task zero, he expects to lose x_0. Hence he would rather do the latter than the former, to narrow the gap by a given amount, if

$$\left(\frac{\lambda}{1-\lambda}\right)[\xi_l x_1 - (1-\xi_l)x_0] > x_0, \text{ or equivalently, } \lambda > \frac{1}{\xi_l(1+r)}$$

[Note that $1/\xi_l(1+r) < 1$ as long as $\pi_l > \pi^*$.]
[†]The fraction π_l of whites invest, so the fraction $\rho_w = \pi_l + (1-\pi_l)p_0$ of them are being put into task one. If the fraction $\pi_b'' \pi_l$ of blacks invests, and if the employer adopts degree of patronization α toward them, he ends up with the fraction $\rho_b = \pi_b + (1-\pi_b)[p_0 + \alpha(1-p_0)]$ of blacks in task one. Compliance with affirmative action requires the employer to ensure that $\rho_w = \rho_b$. Solving this equation we see that, with π_b given, α must be such that

$$\alpha = \frac{\pi_l - \pi_b}{1 - \pi_b} \tag{4}$$

Conversely, to the extent blacks anticipate they will be patronized, their incentive to acquire the skill needed for task one is reduced. Any positive degree of patronization makes a worker's expected gain from investing less than it would have been if his group were merely treated liberally but not patronized. Compared with liberal treatment, a positive degree of patronization raises the chance for a noninvestor to get into task one without affecting the fact that an investor is guaranteed to gain that assignment. Hence, compared with merely liberal treatment, a positive degree of patronization reduces the amount by which investing improves a worker's chances to get into task one and so lowers the fraction of workers who calculate that the benefit of investing exceeds its cost.*

Consider now what happens in the model when, starting from a discriminatory equilibrium, an affirmative action mandate is imposed. Because blacks are a relatively small fraction of the worker population, the employer's best response to the government's policy is to continue being liberal toward whites. Initially he thinks the fractions π_c of blacks and π_l of whites are investing. He therefore anticipates the need for some patronization. However, by patronizing blacks he alters their investment incentives and hence changes the rate at which they acquire the skill needed for task one. This change in black workers' behavior in turn implies that the employer must alter the degree of patronization required for compliance. An "equilibrium under affirmative action" is defined to be a degree of patronization toward blacks together with a rate of investment among them such that (a) when the employer expects that fraction of blacks to invest, he selects the indicated degree of patronization to comply with the government's mandate,

---

*When the employer is liberal but not patronizing, the return from investing is $\omega(1-p_0)$. Let α be the degree of patronization, $0 \leq \alpha \leq 1$. If in addition to expecting the benefit of the doubt, a worker thinks that with probability α he will gain task one even if he fails, then by not investing he has probability $p_0 + \alpha(1-p_0)$ of getting task one. By investing he gets it for sure. So his return from investing falls to $\omega(1-p_0)(1-\alpha)$. Since costs are uniformly distributed, anticipating a degree of patronization α will induce the fraction of blacks π_b to invest, where $\pi_b = \omega(1-p_0)(1-\alpha)$. But since $\pi_l = \omega(1-p_0)$ (see footnote on page 124) we have

$$\pi_b = \pi_l (1 - \alpha) \tag{5}$$

and (b) when blacks expect that degree of patronization, they choose to invest at the indicated rate.*

One equilibrium under affirmative action is obvious: If the employer should come to believe that blacks are investing at rate π_l—the same as whites—he would want to be liberal but not patronizing toward them, and would comply with the government's mandate by doing so. If blacks expect the degree of patronization to be zero they, like whites, would invest at rate π_l. When this equilibrium arises, the employer's initial discriminatory beliefs have been eliminated by the use of affirmative action. This is the ideal outcome predicted by proponents of the policy. The government's insistence on equal representation for each racial group creates a situation in which the opportunities, and so the distributions of skills, for each group of workers are equalized. Having achieved this result, affirmative action policy can "wither away" because the employer's discriminatory beliefs, which justified (for him) the initial unequal treatment of blacks, have been dispelled.

Another equilibrium under affirmative action is less obvious: The employer continues to think blacks invest less frequently than whites. He therefore persists in patronizing them to some degree. But because blacks when patronized have less of an incentive to invest than whites, the employer's belief that patronization is needed becomes a self-fulfilling prophecy. This is not the outcome forecast by proponents of affirmative action. For rather than creating equality of opportunity, the policy in this case leads to a situation in which, to meet the government's requirement of equal representation, the employer favors unskilled blacks. Because non-investing blacks have greater opportunities in this case, the return on acquiring a skill is lower for blacks than for whites and rela-

---

*Formally, an equilibrium under affirmative action is a degree of patronization, α^*, and a fraction of investing black workers, π_b^*, that simultaneously satisfy Eqs. (4) and (5). Simple algebra shows that π_b^* is an equilibrium fraction of black investors under affirmative action if

$$\pi_b^*(1-\pi_b^*) = \pi_l(1-\pi_l), \text{ and } \pi_b^* \leq \pi_l \qquad (6)$$

(It is necessary to require that $\pi_b^* \leq \pi_l$ because the degree of patronization can never be negative.) When $\pi_l \leq 1/2$, Eq. (6) has only one solution, $\pi_b^* = \pi_l$. This is the first equilibrium considered in the text. When $\pi_l > 1/2$, Eq. (6) has two solutions, $\pi_b^* = \pi_l$ and $\pi_b^* = 1 - \pi_l$. This latter is the second equilibrium discussed in the text.

tively fewer blacks invest. So the employer has to continually favor black workers to comply with the government's mandate. In this equilibrium affirmative action, far from withering away, sets in motion a sequence of events that guarantee it will have to be maintained indefinitely.* The incentives for the employer, and hence for black and white workers, are altered by the government's use of a color-conscious strategy in such a way that a racial difference in workers' acquisition of skills is sustained.† This is precisely the unintended negative consequence of racial preferences to which I alluded in the introduction.

It is therefore of some interest to determine which of these two equilibria under affirmative action will actually obtain. At the initial discriminatory equilibrium the employer thinks he needs some patronization, but his use of it alters blacks' investment incentives. As black workers change their behavior, the degree of patronization the employer believes to be necessary also changes. Imagine a process in which the employer and black workers alternately adjust their behavior over a sequence of stages, each party reacting to the behavior observed from the other at the previous stage of adjustment. It is plausible to postulate that the equilibrium reached under affirmative action is the one that eventually emerges from this iterative process of adjustment.

Using simple mathematics, one can show that when $\pi_l \leq 1/2$ this process culminates at the first (obvious) equilibrium described above, and when $\pi_l > 1/2$ it culminates at the second (less obvious) one. Another way of saying this is that *the undesirable outcome obtains under affirmative action if, when facing a liberal employer, the average worker would strictly prefer to invest in the skill needed for task one*. Recall that the average worker will want to invest when facing a liberal employer only if the expected return

---

*This conclusion is true only if the fraction of black investors in this second equilibrium is low enough that the employer would want to be conservative toward them were he not constrained to meet the government's mandate. That is, if $1-\pi_l < \pi^*$.

†The black skill acquisition rate in this equilibrium ($\pi_b^* = 1-\pi_l$) could even turn out to be smaller than in the initial discriminatory equilibrium (π_c). Thus $1-\pi_l < \pi_c$ if $\pi_l + \pi_c > 1$, or equivalently, if $\omega(2-p_0-p_1) > 1$. Hence if the worker's value of getting task one is big enough, and/or the test is sufficiently accurate, then this extreme illustration of the "law of unintended consequences" will in fact obtain in this model.

from doing so exceeds his investment cost. This expected return is greater, the greater is the gain to a worker from being assigned to task one, and the lower is the probability that a noninvestor goes undetected by the test. Thus the higher is the value of assignment to task one, relative to the average worker's investment cost, and the more powerful is the test at identifying noninvestors, the more likely is it that a patronizing equilibrium will arise under affirmative action. The patronizing outcome is also more likely when the disadvantaged group is a relatively small fraction of the total population.

Conclusions

The point of this exercise has been to illustrate, with the aid of formal economic reasoning, that the concerns expressed by some critics of affirmative action should be taken seriously. I have shown, in the context of a simple, stylized model of worker–employer interaction under racial hiring guidelines, that requiring equal representation of minority and majority groups in high-level positions may produce a situation in which the incentives provided minorities to acquire the skills needed to perform adequately in such positions are maintained permanently below the incentives provided majority workers. Whether this outcome occurs depends on such factors as the proportion of the total workforce belonging to the minority group, the advantage to a worker of obtaining a high-level position relative to the average cost in the population of acquiring the skill needed to perform in that position, the relative importance to the employer of assigning skilled and unskilled workers to their most productive positions, and the extent to which the employer can accurately gauge a worker's productivity in a given task before actually employing him there.

This analysis is not an attack on the practice of using preferential treatment as a tool to enhance opportunity for minority workers. Indeed, I have shown that the use of racial preference can sometimes have the desired result. However, departure from color-blind practice by the government need not have these desirable consequences. It is important that we try to understand, in the many concrete circumstances in which preferences are now employed, just when the risks of generating negative unintended consequences of the sort I identify here are worth taking. Thus, I am urging that more empirical research be done on the actual effects of affirmative action. Too often both advocates and critics are content to base their arguments entirely on first principles, without reference to the direct or indirect consequences of this contentious policy. The analysis offered here is meant graphically to illustrate a possibility. Further study is required to identify practically significant cases exemplifying the effects uncovered here.

7

Senate Testimony on the Civil Rights Act of 1990

Mr. Chairman, I thank you for this opportunity to appear before the committee. I have for some years now been writing and teaching about the problem of group inequality in our society. In what follows I will offer a brief survey of the dimensions of that problem, drawn from analyses in the social science literature of the statistical data collected and published by various federal agencies, as I have interpreted them. I hope this survey can provide some context for your deliberations on the proposed civil rights legislation. I would like to stress several points here:

1. While substantial differences in income exist between various ethnic groups, and while discrimination against women and various minority groups in employment has been and continues to be a matter of concern, there is no sound social scientific basis for concluding that the existing economic differences have been caused by, or reflect the extent of, employment discrimination against various groups. Gross statistical disparities are inadequate to identify the presence of discrimination, because individuals differ in many ways likely to affect their earnings capacities that are usually not measured and controlled for when group outcomes are

133

compared. Accordingly, there is no basis for the expectation that antidiscrimination legislation will have anything but a marginal effect on these differences.

2. In the case of blacks, who have arguably experienced the most severely deleterious effects of discrimination in the past, there has been a truly dramatic reduction in the extent of employment discrimination in the period since the passage of the Civil Rights Act of 1964. Moreover, there has occurred over the last four decades a pronounced improvement in the overall relative economic status of black Americans, an improvement that started before the Civil Rights Acts and that is accounted for by beneficial changes in such fundamental economic factors as improved educational attainment, long-term economic growth, and interregional migration, as well as by the diminished extent of employment discrimination. The rate of improvement in the relative earnings of blacks has slowed in the last decade, especially for the youngest cohorts. This is a matter of some concern, which seems to be due to a slowing of the overall rate of economic growth in the United States, as well as to the failure of the quality of education available to black youngsters to continue to improve.

3. Despite the long-term upward trend, there nevertheless remain profoundly troubling racial differences in economic advantage which warrant the attention of this committee and of all Americans. In the case of blacks, the relative labor market gains of individuals have not been matched by comparable gains in the resources available to families. This is because the proportion of families headed by a single parent has risen dramatically among blacks during the same period in which individuals' earnings have improved. As well, the percentage of black children residing in households in which only one parent is present has risen sharply. Poverty rates among such children are disturbingly high. More generally, the emergence of what some have called an "urban underclass" has been noted in many of our cities. Blacks are disproportionately overrepresented in this population, where the problems of drugs, criminal violence, educational failure, homelessness, and family instability are manifest. It is my conviction that these problems constitute the most important and intractable aspect of racial inequality in our time. Unfortunately, these prob-

lems are unlikely to be mitigated by civil rights legislation, because they do not derive in any direct way from the practice of employment discrimination. However, the continued existence of these social problems contributes to the inability of those subject to them to compete effectively in the labor market.

4. I am concerned that the politics of civil rights issues have in the last decade taken on a disturbingly symbolic tone, and have become divorced from the social reality of racial inequality as it actually exists in our society. This trend is reflected, in my judgment, in the public debates over recent Supreme Court decisions, and the extent to which they do or do not reverse the progress in race relations that we have made as a society in the last decades. I am not commenting on the legal correctness of the Court's rulings, but rather on the political meaning that has been attached to them by advocates of minority interests. It is my opinion, as a close student of the socioeconomic trends affecting minority groups in our society, that the danger to minority interests of these developments in the law has been significantly overstated. A far greater threat to the attainment of full social and economic parity for racial minorities is posed by the trends affecting the social, educational, and family life experiences of low-income urban communities. These trends are more difficult to legislate against and do not as readily provide us with villains and heroes. But if they are not reversed, we will continue to face a serious social and political problem of racial inequality in this country for many years to come.

Income Differences and Discrimination

While incomes vary considerably between racial and ethnic groups, one cannot draw conclusions about the extent of discrimination from such differences. Some groups that have been discriminated against in the past nevertheless have higher incomes than groups that are presumed to have benefited from discrimination. For example, Asian Americans have experienced considerable discrimination, yet have incomes often exceeding those of whites. (According to the 1980 census, the family income of Japanese Americans was 30 percent higher than that of whites in 1979.) Discrimination cannot account for this fact, though other factors may be suggested as a plausible explanation. Family income is affected by factors such as the number of family members in the labor force, and the skills that those persons bring to the labor market. Therefore, family structure (whether families consist of husband–wife couples with children, or mothers raising their children alone, for example) will be an important determinant of group differences in family incomes. Also, some groups may exhibit a greater amount of family work effort than others, even when the structure of families is similar. For example, 71 percent of Filipino families have two or more earners, compared to 55 percent of white American families. (This consideration is important in accounting for the relative family incomes of Chinese, Japanese, Korean, and Cuban families as well.)

Individual skills are also important in accounting for differences between groups in income. Educational attainment varies considerably by race and ethnicity. In 1980 only 58 percent of Hispanic men aged 25 to 29 had completed high school, compared to 89 percent of Asian men and 73 percent of black men. If one compares the earnings of minority individuals relative to that of whites, varying the degree of educational attainment, it becomes clear that differences in education contribute in a major way to group income differences, because the ratio of minority to white earnings is consistently higher among persons with the same amount of education than it is among all persons. For example, in the 1980 census black men aged 25 to 34 are recorded as having hourly earnings at 84 percent of the level of whites. Yet for men with twelve years of schooling, relative black hourly earnings were 87 percent of those for whites; among men with sixteen years of schooling, relative black earnings were 90 percent of those for whites. Moreover, there are differences in school achievement among persons with the same years of schooling that are likely to explain some earnings differences. These differences, reflected in part by variation across groups in students' performance on achievement tests, may be attributed to differences in the quality of schools attended by group members, as well as differences in the education and income of students' parents.

The problem of inferring discrimination from earnings differentials is further illustrated by reference to the relative earnings of women in various ethnic groups. Among women aged 45 to 54 with a college education, for example, blacks earned roughly 13 percent more than whites in 1979, despite the fact that they probably experienced more labor market discrimination. Some economists have attributed this fact to the greater work experience and labor market attachment exhibited by black women. Labor force participation rates have traditionally been higher among black women than among whites, and black women have been more likely to work while their children are young, a fact which may derive from the higher probability that a black woman would be the sole support of her children.

It is not possible here to offer a complete discussion of the factors determining individual earnings, nor of the reasons why earnings might differ between groups. The preceding discussion is intended to suggest, however, that employment discrimination is but one (and by no means the most important) of these factors, and that the tendency to conclude that discrimination is a problem from the mere fact that groups have differing incomes should be resisted. This point is underscored by the fact that, even within groups usually treated as a single aggregate for the purpose of discussing the existence of discrimination, one can observe significant differences in economic experience. Black American families of West Indian descent fare much better than do blacks overall, with incomes comparable to those of whites. And among white men, the group usually offered as a basis of comparison for the purpose of measuring the well-being of others, there are significant differences that presumably cannot be explained by discrimination. For example, even after adjusting for education, geographic region, and other factors, Jewish men were found in a recent Civil Rights Commission study to earn about 15 percent more, and Italian men 6 percent more, than white men of British descent.

Economic Progress of Blacks and the Significant Remaining Inequality

There has been significant improvement in the earnings experience of employed black workers over the period 1940–1980, as documented by the decennial census data. This improvement is both absolute and relative to the earnings of comparable whites. This improvement began well before the onset of the civil rights legislation of the 1960s. It is explained in part by the shift of black workers out of agriculture, where they were concentrated prior to World War II; by the migration of blacks from countryside to city, and from South to North and West, that has occurred in this period; by the improvement in the quality and quantity of education attained by black workers, and by a decline in labor market discrimination against black workers. The pace of improvement historically has been greatest when the overall rate of growth for the economy has been greatest (during the 1940s and 1960s, for example), and appears to have slowed during the 1980s. This improvement has been relatively greater for more educated and younger workers. However, since 1960 the gains in relative earnings among employed blacks have been accompanied by a pronounced downward trend in the labor force participation rates of black men, a trend that accelerated during the 1970s. Family incomes have not improved among blacks relative to whites in a manner comparable to the change in the earnings of employed individuals.

These earnings gains are reflected in the following data (estimated annual earnings of fully employed men in constant 1987 dollars):

Mean Male Income by Race

Year	Whites	Blacks
1980	28,212	20,480
1970	28,075	18,078
1960	21,832	12,561
1950	15,677	8,655
1940	11,441	4,956

Source: Smith and Welch, "Black Economic Progress After Myrdal," *Journal of Economic Literature*, June 1989.

These average gains have not, however, been enjoyed equally by all black workers. In the past quarter century, earnings inequality within the black population has increased. Since 1959 inequality among black men has been greater than among white men, with the bottom 40 percent of black men earning about 8 percent of total black male earnings in 1959 but only 5 percent in 1984; and with the top 20 percent of black men earning about one-half of total black male earnings in 1959 but roughly 60 percent by 1984. This increasing inequality is due in large part to the fact that an increasing proportion of black men report no labor market earnings at all, because they are unemployed or not in the work force. Among black men 24 years old the proportion unemployed, out of the labor force, or in jail rose from 13.8 percent in 1950 to 19.8 percent in 1960, 21.1 percent in 1970, and 28.2 percent in 1980; for men 35 or 36 years old the proportions were 13.5 percent in 1950, 17.1 percent in 1960, 13.7 percent in 1970, and 20.3 percent in 1980. Note the sharp rise during the 1970s.

Family income has also become more unequal among blacks. For example, the proportion of black families with incomes over $35,000 (in 1986 dollars) grew from 15.7 percent to 21.2 percent in the period 1970–1986. The proportion with incomes in excess of $50,000 increased from 4.7 percent to 8.8 percent in the same period; yet the proportion of black families with income of less than $10,000 also grew, from 26.8 percent to 30.2 percent. Among two-parent households with children, black earnings rose 4 percent between 1973 and 1984, while white earnings fell 4 percent. Earnings for female-headed households fell for both blacks and whites (by 9 percent and 8 percent, respectively), but there are significantly more black single-parent households than white. Moreover, better-educated blacks have gained more than less-educated blacks from the improvement in relative black earnings. Annual earnings of college graduates rose by 6 percent among black males relative to whites between 1969 and 1984; for those with eight to eleven years of schooling, the relative gain was 2 percent, but among high school graduates blacks' relative earnings actually fell by 5 percent over this period.

While there is much debate about the causes of these offsetting negative trends, particularly about the decline in labor market participation of black men in the last twenty years, it seems clear that employment discrimination is not a major factor. Most of the discussion has focused on the effects of benefit programs on labor force participation among black men, and on the decline in industrial employment in the urban areas in which blacks are most concentrated. I do not take a position here on this issue, but merely stress that the phenomenon is a complicated one involving many factors.

One feature of the current socioeconomic situation of blacks requires particular emphasis, though, and that is the decline in the two-parent household as a context for child rearing. This phenomenon has direct implications for the incidence of poverty among children, and consequently for the prospects of continued improvement in the relative economic position of blacks in the future. Again, it is not possible here to review this situation in detail, but a general impression is conveyed by the following statistics. Between 1960 and 1988 the percentage of black women aged 15 to 44 married with a spouse present declined from 51.4 percent to 29.1 percent; there was also a decline for whites, though not as pronounced (from 69.1 percent to 54.5 percent). Over the same period, the percentage of children living with a married couple fell among blacks from 67 percent to 38.6 percent, while the percentage of black children living with a never-married parent rose from 2.1 percent to 29.3 percent. These startling numbers suggest the magnitude of the profound change in family structure among blacks that has been going on now for more than a quarter century. No one really understands why these changes are occurring, though a proximate cause may be identified in the rising fertility rates during the last decade among never-married black women, along with the declining birthrates among married black women, which have been falling for three decades. In any event, by 1988 the percentage of births among blacks that occurred to unmarried women had risen to 61.2 percent. Every study of the relationship between family structure, childhood poverty, and subsequent social mobility of children suggest that this trend bodes ill for the continuation of historic improvements in the relative economic status of black Americans.

The Politics of Race

Matters of race inevitably produce strong feeling when they arise in American politics. The sense that the wounds of the past are being reopened by a Supreme Court bent on reversing historic gains is sure to induce alarm among all concerned for social justice. The continued existence of visible and abject urban poverty disproportionately afflicting blacks, together with the presence in national government of a series of relatively conservative administrations, has fueled this concern. There are vast disparities in material condition separating the inner-city black poor from the rest of the nation. This inequality has caused public discourse on matters concerning race to be tense, angry, and too often unproductive.

Our nation does face a serious challenge in the area of race relations, but it is important to be clear about just what the challenge is, and what it is not. In my view, the problems of the so-called black underclass cannot be usefully ascribed solely to white racism, and they will not yield to political interventions in the form of stronger civil rights legislation. Over the last quarter century we have witnessed a disquieting loss of coherence in lower-class black urban society. The social disintegration has proceeded even as the civil rights movement has achieved many of its aims, and as the size and influence of the black middle class has grown impressively.

While we must find ways effectively to address the problems of the inner-city poor of all races, I believe it will be helpful to bear in mind how limited a role civil rights legislation now plays in impacting the overall situation of the black poor. This, of course, is not to say that civil rights are not important in their own right. Nevertheless, it seems to me that the intensity and emotion that surround debate on this bill derive from the symbolic importance which the civil rights issue has assumed as an indicator of general concern for the condition of racial and ethnic minorities in our society. To the extent that this focus on civil rights legislation as a remedy for the more general problem of racial inequality crowds from the public agenda a consideration of the broader causes of that inequality, I believe that long-term progress on the fundamental problem will be retarded.

II
Can We Talk?

8

Self-Censorship
in Public Discourse
A Theory of Political Correctness
and Related Phenomena

The great enemy of clear language is insincerity. When
there is a gap between one's real and one's declared aims,
one turns as it were instinctively to long words and
exhausted idioms, like a cuttlefish squirting out ink. . . .
Thus political language has to consist largely of
euphemism, question-begging and sheer cloudy vagueness.

—George Orwell
"Politics and the English Language"

Putting the PC Debate in Perspective

"Political correctness" (PC) is an important theme in the raging
cultural war that has replaced the struggle over communism as the
primary locus of partisan conflict in American intellectual life.
Starting on the campuses over issues like abortion, affirmative
action, multicultural studies, environmentalism, feminism, and gay

The author thanks Thomas Schelling, without whose encouragement this chapter would never
have been written.

rights, the PC debate has spread into newsrooms, movie studios, and even the halls of Congress. Critics, mainly on the right, claim that only the "correct" views on these and other sensitive issues can be expressed—on campus, in print, on film, or in electoral politics—without evoking extreme, stifling reactions from activists seeking to make their opinions into an enforced orthodoxy. They cite a litany of woes about how, in venues where the left is most powerful, those expressing even mildly divergent views are treated poorly. In response, liberals call these charges overblown and insist that their efforts to hold people accountable for what they say and write are justified by legitimate moral concerns.

We can usefully distinguish two levels on which disagreement occurs. At the primary level, partisan arguments on certain questions divide public opinion: how bad is the "date rape" problem, and what should be done about it? What texts are canonical, and are non-Western cultures adequately represented among them? What causes the violence among young black men in the cities and how can it be reduced? What is the nature and moral standing of homosexuality? Disagreement on these substantive matters stems from the different values, factual judgments, and theoretical frameworks that people employ to analyze the world around them. These disagreements are inevitable and healthy. They have the potential to engender constructive exchanges from which all participants can learn and better public policies can emerge.

At a secondary level, though, a contentious discussion is taking place over the very nature of primary discussions: are speakers treated respectfully regardless of the popularity of their views? Are some opinions given privileged access to the media? Are people candid in their arguments? Who can talk about what topics, and when, without violating some unspoken canon of decency? Do advocates of one position seek to prevent or discredit the expression of opposing ideas? Do some arguments so offend the sensibilities of some citizens that they should be preemptively excluded from public debate?

These two levels of debate can become confused. Some complaints about PC are, upon examination, really laments that within a certain community of discourse the complainer's views are unpopular. The most serious questions raised in the PC debate, however, focus on the secondary level just mentioned. The fundamental issue is whether the climate for the voicing of opinion in important forums (and the universities are by no means the only forums of interest) continues to permit a constructive, informative dialogue on vital matters of common concern. Increasingly, there is reason to doubt that this is so.

Unlike much that has been written on this topic, I will not waste time in this chapter telling "horror stories" about the excesses of PC zealots, or lamenting their influence on the campuses.[1] Instead, I will endeavor to lay bare the underlying logic of political correctness—to expose the social forces that create and sustain movements of this sort. Two preliminary observations will help to set the stage for the analysis.

First, though political correctness is often spoken of as a threat to free speech on the campuses (and this is indeed the case when it results in legal restrictions on open expression, as with formal speech codes), the more subtle threat is the voluntary limitation on speech that a climate of social conformity encourages. It is not the iron fist of repression, but the velvet glove of seduction that is the real problem. Accordingly, *I treat the PC phenomenon as an implicit social convention of restraint on public expression within a given community.* Conventions like this can arise because (1) a community may need to assess whether the beliefs of its members are consistent with its collective and formally avowed purposes, and (2) scrutiny of their public statements is an often efficient way to determine if members' beliefs cohere with communal norms. This need to police group members' beliefs so as to ferret out deviants, along with the fact that the expression of heretical opinion may be the best available evidence of deviance, creates the possibility for self-censorship: members whose beliefs are sound but who nevertheless differ from some aspect of communal wisdom are compelled by a fear of ostracism to avoid the candid expression of their opinions.

Secondly, despite the attention that has been given to recent campus developments, the phenomenon of political correctness, understood as an implicit convention of restrained public speech, is neither new nor unusual. Indeed, pressuring speakers and writers to affirm acceptable beliefs and to suppress unacceptable views is one of the constants of political experience. All social groups have norms concerning the values and beliefs appropriate for members to hold on the most sensitive issues. Those seen not to share the consensus view may suffer low social esteem and face a variety of sanctions from colleagues for their apostasy; heretics are unwelcome within the councils of the faithful. Communists and their sympathizers paid a heavy price for their "incorrect" views during the early years of the cold war. "Uncle Toms"—blacks seen as too eager to win favor with their white "overlords"—are still treated like pariah by other blacks who greatly value racial solidarity. Jews critical of Israel or Muslims critical of Islam (like Salman Rushdie) may find that they "can't go home again."

Therefore, a theory of contemporary political correctness problems should be broad enough to address these related phenomena. I sketch here an approach that I believe meets this requirement. My theory is based on a conception of political communication that stresses strategic considerations. From this point of view, people engaged in primary-level debates over policy questions must also—at the secondary level, if you will—consider how their interests are affected by the specific manner in which they express themselves. The next section develops the main ideas along this line. This strategic approach is then applied to explain how conformity in public speech emerges as a stable behavioral convention within a given community. A later section reviews some historical examples of censored public discussions, and this is followed by a discussion of some broader implications, for both the style and the substance of policy debates, of the kind of expressive behavior identified here. A special effort is made throughout to shed light on some of the more problematic features of public rhetoric on race-related issues in the United States.

Strategic Behavior in the Forum

George Orwell's skepticism about political rhetoric, elaborated in his essay "Politics and the English Language" (quoted at the beginning of the chapter), has much to recommend it. Political communication—the transmission of ideas and information about matters of common concern with the intent to shape public opinion or affect policy outcomes—is tricky business. Both those sending and those receiving messages must be wary. Senders want to persuade or inform via spoken and written words. They strive to convey their intended message while avoiding misinterpretation or discovery of their true purposes. Receivers want to distill from incoming rhetoric information useful for forming an opinion or making a decision, but they do not want to be manipulated or deceived. In order to be effective, both parties need to behave strategically. Naive communication (where a speaker states literally all that he thinks, and/or an audience accepts his representations at face value) is both rare and foolish in politics. A political speaker's expression is more often a calculated effort to achieve some chosen end; and an audience's *impression* of the speaker is usually arrived at with an awareness that this is so.

Recall the oratorical confrontation in Act III, Scene 2 of Shakespeare's *Julius Caesar.* Caesar has been murdered by a group of conspirators that includes Brutus. Antony, close to Caesar and no part of the conspiracy, is outraged and bent on revenge. Brutus goes before the crowd to explain his actions, saying Caesar was ambitious, a man who would be king, a potential tyrant who had to be stopped for the sake of the republic. "Not that I loved Caesar less, but that I loved Rome more," he declares, relying on his reputation for honor and decency to sway the crowd. He argues directly; his speech is naive, guileless, literal. He seems to prevail as he takes his leave. Then Antony rises, saying, "Friends, Romans, countrymen, lend me your ears. I come to bury Caesar, not to praise him." This, of course, is not true. He praises Caesar profusely, reminding the audience of Caesar's greatness in war, of his kindness and generosity in peace ("Ambition should be made of sterner stuff!"). As for his view of Brutus and the others, he does not overtly disparage them; he seems to accept their stated motives: "Brutus says Caesar was ambitious, and Brutus is an honorable man." He never reveals that revenge is his own motive, and the assembled citizens seem to take Antony at his word. Yet by its end, his powerfully manipulative oration has made the words "honorable man" in reference to Brutus mean exactly their opposite, and defense of Brutus by anyone in the crowd has become impossible. Shortly, civil war breaks out. Shakespeare shows us here the potential for political gain through strategic expression, and also the dangers—for an advocate, as well as for the public good—of naive behavior in the forum.

I want to explore how the form and substance of collective deliberations on sensitive issues are affected by strategic behavior in the forum. There is always some uncertainty when ideas and information are exchanged between parties who may not have the same objectives. Each message bears interpretation. There is no such thing as context-free expression; we are inevitably reading and writing "between the lines." Because political rhetoric engages interests, expresses values, conveys intent, and seeks to establish commitment to certain courses of action, the risk of manipulation is particularly great in political argument. When people address us in the forum, we must consider what they will do if they get power, decide whether they can be trusted, and wonder, "What type of person is it who would speak to me in this way?"

Erving Goffman has brilliantly analyzed the dilemmas and complexities of communication in the face of this kind of bilateral calculation.[2] Goffman in effect reduces the "game" played between two parties to an interaction—a sender, who expresses himself in some way, and a receiver, who takes in and reacts to that expression, forming an impression of the sender.[3] We might for our purposes think of the sender as a political speaker participating in public debate, and the receiver as a member of the audience who must form an opinion on some controversial matter. Or the sender might be a professor lecturing on American race relations, and the receiver a minority student drawing conclusions about the professor's sensitivity and commitment. The sender has views or values that are not directly knowable by the receiver but that, if known, would significantly alter the receiver's construction of the "meaning-in-effect" of any expression.[4]

The sender may want to signal—that is, credibly but indirectly convey—that he holds a certain point of view, or he may want to disguise the view he really holds. Knowing that these possibilities exist, the receiver will search each expression for evidence of their sender's true motivations and beliefs. From this perspective, using Goffman's terminology, each act of political communication is a small *performance* that bears close interpretation. Its meaning-in-effect—the impression in the receiver's mind to which it gives rise—may depend very much on context and, in particular, on what other senders whose values and beliefs are already known to the audience have been transmitting.

When speakers are choosing words intended to stimulate a particular response, strategic listeners cannot simply accept the literal content of an expression as its meaning-in-effect. To take the speaker literally is to behave naively, and thus to risk being deceived. Sophisticated listeners must look behind what is spoken or written, in an effort to discern all that is implied by the act of speaking or writing in a given way.

The sender of a public message intended to shape opinions and influence policy may have ultimate aims that are not apparent to his audience. And yet, because that sender's values, ideals, and intentions will shape the strategy he adopts in the forum, a proper decoding of his message requires knowledge of his ultimate aims. For this reason, interpretation of political expression essentially involves making inferences from the expressive act about the sender's motives, values, and commitments. *The search for "true" meaning entails judging the character of speakers*—asking whether they really believe what they say and whether they hold unexpressed views that, if known to us, would affect our reception of their arguments.

At the same time, a skillful speaker will structure his message mindful of the inferences that listeners are inclined to make. He will try to use the patterns of inference established within a given community of discourse to his advantage. He will avoid some expressions known to elicit negative judgments or associations, and he will deploy others known to win favor with his audience or to cast him in a positive light. Thus, in the context of political communication, speakers and listeners, or writers and readers, play an "expression game." The appropriate behavior for every party depends on the strategies being used by all the other "players." An "equilibrium" in this game can be thought of as a convention governing the rhetoric used by senders, and the strategies of inference and interpretation employed by receivers, such that each party is content to behave as he does, given the pattern of behaviors adopted by all of the others.

Take this chapter as a case in point. It is public and political, despite the academic veneer. To address the subject of "political correctness," when power and authority within the academic community is being contested by parties on either side of that issue, is to invite scrutiny of one's arguments by would-be friends and enemies. Combatants from the left and the right will try to assess whether a writer is for them or against them. How a chapter like this is read and evaluated, what in it is taken seriously and what dismissed out-of-hand, depends for many readers on where they presume the writer is coming from—what they take to be his ulterior motives. This assessment, in turn, is based not simply upon words on the page but also on whatever else can be learned about the writer's character and commitments. One way to gain insight into the writer's values is to measure his treatment of certain sensitive themes against the standard set by others whose values may be known.*

It is even possible that some readers, based on what they think they know about my opinions from reading other things I have written or from knowledge of my general reputation, approach this chapter with a strong prior assessment of the "real" purposes of my argument—a neoconservative apology for the status quo, let us say. Knowing that I may be read in this way (which can either aid or damage my credibility, depending on the reader), I will edit my writing, perhaps unconsciously, so as to avoid conveying the "wrong" (that is, unintended, even if accurate) impression. I can pander to the presumed prejudices of my audience, denounce them, or strive to dispel them, but I ignore them at my peril.

Although this chapter is an argument about how we argue in public, the discussion also engages substantive matters of controversy. Because I am particularly interested in the structure of public discussion in the United States on racial issues, I occasionally point to those issues to illustrate general principles developed in the argument. For example, I refer to troubling aspects of the public debate on affirmative action. Some readers may question my motives for using these illustrations, suspecting that my argument about deliberative process is really a disguised argument about

---

*Thus, the fact that I use the male form of the third-person pronoun ("he," "him," "his") when a gender choice is unavoidable will not go unnoticed. My declaration here that this choice was taken at random and adhered to for consistency's sake will, I fear, avail me little with some readers. This is especially so if the use of the female pronoun has become a convention among other men writing on these issues.

substance. They may take my observation that discussion of affirmative action is not always fully candid as an indirect attack on the policy itself. They may impute to me a hidden agenda. This possibility has implications for the form of argument that I should make here if I want to succeed in communicating my general ideas.

I must tread carefully as I try to express my particular "truth." If you will read between the lines for my true meaning (my actual, if not fully expressed, sentiments), then I am determined to write between the lines—avoiding or embracing certain code words, choosing carefully my illustrative examples, concealing some of my thinking while exaggerating other sentiments—so as to control the impression I make upon my audience. I want to write persuasively, but is that really different from manipulation? You want to be informed, or perhaps entertained, but you certainly do not want to be fooled.*

There Is No (Entirely) Free Speech

From this strategic perspective a regime of political correctness may be viewed as *an equilibrium pattern of expression and inference within a given community where receivers impute undesirable qualities to senders who express themselves in an "incorrect" way, causing senders to avoid such expressions.* To illustrate, if known enemies of progressive ideals regularly make a certain argument, then one who wants to be seen as standing on the right side of history cannot make a similar argument without the risk of being labeled a reactionary. In a social environment where there are some real racists, and proponents of diversity insist that blacks be referred to as African Americans and American Indians as Native Americans, a speaker who eschews that terminological fashion in the course of an otherwise admirable argument invites the conclusion that he is intolerant of ethnic difference. His more prudent course is to use the politically correct terms, even when he prefers

---

*In a lecture, where communication is by spoken word, my options for strategic behavior are greatly expanded. I can use my inflection of voice, posture, gestures, and physical appearance, as well as some carefully chosen words delivered with mock spontaneity, to manage the impression I convey.

not to. In a south Florida enclave, where hatred of Castro is universal, to argue that the normalization of relations with Cuba should be studied amounts to announcing that the arguer cares nothing whatever about remaining in good standing with his fellows. And in a nearby precinct, where reaction against the Cuban immigration runs high, to question the wisdom of making English the state's official language has a similar meaning-in-effect.

In economics, Gresham's law holds that when two types of currency circulate and one is intrinsically more valuable (say, gold instead of silver, despite an equivalent face value) people hoard the good money and make purchases with the bad. Soon only the bad money remains in circulation. Similarly, people with extreme views can drive moderates, who want to avoid the reputational devaluation of being mistaken as zealots, out of a conversation. In effect, the moderates "hoard" their opinions; hence, the public discourse on some issues (perhaps abortion, for example) can be more polarized than is the actual distribution of public opinion.

What forces, we should ask, could create and sustain such patterns of inference? Note that in the examples above what might be called an "ad hominem impulse" determines the audience's response: they ask what type of person would say such a thing, rather than whether this argument has merit. Ad hominem reasoning lies at the core of the political correctness phenomenon. A speaker's violation of protocol turns attention from the worth of his case toward an inquiry into his character, the outcome of which depends on what is known about the character of others who have spoken in a similar way. When sophisticated speakers are aware of this process of inference, many of them will be reluctant to express themselves in a way likely to provoke suspicion about whether their ultimate commitments conform with their community's norms.

Ad hominem inference, though denigrated by the high-minded, is a vitally important defensive tactic in the forum. When discussing matters of collective importance, knowing where the speaker stands helps us gauge the weight to give to an argument, opinion, or factual assertion offered in the debate. If we know a speaker shares our values, we more readily accept observations from him that are contrary to our initial sense of things. We are less eager to dismiss his rebuttal of our arguments, and more willing to believe facts reported by him that have unpleasant implications.* The reason for all of this is that when we believe the speaker has goals similar to our own, we are confident that any effort on his part to manipulate us is undertaken to advance ends similar to those we would pursue ourselves.† Conversely, speakers with values very different from ours are probably seeking ends at odds with those that we would choose if we had the same information. The possibility of adverse manipulation makes such people dangerous when they are allowed to remain among us undetected. Thus, whenever political discourse takes place under conditions of uncertainty about the values of participants, a certain vetting process occurs in which we cautiously try to learn more about the larger commitments of those advocating a particular course of action.‡

If, by the various means available, an individual is discovered not to share in the deepest value commitments of a particular community, the reaction may well be to exclude that person from participation in future deliberations, and to disparage him publicly for his deviance. The social ostracism, verbal abuse, extreme disap-

---

*For example, many readers are more confident about the accuracy of news reported in a paper whose editorial opinions they share, despite the fact that reporting and editorial functions are strictly segregated at reputable papers.

†Crawford and Sobel (1982) show that, taking due account of the incentive for strategic expression, information will be conveyed from sender to receiver in proportion to the similarity of their views about how that information should be used.

‡The particular reason for seeking out deviants identified here—a desire to avoid being fooled or manipulated in collective deliberations—is not the only, or perhaps even the most important motive. Thus Kurtz (1983) suggests other factors that may drive the "hunt for heretics." One is a community's need to establish a distinctive identity and to maintain group solidarity: "Group solidarity is seldom strengthened by anything as much as the existence of a common enemy, and the heretic, as a 'deviant insider,' is close at hand." Another is the need of elites in a community to justify their positions: "Through the labeling and suppression of heresy, institutional elites can rally support for their positions through battle with a common enemy."

Howe (1982) recalls how the search for a common enemy led various left-wing political groups in the 1930s and 1940s to be obsessed with ideological purity: "The political sect has to pin everything on the rightness of doctrine. The party line becomes its most precious good. To call into doubt even an inch of that line is to endanger its survival, so that, in a way, it is quite right to cast out heretics. In a sect, heresy is never incidental." Factors such as these may be at work in the contemporary political correctness movement.

Most of my argument, however, does not turn on the particular reasons that groups strive to maintain conformity. What matters is that they do so, using the expressive content of political speech to identify deviance.

proval, damage to reputation, and loss of professional opportunity which can occur when one is judged to be deviant from some strongly held moral consensus are very unpleasant experiences. When there is broad agreement concerning what are acceptable and unacceptable opinions, prudent persons will conduct themselves so as to avoid giving gratuitous offense to received orthodoxy. Those who speak in flagrant violation of the conventional wisdom must know the risks they are taking, and must therefore be acting in full recognition of the possible consequences. Being sanctioned for the expression of disapproved opinions seldom befalls someone by accident; it is more often the result of freely choosing to say the disapproved thing. It is probable that real deviants within a given community—those who are in fact "incorrect" in their political sensibilities and who do not share the moral consensus of the community on the issues in question—find the prospect of ostracism less distressing than those who agree with the broad outlines of the consensus, though perhaps not with its every detail.

Crucial to my argument, then, is the following syllogism. Suppose that (1) within a given community the people who are most faithful to communal values are by and large also those who want most to remain in good standing with their fellows, and (2) the practice has been well established in this community that those speaking in ways that offend communal values are excluded from good standing. Then, (3) when a speaker is observed to express himself offensively, the odds that the speaker is not in fact faithful to communal values, as estimated by a listener otherwise uninformed about his views, are increased.

That (3) follows from (1) and (2) is a simple consequence of rational inference by listeners, given rational behavior by senders. But this reasoning implies that sanctions against some forms of expressions could become a self-sustaining convention. Assuming a positive association between fidelity and sociability, there could easily exist an equilibrium of the communal expression game in which apostates are identified by their differential willingness to utter phrases known to be associated with disapproved belief. If it is commonly known that morally suspicious speech invites sanction, and if sanctions cause greater harm to those who really share our values than to those who do not, then the very fact that someone chooses to utter the disapproved phrases suggests that the speaker probably does not share the consensus. Suspicious speech signals deviance because, *once the practice of punishing those who express certain ideas is well established, the only ones who risk ostracism by speaking recklessly are those who place so little value on sharing our community that they must be presumed not to share our dearest common values.*

It is in this sense that I can say that there is no entirely free speech. Anyone speaking out on a controversial matter pays the particular price of having others know that he was willing to speak, in a certain way, under a given set of circumstances. When listeners know that not everyone would be willing to pay that price, and specifically that "true believers" are less likely than apostates to risk incurring the community's wrath, they can make empirically valid inferences about reckless speakers. Norm-offending speech, then, conveys more than just literal meanings. Anticipating these inferences, and wanting not to be seen as deviant, prudent true believers may elect to say nothing that risks offending collective norms. By doing so, they leave the field clear for the apostates, thereby creating the meaning-in-effect that norm-offending speech identifies deviant belief. In a circumstance of this kind, a climate of self-censorship can become entrenched.*

Such self-censorship is the hidden face of political correctness. For every act of aberrant speech seen to be punished by "thought police," there are countless other critical arguments, dissents from received truth, unpleasant factual reports, or nonconformist deviations of thought that go unexpressed (or whose expression is distorted) because potential speakers rightly fear the consequences of

---

*Essential to sustaining this equilibrium pattern of inference is the consensus which obtains within a given community that some expressive acts convey normative, as well as literal, meanings. That is, receivers know that the senders know that receivers think these words are offensive, callous, reactionary, suspicious, indicative of "softness," associated with disloyalty, and so forth; it is common knowledge that such speech has a negative connotation, even when that is not the sender's literal intent. Thus when an outsider, by the inappropriate use of some loaded terms, makes a *faux pas*, we exempt him from a judgment about values initially, because we allow that he may not have known the rules. We say, "perhaps he didn't mean it the way it sounded." His words cannot possibly have the same effective meaning for us when we cannot be sure that he knew how we might interpret them.

a candid exposition of their views. As a result, the public discussion of vital issues can become dangerously impoverished, as the following examples illustrate.

Examples of Censored Public Discourse

An Incorrect Discussion of the Holocaust

Let us look briefly at the important case of Phillipp Jenninger, once the president of the Parliament in what used to be West Germany. Jenninger was forced to resign in November 1988 following a speech he gave at a special parliamentary session marking the fiftieth anniversary of *Kristallnacht* ("Night of the Broken Glass"). In that speech he rendered an account of events leading up to the infamous evening in 1938 when German Jews were set upon, their property destroyed, and their lives taken—a night that many historians mark as the beginning of the Holocaust. An uproar was created by the fact that many in his audience construed Jenninger's brutally frank account of prevailing attitudes among Germans in the 1930s as a disguised defense of Nazism.[5]

Paradoxically, all agreed that Jenninger had for many years been an opponent of totalitarianism of all stripes, a fierce anti-Nazi, and an arch supporter of Israel. No one accused him of being anti-Semitic. Even before his speech had ended, however, there were demonstrations of anger from some in the audience who, finding his words profoundly offensive, rushed ashen-faced from the chamber. Yet virtually all reviewers who examined the speech concluded that Jenninger had said nothing untrue, malicious, or defamatory; he simply said things that some people did not want to hear in a manner that they were unwilling to tolerate.

The context of Jenninger's remarks, and perhaps more importantly the voice he employed during a part of the speech, made his utterances impossible for many Germans to accept. According to one analyst, his mistake was that he had such confidence in his reputation as a friend of Jews and of Israel that he believed he did not need to use the subjunctive mood, or some other grammatical distancing device, when making what would otherwise be perceived as noxious statements.[6]

Jenninger began with a forthright condemnation of Nazi vio-lence:[7]

> What took place 50 years ago today in Germany had not been seen in any civilized country since the Middle Ages. . . . The violence . . . was a measure planned, instigated, and promoted by the government . . . The German people remained largely passive . . . Everyone saw what was happening, but most people looked the other way and remained silent.

He was equally direct, however, in conveying the positive percep-tion that most Germans had of Nazi leadership. At one point Jen-ninger imagined, as though he himself were thinking out loud, how a typical German citizen must have viewed the political successes of Hitler after the nation's humiliating defeat in World War I:

> There is hardly a parallel in history to Hitler's series of political tri-umphs in those first years. The reintegration of the Saar; . . . a mass arms build-up; . . . the occupation of the Rhineland; . . . the "annexa-tion" of Austria, creating the "Grossdeutsches Reich"; and, finally, only a few weeks before the November pogroms, the Munich Agreement, the partition of Czechoslovakia. The Versailles Treaty was now really only a scrap of paper. . . . The German Reich had suddenly become the hegemonial power of the old continent.

And perhaps most seriously, using a matter-of-fact tone meant to convey that these opinions were not at all extraordinary for the time, Jenninger vividly called to mind the suspicion of and con-tempt for Jews that many Germans felt:

> And as for the Jews: hadn't they in the past arrogated a role unto them-selves that they did not deserve? Wasn't there a need for them to finally start accepting restrictions? Hadn't they even perhaps merited being put in their place? And, above all, didn't the propaganda—aside from wild exaggerations not to be taken seriously—correspond . . . to peo-ple's own suspicions and convictions?

Nevertheless, Jenninger's overriding purpose clearly was to engage in a serious moral discourse. For he dealt directly with the horrors that were to come, seeing in them the unavoidable conclu-sion of the Nazis' political logic:

> After this the death factories were built. . . . The offenders replaced the executioner with grotesquely exaggerated industrial methods of vermin

control—in keeping with what they said regarding the need to "exter-
minate vermin." We do not want to close our eyes to this last and very
horrible fact. Doestoevski once said, "If God did not exist, everything
would be permitted." . . . [This] turned out to be a prophetic anticipation of the political crimes of the twentieth century.

Jenninger went on to quote from an SS man's account of the
machine-gun mass killing of many hundreds of Jews—a soldier sits
idly, smoking a cigarette, legs dangling over the edge of a huge pit
that is being filled with the bodies of Jewish victims. Even on the
printed page, the passage is shocking. That, of course, is what Jenninger intended. Yet by speaking in this way he was doubly offensive, paying insufficient deference to the sensibilities of the
descendants of either the victims or the perpetrators of the Holocaust. Telling this particular unpalatable truth in the way that he
did violated an unannounced but commonly understood taboo, and
this cost him his political career.

Phillipp Jenninger's experience illustrates a complex social reality. His personal sentiments, as evidenced by a lifetime in politics,
could not have caused his downfall. On the contrary, it was his liberal reputation that led him to believe he could get away with such
graphic truth-telling.* And though everyone acknowledged the literal truth of his claims, in the end this seemed not to matter. Many
even affirmed the importance of his evident goal with the
speech—encouraging modern Germans to look candidly at their
history, the better to avoid repeating it. Still, by violating a taboo
against any expression that might be construed as sympathetic
with this period in German history—by offending an etiquette of

---

*Thus, this particular example does not exactly fit the theory sketched on pp. 153–158. Some in
the audience may have known that Jenninger was no Nazi sympathizer, but thought that he had
to be punished for sounding like one or else the real neo-Nazis would gain authority to speak
more freely. This view would explain why Michael Fuerst, deputy chairman of the Jewish Council in Germany, was also forced to resign his position after saying publicly, "I welcome that [Jen-
ninger] described in full clarity what was happening in Germany between 1933 and 1938,
especially the fact that everything that Hitler did was strongly supported by the masses of all
Germans." Jenninger's reckless talk was not to be welcomed. That other Germans might begin
openly to speak in this way was precisely the problem.

discourse that prevents the full truth of the period from being faced, failing to limit himself to the platitudes that (though showing due deference to collective sensibility) cannot possibly advance the moral discussion—he committed an unforgivable offense.

Jenninger, it could be said, suffered the wrath of political correctness. But glibly comparing this event with the problems of dissenters from some campus orthodoxy risks missing its true significance. The limitation on public discourse that Jenninger's fate underscores is a profound phenomenon that reflects powerful social forces at work in many other contexts. Analyzing these forces is far more valuable than taking comfort by denouncing their consequences.

The case at hand illustrates how *the effective examination of fundamental moral questions can be impeded by the superficial moralism of expressive conventions. If exploring an ethical problem requires expressing oneself in ways that raise doubts about one's basic moral commitments, then people may opt for the mouthing of right-sounding but empty words over the risks of substantive moral analysis.* The irony here is exquisite. For though the desire to police speakers' morals underlies the taboo, the sanitized public expression that results precludes the honest examination of history and current circumstance, from which genuine moral understanding might arise. As we shall see, discussion of racial issues in the United States is plagued by a similar problem.

Another point worth noting is that Jenninger was apparently unable to create sufficient space between his spoken words (which in some of the most offensive passages were not even his words, but rather those of some long-defunct propagandist) and his intended meaning. He failed to bracket or frame his utterances about realities of the Nazi era in such a way that the listeners could clearly distinguish between a recounting of others' feelings and an expression of his own. Once he began to talk in a certain way, the words had a life and meaning of their own, uncontrollable by any explicit qualification that he might have issued. I will elaborate in the next section on the fact that it is often not possible to exempt oneself from punishment for deviant speech by a simple declaration of innocuous intent.

The Sanctions "Debate"

In the latter half of the 1980s we all knew that solidarity with the struggle of blacks in South Africa required the U.S. government to impose trade sanctions against that nation, and American universities to divest themselves of stock in companies doing business there. Nobel laureate Desmond Tutu, Reverend Allen Boesak, spokesmen for the African National Congress, and black American antiapartheid activists repeatedly said so. People genuinely committed to justice did not become entangled in arcane technical arguments about the effects of economic boycotts. Nor were they unduly concerned about the possible deleterious impact of sanctions on black South Africans, since the most visible proponent of *that* argument was the racist government. Remarkably, even those South Africans who had spent a lifetime fighting apartheid but opposed sanctions because they thought the policy would do more harm than good (Helen Suzman, for example) were not taken seriously by American activists.

Because President Reagan's policy of "constructive engagement" was universally viewed by campus activists as morally bankrupt, few college administrators openly countered demands for divestment with the plausible claim that, instead of selling stocks, the institutions could accomplish more by being constructively engaged (through educational exchanges and the like) with the South African people. Moreover, even to propose an analysis of the impact of sanctions, with the judgment about their advisability contingent upon the outcome, was to tread on politically dangerous ground. There was a consensus among decent people of the need to stand in solidarity with victims of racism.

Consider the dilemma of a politically liberal university president during this period. Whether or not he believed in the efficacy of the sanctions policy, he could not credibly claim to be ignorant either of what this action had come to mean or of the students' knowledge of *his* knowledge of its meaning. If he nevertheless chose to resist student demands for radical change in university investment policies, calling divestment a well-intentioned but unwise policy for the university, then he must have intended that the students draw the inference that he was an obstructionist.

Most college administrators and trustees dubious about the morality or wisdom of divestment found the prospect of this reaction from students to be unpalatable.

It is plausible to suppose that those college presidents with a greater than average commitment to the fight against racism would also have been more concerned than the typical administrator about adverse student reaction. Thus, though they may have thought divestment unwise, such people, not wanting to risk damage to their reputations as good liberals, would have succumbed early to student pressures to divest. Over time, those college administrators openly resisting divestment came more and more to consist of persons who, by their other public utterances and actions, had given evidence of a lack of fidelity to progressive causes. This made it even more difficult for their genuinely progressive, but dubious, colleagues to voice their doubts about divestment or, for that matter, about the tactics (tents on the campus green, occupation of administrative offices) employed by student protesters promoting the policy. In the end, resistance to the sanction policy became an accurate signal of lack of commitment to the liberal cause, since the liberals who doubted the virtues of the policy had censored themselves, while conservatives continued openly to oppose the policy.* This process took place not just on campuses, but in legislatures and on op-ed pages as well.†

An important consequence of these developments was that sustained rational discussion of the many complex ethical and political considerations raised by the sanctions policy, and by the tactics used to promote it, simply did not take place on the campuses in those years. Decisions were taken without the benefit of a full analysis and debate. This highlights an elemental, and potentially dangerous, logic that can operate in a climate of self-censorship:

---

*Some prominent voices against the policy—David Riesman, Clark Kerr, and Alan Pifer, for example—had solid reputations as liberals. I only claim that open opposition to the policy was more likely to be observed, the further to the right of the political spectrum one moved.

†In due course, cities and towns across the United States enacted their own sanctions policies, refusing to deal with businesses tainted by association with South Africa. Union pension funds developed divestment programs. Companies adhering to the so-called Sullivan principles and providing substantial benefits to black workers and their families in South Africa eventually found it impossible to justify their presence there.

A certain course of action is imbued with a symbolic meaning-in-effect, quite apart from the real-world consequences of its pursuit. Expression of doubt about the wisdom of this course of action is suppressed because dissenters want not to be labeled as deviant from some communal norm. As a result, the policy is pursued willy-nilly, and on a broad scale, with perhaps benign but perhaps disastrous consequences. Since the alternatives are never properly studied, one cannot be sure. In any case, the consequences, which should be the primary consideration, become subordinated to the goal of expressing virtuous sentiments.

I am not arguing that the sanctions policy was disastrous, merely that it was often pursued without due consideration of its objective consequences or, sometimes, in spite of what were thought to be the likely results.* Perhaps as important to the universities, decisions about the handling of student protests on behalf of the policy were colored by a concern for the negative symbolism that applying discipline in that context was sure to have. The inaction of those years set precedents that have outlived the sanctions "debate."

Moreover, instead of a university's decision on divestment, consider a nation's decision about whether to wage war, or a union's decision about whether to strike. The same dangerous logic well might apply; opposition to a proposed course of action could take on a meaning-in-effect that precludes vigorous deliberation on its merits. Yet the result could be that enormously harmful actions, affecting millions of lives, will be wrongly undertaken.[8]

A Classic Political Witch Hunt

As a final illustration, consider the climate of opinion that must have prevailed in a congressional hearing room in the 1940s and 1950s, when investigations into the loyalty of prominent Ameri-

---

*Conveniently, the policy was painless for its American advocates, though it may have been a disaster for some black South Africans. The logic of this argument also applies to the sanctions debate *within* South Africa.

cans were openly conducted. It was commonly understood at the time that the United States faced a formidable adversary in a cold war, and that many U.S. citizens sympathized with the espoused ideals of this adversary. It was thought entirely appropriate that steps be taken to protect our national interest against possibly disloyal acts by these misguided souls. Some of these steps, to be sure, raised constitutional questions, but one had to weigh the relative importance of liberty and security. After all, there were real communists among us, committed to advancing the agenda of the Soviet Union. Besides, who exactly were these people voicing such vehement procedural objections to the employment of reasonable safeguards against possibly damaging breaches of security? Just what kind of person would, under the circumstances, nitpick about the civil liberties of a few communists and their fellow travelers?

The Soviet Union was expanding rapaciously in eastern Europe; the "reds" had taken over in Beijing; the State Department had apparently been infiltrated; and atomic secrets had been stolen. Under these circumstances, what kind of people quibbled over such details as whether a line of questioning entirely comported with some standards of due process? Could we not infer something about their values from their refusal to name names, or their willingness to speak openly on behalf of an accused? Perhaps those objecting to our methods of inquiry should themselves be sanctioned.*

In such a climate, an anticommunist civil libertarian who does not want to be mistaken for a fellow traveler might find silence to be the wisest course. And those bent on ferreting out the deviants might find that they can say just about anything, about just about anyone, without being called to account for it. The more widespread the silence among unquestionably loyal Americans, and the more prominent the fellow travelers among those protesting the witch hunt, the more reliably does the fact of protest provide a signal about political belief. A demagogue like

---

*Mindful of my own "Jenninger problem" I hereby declare, for what it may be worth, that this account does not express my personal views but describes the hypothetical views of a "typical American" in the early cold war period.

Senator Joseph McCarthy of Wisconsin could enjoy a prolonged career under such circumstances. When people, once having become targets, can be smeared with lies and innuendo ("I have in my hand a list of names"), and when guilt can be based on a decades-old association with a suspicious cause, caution must be the rule of the day. Such caution plays right into the hands of the demagogues.

A generic problem with conventions of signaling values is the ease with which they can be abused by partisan opportunists. When listeners are keen to discern a speaker's basic values on a crucial issue, a speaker has to worry that his political enemies will, by distorting or misrepresenting his expressions, falsely depict him as being morally unsound. He has to take care, in other words, not to be smeared. To minimize this risk the speaker may need to avoid some issues altogether, or to speak only in the most circumspect and indirect way, especially if he is criticizing the consensus view. Pointed remarks on a sensitive topic lend themselves to caricature and distortion. Thus, and again ironically, the public's heightened moral sensitivity (together with a political climate of intense partisan conflict) may actually result in a lower level of effective moral discourse, as the making of nuanced arguments and the drawing of fine distinctions become too risky for political speakers.

The smear campaign as an instrument of political warfare was made famous during the McCarthy period. This had a clear and lasting effect on the formulation of foreign policy. Arguments about relations with communist China, for example, were encumbered with a host of collateral meanings, thereby inhibiting public discourse.* Moreover, unprincipled conservatives tried to pin the "commie" label on political enemies whose real offense was the

---

*Consider the case of Phillip Jessup, nominated for a diplomatic post in the 1950s by President Eisenhower, but rejected by the Senate because some years earlier he had attended a conference on whether U.S. China policy should be reconsidered. Indeed, it took two decades for that policy to be accommodated to reality by the staunch anticommunist Richard Nixon, who had "natural cover" against the claim of deviance.

holding of liberal views on domestic policy.* More recently, the public's desire to infer a political figure's true values on race and gender issues has been exploited for partisan purposes in this way. Nominees of Republican presidents, often lacking the benefit of a track record giving them credible "cover" against the charge of being racists, have been especially vulnerable to this sort of smear tactic.†

Implications for the Character and Effectiveness of Public Debate

The Futility of Protesting Too Much

All of these examples illustrate an important feature of regimes of tacit censorship: one cannot break their grip through a simple declaration of sincerity ("Despite my violation of the norm, please

---

*Support for the New Deal was often raised in this context. Consider the comment of Senator Hugh Butler of Nebraska about former secretary of state Dean Acheson, after Acheson publicly supported Alger Hiss: "I watch his smart-aleck manner and his British clothes and that New Dealism, everlasting New Dealism in everything he says and does, and I want to shout, 'Get out, Get out. You stand for everything that has been wrong with the United States.'" [Quoted in Navasky (1980), p. 21] Evidently, there was more going on here than just the fight against communism.

†The 1987 campaign against Robert Bork's Supreme Court nomination is a classic case. It was launched with a speech by Senator Edward Kennedy describing Bork's America as "a land in which women would be forced into back-alley abortions, blacks would sit at segregated lunch counters, rogue police could break down citizen doors in midnight raids." This gross distortion was part of a calculated rhetorical strategy that in due course prevailed. The strategy was spelled out with remarkable candor in a memorandum circulated among anti-Bork interest groups: "To offset the White House's emphasis on Bork's intellectual qualifications, opponents need to imprint his nonjudicious turn of mind with such labels as: closed minded, . . . insensitive, prejudicial, . . . injudicious, rigid, cold and indifferent, lacking empathy, flaming and inflexible, [and] insensitive to injustice." (Advocacy Institute, "The Bork Nomination: Seizing the Symbols of the Debate," July 14, 1987, pp. 5–6)

I am aware that many readers will object to my mentioning this episode in the context of McCarthyism. My point, however, is analytical, not political. I mean only to show how the smear—defined as the misrepresentation of a political figure's expression so as to cast him in morally dubious light before the public—is a ubiquitous tactic of partisan politics.

Smears of Democratic presidents' nominees have also occurred. Just after Bill Clinton withdrew the nomination of Lani Guinier to head the Justice Department's civil rights division, an issue of the conservative *American Spectator* trumpeted the fact that Guinier's father had been close to the Communist party in the 1940s and 1950s!

understand that my values are pure"). Reliance on such literal claims is a common mode of naive behavior in the forum. The act of making the claim may itself become a signal of the claimant's deviance. When a form of expression has the meaning-in-effect that those speaking in this way are likely to have incorrect values, overt demands for credulity or complaints about the limits being placed on freedom of expression quickly become futile. Conventions of tacit restraint in public expression are made more durable by the fact that they do not themselves easily become objects of criticism, since it is often the "truly deviant" who have the greatest interest in criticizing them.

Meta-argumentation—arguing at the secondary level about the form that primary arguments should be allowed to take in the community—can become the refuge of scoundrels seeking to avoid the righteous condemnation that their morally dubious expressions have earned. And it is indeed the case that complaints about the PC "reign of terror" on campuses, even when not exaggerated, have had little effect on the administrators, professors, or student activists enthusiastic about one or another of the so-called correct causes. Complaints about liberal PC, though divorced from explicit advocacy for any policy position, nevertheless have the faint but distinct odor of conservatism about them.

We all know the phrase "Some of my best friends are [name of group], but . . . ," as in "Some of my best friends are blacks, but their affirmative action claims have gone too far," "Some of my best friends are Jews, but Israel's policies are barbaric," and so forth. Note that this verbal construction is no longer used literally; instead it now serves as a sarcastic reference to people who unsuccessfully affect a concern for values they do not really share. The strange career of this expression—its literal meaning being overtaken by a symbolic one—highlights the fact that strategic political expression has become much more salient in American public life.

Literal use of the phrase is now patently naive. Though the purpose of the "Some of my best friends . . ." clause is to spare the speaker ill judgment about his values when the "but . . ." clause is spoken, it serves instead to alert listeners that a bigot's statement is about to come. Listeners know that the speaker is aware that people making such statements are suspected of racism (or anti-

Semitism, misogyny, sympathy for communists, homophobia, and so on); after all, issuing the qualification acknowledges the suspicious nature of such talk. What type of person, the listener then asks, requests this exemption?

For example, those who genuinely value racial equality know that even if they harbor reservations about affirmative action, in the interest of supporting a good and decent policy they ought not to utter them. And those less interested in racial equality can be relied upon to see no such constraint. So not only will "progressives" abstain from criticizing affirmative action, they will also not complain about not being able to express their criticisms!

About the person arguing for the right to tell a racial joke, prefacing his argument with "Some of my best friends are blacks, but . . . ," we say to ourselves that this person protests too much. Under a convention of restrained public expression, prudent people do not protest at all for the right to say imprudent things.

Strategic Imprecision

In "Politics and the English Language" Orwell, describing the poor state into which political writing had fallen in postwar England, observed the following:

> The word *Fascism* has now no meaning except in so far as it signifies "something not desirable." . . . A word like *democracy* not only [has] . . . no agreed definition, but the attempt to make one is resisted from all sides. It is almost universally felt that when we call a country democratic we are praising it: consequently the defenders of every kind of regime claim that it is a democracy, and fear that they might have to stop using the word if it were tied down to any one meaning. Words of this kind are often used in a consciously dishonest way. . . . The person who uses them has his own private definition, but allows his hearer to think he means something quite different.

This is an insightful observation, directly relevant to the present discussion. It is clear that ambiguous and imprecise expression is a valuable tactic for the strategic speaker. By expressing himself in generalities a sender allows various receivers to impute their own, possibly inconsistent meanings to his pronouncements. With a euphemism well chosen for its vagueness, a speaker can say palatably (that is, in a manner consistent with extant communal norms) what might offend some listeners if it were said more incisively. The circumlocution may be intended to deceive, or merely to obscure, but in either case the result is a debasement of the currency of public discourse.

Consider, for example, some uses of the term "minorities" in contemporary American public speech. The speaker may actually mean "blacks" but find that term embarrassingly specific. (This is usually the case when the reference is to some aspect of urban life that has negative connotations.) Or, as in the phrase "women and minorities," the speaker may hope by the use of words alone to create a coalition of interests in the listener's mind when none exists in fact. Or, finally, consider a recent addition to the progressive lexicon, "disadvantaged minorities." One finds this phrase used in educational philanthropy circles when the speaker really means "nonwhites, excluding Asians"—never mind the fact that many Asians are disadvantaged. Imagine the uproar were a foundation candidly to announce a scholarship program intended to help "nonwhite persons belonging to groups that perform poorly on standardized tests." So the strategic speaker sacrifices honesty and accuracy by declaring instead that the program is aimed at "disadvantaged minorities." (A variation on this theme is the "underrepresented minority"—though these days talk of any minority group being overrepresented is unheard of.)*

Such linguistic imprecision impairs analysis. But that is often its purpose. The person who utters the phrase "women and minorities" may want not to reckon with the fact that the majority of women, being married to white men, share significant resources

---

*It was not always so, witness the limits which many institutions imposed on Jewish enrollments earlier in this century—limits openly justified by a concern about Jewish "overrepresentation." When, in the late 1970s, the applications of Asians to elite colleges and universities began to grow more rapidly than their enrollments, no similar justification of restricting the access of these superbly qualified students could be made. In fact, what appear to have been informal ceilings on Asian admissions were swept away as complaints about the disparity between acceptance rates of Asian and white applicants were made public. Indeed, the combination of minority status with outstanding academic performance among Asian Americans, has proved profoundly unsettling to the practice of affirmative action in college admissions. See Takagi's excellent study of these developments (1992).

and fundamental interests in common with their putative oppressors. An advocate for "diversity" may prefer not to be explicit about which differences are included and which (religious and political beliefs, for example) are excluded from that advocacy. No sane person could relish the task of explaining to poor but studious Vietnamese immigrants why they do not qualify for some "minority" scholarships. And if one wants to accommodate more "underrepresented" black and Hispanic students at a university by admitting fewer whites, but not fewer Asians, then one surely would rather not dwell on the statistical overrepresentation of the latter.

Another way in which the lack of clear language can be helpful is illustrated by *the use of emblematic speech to signal moral values.* The speaker advertises his beliefs by using words in a way that, for political or aesthetic reasons, someone not holding that belief would never emulate. Then the speech act has the effect of waving a banner: "queers," "at-risk group," "institutional racism," "fascist America," "differently abled person." When words are spoken in a given manner only by those holding a discrete set of opinions, their use in this way signals that the user adheres to that party's line.

Two strangers conversing on an airplane will feel each other out to learn if they have similar views on matters that otherwise would be better to avoid. Such conversations involve the tentative and halting display of one's position by use of emblematic speech. Each speaker, seeking recognition and reinforcement, looks for the positive feedback that encourages the candor possible only among the like-minded. The dialogue may evolve into an intense and intimate exchange, or it may lapse into vague and meaningless banter, depending on what the speakers are able to learn about one another. If real communication eventually occurs, the path to it will have been paved by overtures of calculated imprecision.

Alternatively, consider a political speaker addressing a crowd in the forum. If the significance of some words as signals of belief is known only to insiders, their use in public allows the speaker to convey a reassuring message to some listeners ("I share your values") without alarming the others. These words are *coded emblems of belief.* A racist politician might use code words such as "welfare queen," "criminal element," and "states' rights" to appeal to like-minded voters, while maintaining what in the intelligence world is called "plausible deniability" of this motive: if challenged, the speaker exploits the code words' ambiguity of meaning and claims that he intended no offense. Once words become emblems in this way, speakers with different values who want not to risk being misunderstood must abandon their use altogether.

Multiple Audiences

The use of code words is characteristic of a situation where the speaker faces multiple audiences—distinct communities of listeners that do not share communal norms. This situation is rich with strategic possibilities. The presence of distinct audiences may lead to more candid expression, as each group keeps the speaker honest on issues of concerns to the other.* Or, if one audience is naive and the other sophisticated, a duplicitous speaker may "talk over the heads" of the naive listeners to get his true message across to those "in the know."† Another possibility, frequently observed with discussion in mixed company, is that standing to address an issue is restricted to a certain class of persons who have "natural cover." These are people who, because of their group identity, are not immediately presumed to have malign motives for expressing themselves in a potentially offensive way.

Thus blacks, but not whites, can make movies or report news

---

*A corporate executive discussing his firm's financial status with bankers and union leaders both in the room is more credible with each by virtue of the presence of the other: he wants the bankers to think the firm is doing well and the union leaders to think it is doing poorly, and both parties know this! See Farrell and Gibbons (1989). A similar logic constrains the chances of rhetorical manipulation when a politician commits himself to giving *exactly the same speech* on racial issues to both a black and a white audience, as Bill Clinton did during the 1992 presidential campaign.

†Thus Strauss (1952) argues that by "writing between the lines" some medieval philosophers engaged in criticism of the status quo without provoking a charge of heresy. They disguised their arguments so they would not be understood by lay authorities, but could still be grasped by other philosophers: "[A] man of independent thought can utter his views in . . . print without incurring danger, provided he is capable of writing between the lines. . . . For the influence of persecution on literature is precisely that it compels all writers who hold heterodox views to develop a peculiar technique of writing, the technique which we have in mind when speaking of writing between the lines." (p. 24) Very much in keeping with the spirit of this chapter, Strauss goes on to draw implications for how these texts should be read from his presumptions about how they were written. His theory of reading rests fundamentally upon the fact that the philosopher speaks to multiple audiences.

stories on the problem of skin-color prejudice that continues to affect African American society. Women, but not men, can publicly question whether in a given case the charge of date rape has been manufactured on the morning after by a "victim" who wishes she had made a different decision about sexual intimacy the previous night. The censorship in these cases is partial; those who have "cover" express themselves freely, whereas those who lack it must be silent. When the combination of an ascriptive trait with an offending expression is necessary to mark the speaker as "bad," words spoken in mixed company have a meaning-in-effect that is contingent upon who has spoken them. A white is taken to be a racist if he says "nigger," but blacks use the term all the time. Used by blacks, its meaning ranges from an endearment to an epithet, but for whites—whatever their intent—it can only be an epithet.

When the effective meaning of some expression is contingent on both the speaker and the audience, then the rules of permissible expression in mixed company will generally differ from those applicable to homogeneous gatherings. Men talking among themselves have rules concerning what can decently be said about women, but these are generally less restrictive rules than the ones governing a mixed conversation. This is one reason why the "token woman" (the only one at a table of men) can be more than marginally significant. She may have only one vote, but by her presence, and without saying a word, she can profoundly influence the tone and substance of the debate by narrowing the boundaries of legitimate discourse.*

Notice also that when the rules of permissible expression vary with the audience, prudent speakers must be sure to remember to whom they are speaking at any moment. And they must also worry about how an expression made in one context will "sound" in another. Indeed, a common source of political gaffes is the rendering in public by the news media of a remark made in a private setting where different rules applied. For example, during the 1984 presidential campaign, Jesse Jackson referred to New York City as

---

*Men as well as women will apply the stricter rules. Thus a man can be condemned by other men for saying something in the presence of women that is commonly said in their absence. Yet it would be a mistake to dismiss this as an unfair double standard, since with a different audience the same words do not have the same effective meaning.

"Hymietown" while speaking to an all-black audience of reporters and staff. While the remark should not have been said even there, Jackson's intention was probably less malign than the anti-Semitic meaning ascribed to the comment after it became public. Still, once the comment was revealed, the ad hominem query—what kind of person speaks, even privately, in this way?"—became irresistible.*

An interesting feature of multiple audience situations is that sometimes it is insiders, not outsiders, who are specifically forbidden to voice certain opinions or address certain issues in mixed company. "Washing dirty linen in public" refers to injudicious speech by an insider that is taboo in mixed company but would be appropriate if no outsiders were present. This can be speech—criticism of one's group, especially—in which outsiders routinely engage. The taboo may derive from a concern that outsiders will misinterpret the information, a fear that the insider's words will be exploited by outsiders against the group's interest, or a worry that outsiders will feel legitimized in their own criticism of the group once an insider has confirmed it.

In general, conflict or competition between groups in an audience changes the strategic implications of critical expression. If a partisan opponent criticizes our party, we respond by saying that the critic does not know what he's talking about, and in any case seeks only to discredit us. If one of our own makes the same criticism, no such defense is available, and moreover, our opponents are emboldened to make some points of their own. The insider critic is more persuasive than the outsider because he has superior information about group functioning, and his criticism is more likely to be motivated by a genuine concern for the group's welfare. For these reasons groups often try to discourage insider criticism by punish-

---

*Most "racist" remarks discovered to have been made by public figures have this character. While this does not excuse the offender, it sharpens our understanding of the offense, which more often is one of naivete than of malice. Yet because the malign are more likely than the benign to overlook the fact that some expression might offend an unintended listener, calling such gaffes racist is consistent with the logic of strategic inference.

ing the members who engage in it—a tendency that has important implications for the ethics and efficacy of public discourse.*

I am often struck by the intensity of critical debate among black Americans over such issues as the social problems of the so-called underclass—when that debate takes place out of the hearing of whites. The same theme being explored by a black speaker in mixed company causes other blacks to severely sanction the deviant. If, for example, a white gives voice in mixed company to his fear of criminal victimization, he may be perceived as criticizing blacks (and that may be his intent). This perception will be enough to keep some, but not all, whites from expressing their fear. But if a black person in that audience supports or confirms the white person's feeling, when everyone knows that complaint over the "criminal element" has racial connotations, he courts serious trouble with other blacks. So does the black who worries publicly about the fairness of affirmative action.

Both are expressing themselves in ways that cause their fellows to question their basic commitments. By departing from the

---

*Discouraging insider criticism can have significant costs, a point explored at length in Hirschman's important book (1970). Precisely because it is rooted in familiarity with and concern for the group, such criticism can be compelling, but also painful, to hear. Yet when insiders are not permitted to voice their dissatisfactions, they may exit—that is, withdraw from active participation in the public life of the group—leaving the discussion to the contented and forestalling needed reform. Hirschman stresses, therefore, the importance of loyalty: a speaker's willingness to stay and argue over how the group should conduct its affairs, even at great personal cost to himself. This is to be distinguished from blind loyalty, the reflexive and uncritical endorsement of one's communal norms captured in the phrase "my country, right or wrong."

The loyal political critic in a multiple audience environment faces the dilemma that, to be effective, his interventions must be spoken publicly and heard by friends and enemies alike. Walzer (1988) describes this dilemma in his wise and elegant study of social criticism: "Intimate criticism is a common feature of our private lives; it has its own [implicit] rules. We don't criticize our children, for example, in front of other people, but only when we are alone with them. The social critic has the same impulse, especially when his own people are confronted by hostile forces. . . . But the social critic can never be alone with his people; there is no social space that is like familial space, and so the critic's intimacy can't take the form of private speech; it can only shape and control his public speech. A certain forbearance qualifies or alternates with his stringency. He must speak, however, and speak out loud so long as there is any hope that he will be listened to among his own people. . . . The silence of the connected social critic is a grim sign—a sign of defeat, a sign of endings" (pp. 151–52).

convention of restrained expression, they are seen as violating a cardinal principle of group loyalty. (Though, as Albert Hirschman has noted, the willingness to deviate in the face of sanctions for the sake of the group's welfare, as one understands it, might be seen as an expression of true loyalty.) It is therefore not surprising that these deviants are often accused of being racially inauthentic. Breaking the no-group-criticism-in-mixed-company taboo raises in the minds of "blind loyalists" the question of whether the critics are "genuinely" black.* And yet, as Michael Walzer has observed, serious political analysis in a democracy cannot take place in private—among blacks alone, out of whites' hearing. So, by making racial authenticity contingent on rhetorical conformity, the blind loyalists succeed in diminishing the vitality of the American political forum.

Forbidden Facts

French intellectual Jean-Francois Revel, lamenting the difficulty of keeping the truth about the Soviet Union before the western European public, observed that "it is around the circulation of facts that the taboos are strongest in the evolution of public information and debate into national policy. . . . As a rule, concern that a fact might influence public opinion in a way we dislike overrides our curiosity about it and our honesty in making it known."[9] Revel identified three reasons for these taboos: (1) Leftists who embraced socialist ideals saw criticism of the Soviet Union as a disguised attack on socialism; thus they avoided it themselves and looked askance at people willing to sound the alarm. (2) Conservatives seeking a more militaristic posture justified their policy arguments by characterizing the Soviets as aggressors. So, to counter their arguments, evidence of Soviet aggression had to be denied. (3) The prospect that the nuclear superpower to the East might actually pose a threat to the European democracies was so frightening that

---

*Thus conservative Supreme Court Justice Clarence Thomas was described by a black legal scholar critical of his nomination as "black on the outside, but white on the inside." Carter (1991) discusses with insight some of the problems with the notion of racial authenticity implicit in these remarks.

many people simply preferred to deny the reality of the threat, hiding their heads in the sand.

These observations are relevant to our general analysis of censored public discussion. Notice that points (1) and (2) above both involve strategic factors: if reporting a fact symbolizes that the reporter has bad values, or strengthens the hand of those on the wrong side in a public debate, then prudent people do not report that fact. If some truth about the world is inconsistent with a firmly held communal value, listeners may punish the messenger who asserts that truth, reasoning that only someone who disdains the value would act so as to undermine it. Anticipating this punishment, investigators will not only be dissuaded from saying what they know, but also from asking questions that might have unpleasant answers. When rhetoric about facts in this way comes to signal one's values on an important ethical matter, the identification and analysis of significant social problems can be impeded.

This problem is classically illustrated in the historic conflicts between religion and science. Galileo was forced by the Church to recant his views; Christian fundamentalists have attacked the teaching of evolution. But in our time, other, secular motivations for suppressing facts and limiting analysis loom larger. Scientists looking into the genetic basis, if any, for gender or racial differences in behavior have met with vocal opposition from "women and minorities" who regard the very act of such speculation to be evidence of bigotry. The search for biological factors influencing violent behavior has been denounced as racist, though this plausible hypothesis has no evidently racial connotation.* Ironically, the speculation that sexual preference is *not* rooted in biology has been denounced as well by the very same people.

Consistent with my theory that expression is often curtailed for fear of offending communal norms, one finds that the pressure on

---

*Frederick Goodwin was forced out as director of the Violence Initiative of the National Institute of Mental Health in 1992 for suggesting publicly that study of the aggressive behavior of male primates in the wild might shed light on problems of violence in human societies. In a fatal error, he used the words "monkeys" and "inner cities" in adjacent paragraphs. In a resignation letter to President Bush he said, "I am appalled to see the way in which complex and important scientific issues can become distorted when they enter into the political arena during an election year." See Miller (1992) and Sagarin (1980).

researchers not to carry out an investigation, or to withhold its findings, often originates from *within* scientific communities rather than without.[10] This is especially so in the social sciences. Sociologist James Coleman, perhaps the world's leading scholar of educational policy, recalls that in 1976 the president and a number of prominent members of the American Sociological Association tried to have him censured for the "crime" of discovering, and announcing, that citywide busing for school desegregation purposes caused white flight. This claim had been denied for years prior to Coleman's research, and far-reaching social policies had been erected on the presumption that it was not true. When Coleman presented his work at the ASA meetings that year, the corridors outside of the lecture hall, and the wall behind the podium from which he had to speak, were covered with posters displaying (along with his name and the title of his talk) Nazi swastikas and other epithets suggesting that he was a racist.[11] We now know that Coleman had been right, and that the taboos "around the circulation of facts" then prevalent among American sociologists have had seriously deleterious consequences.*

Some areas of social science inquiry are so closely linked in the public mind to sensitive issues of policy that an objective, scholarly discussion of them is now impossible. Instead of open debate where participants are prepared to be persuaded by arguments and evidence contrary to their initial presumptions, we have become accustomed to rhetorical contests where competing camps fire volleys of data and tendentious analyses back and forth in an effort to win the battle of public opinion. Sometimes the press is an active participant in these struggles, selectively reporting the findings that confirm the politically correct point of view. Issues of race, gender, and sexual preference are particularly susceptible to this process of politicization.

Investigators identifying with certain groups advocate particular approaches to their disciplines—a feminist, or a black, or gay

---

*Some years later, when lecturing on their important treatise *Crime and Human Nature* (1985) in the shadow of Harvard University, Richard Herrnstein and James Q. Wilson were drowned out by students chanting, "Wilson, Herrnstein, you can't hide. You believe in genocide!"

approach to history, sociology, economics, anthropology, and so forth. This fragmentation—now well advanced and seemingly irreversible, whatever one may think of it—is closely connected with the fact that *public rhetoric in many areas of the social sciences is self-consciously undertaken as a multiple-audience conversation.* The disciplines are not insular venues of discourse, governed by internal norms of scholarly expression accepted by all who have been trained to do research in the field. Not only do social scientists address each other, they participate in a larger discussion with extrascientific implications. Perhaps it was ever thus, though growth of the regulatory and welfare state has undoubtedly enlarged the extent to which scientific expression has political consequences.

The notion of "objective research" (on the employment effects of the minimum wage, say, or the influence of maternal employment on child development) can have no meaning if, when the results are reported, other scientists are mainly concerned to pose the ad hominem query ("Just what kind of economist [or sociologist, or other professional] would say this?") Not only will investigators be induced to censor themselves, the very way in which research is evaluated and consensus about "the facts" is formed will be altered. If when a study yields an unpopular conclusion it is subjected to greater scrutiny, and more effort is expended toward its refutation, an obvious bias to "find what the community is looking for" will have been introduced. Thus, the very way in which knowledge of the world around us is constituted can be influenced by the phenomenon of strategic expression.

Conclusion

There are many questions that remain to be investigated. Why do certain issues seem to be especially effective vehicles for the tacit communication of the values of those who speak and write about them? Who, if anyone, chooses the vocabulary of symbolic expression? When is political correctness—understood as consensual restraint on public expression in a community—beneficial? (I have mainly discussed its problematic nature.) What can be done to reverse a regime of rhetorical reticence once it has been established? What are the responsibilities of individuals within a community whose public discourse on important matters lacks in candor? Is there a role for courage and heroism?

These are matters of great seriousness, raising ethical as well as political questions. Who, we must ask, will speak for compromise and moderation in negotiations, when to speak in this way is seen to signal a weak commitment to "the struggle"? Who will declare that the emperor is naked when a leader's personal failings hurt the movement? Who will urge, under pressures of economic or electoral competition, that the old ways of doing business in our company or our party require reexamination? Who will report the lynchers, known to everyone in town despite their hooded costumes? Who will expose the terrorists, or denounce the haters, once terror and hatred have become "legitimate" means of political expression? Who will insist that we speak plainly and tell the truth about delicate and difficult matters that we would all prefer to cover up or ignore? How can a community sustain an elevated and liberal political discourse when the social forces that promote tacit censorship threaten to usher in a dark age?

One of the finest statements ever written on these questions, I believe, is Vaclav Havel's essay "The Power of the Powerless."[12] Confronting the overarching repression of the "post-totalitarian system," Havel describes the existential and ideological features of late communism that gave the dissidents their power. "Between the aims of the post-totalitarian system and the aims of life there is a yawning abyss," he writes. While life moves toward "fulfillment of its own freedom," the system demands "conformity, uniformity and discipline." The system is permeated with lies: workers are enslaved in the name of the working class, the expansion of empire is depicted as support for the oppressed, denial of free expression is supposed to be the highest form of freedom, rigged elections are the highest form of democracy, and so on. For the system to continue, individual citizens must choose to "live within a lie." The dissident who quixotically refuses to go along with the program, defiantly attempting to "live within the truth," is profoundly subversive: "By breaking the rules of the game, he has disrupted the game as such. He has exposed it as a mere game. . . . He has said that the emperor is naked. And because the emperor is in fact naked, something extremely dangerous has happened."

Thus the struggle between the "aims of the system" and the "aims of life" takes place not between social classes, or political parties, or aggregates of people aligned for or against the system. Rather, this struggle is fought within each human being:

> The essential aims of life are present naturally in every person. In everyone there is some longing for humanity's rightful dignity, for moral integrity, for free expression of being and a sense of transcendence over the world of existences. Yet, at the same time, each person is capable, to a greater or lesser degree, of coming to terms with living within the lie. Each person somehow succumbs to a profane trivialization of his or her inherent humanity, and to utilitarianism. In everyone there is some willingness to merge with the anonymous crowd and to flow comfortably along with it down the river of pseudo-life. This is much more than a simple conflict between two identities. It is something far worse: it is a challenge to the very notion of identity itself.

Truth, Havel concludes, has its own special power in the post-totalitarian system: "Under the orderly surface of the life of lies, therefore, there slumbers the hidden sphere of life in its real aims, of its hidden openness to truth."

While I certainly do not intend to compare the constrained expressive environment of a politically correct college campus with the systematic extirpation of dissent characteristic of the totalitarian state, I nevertheless find the moral dimensions of Havel's argument relevant to the dilemmas faced by individuals in our own society. Conventions of self-censorship are sustained by the utilitarian acquiescence of each community member in an order that, at some level, denies the whole truth. By calculating that the losses from deviation outweigh the gains, individuals are led to conform. Yet by doing so they yield something of their individuality and their dignity to "the system." Usually this is a minor matter, more like the small sacrifices we make for the sake of social etiquette than some grand political compromise. But, as I hope I have made clear, circumstances arise when far weightier concerns are at stake. The same calculus is at work in every case.

How, then, are the demagogues and the haters to be denounced? How can reason gain a voice in the forum? How can the truth about our nation, our party, our race, our church come to light when the social forces of conformity and the rhetorical conventions of banality hold sway? How can we have genuine moral discourse about ambiguous and difficult matters (like racial inequality in our cities, or on our campuses) when the security and comfort of the platitudes lie so readily at hand? Though it may violate the communal norms of my economics fraternity to say so, I believe these things can be achieved only when individuals—first a few, and then many—transcend "the world of existences" by acting not as utilitarian calculators, but rather as fully human and fully moral agents determined at whatever cost to "live within the truth."

9

Leadership Failure
and the Loyalty Trap

Since the late 1960s black American intellectuals and politicians have fallen prey to what amounts to a conspiracy of silence about the social and moral condition of the black lower classes. We return with trepidation to the places where we were born and raised, now communities unlike any we had known; we look despairingly at the tenements that once housed poor families in dignity but no longer do; we remain bewildered by the profound changes that have occurred in less than a generation. Yet we are unwilling to voice that bewilderment forthrightly, or to ask of today's residents, "How can you live like this?" We are participating in a conspiracy.

We have tolerated incompetence in the social and political institutions serving this population, because its source has been black. We have made excuses for and sometimes even glorified the supposedly rebellious actions of thugs, although those thugs have made poor black people their victims. We have strained our imaginations, and our fellow citizens' credulity, to find apologies for the able-bodied, healthy, and intelligent young men who father children and then walk away from the responsibility to support them. We have listened in silence, or sometimes with enthusiastic encouragement, to middle-class young black men and women at the best colleges and universities explain, in the terms of an ideology of "racist exploitation" that was not even valid in the 1960s and is much less so today, their failure to make full use of the opportunities presented to them. In the name of racial loyalty, and in an effort to keep alive the sense of oppression that fueled the revolts of our youth, we have engaged in an almost criminal abdication of responsibility.

Moreover, we have encouraged and enforced the exclusion from good standing in our ranks of those few (often called "bourgeois elitists," though their origins are usually lower working class) who have had the insight and courage to object to this transparently inadequate series of rationalizations. But it has been the black poor, not ourselves, who have paid the price for this folly.

We have embraced a false, enervating conception of racial loyalty. While it avoids giving aid and comfort to the enemy (that is, to the "white man"), it requires that we ignore the dictates of our forebears' traditions and deepest values. Seduced by the moral relativism that emerged triumphant in the 1960s, we blacks in the best position to do so now find ourselves without the will or self-confidence to provide direction and set standards for our people. We have lapsed into the absurd posture of identifying true commitment to the cause with being uncritical of a person's deeds, however despicable, if that person is black. We act as if the historical fact of slavery and the associated culpability of America have endowed blacks with a fully paid insurance policy excusing whatever behavior ensues. Every personal failing of a black, even the illegal behavior of corrupt politicians, becomes evidence of the racism of whites. And every black individual who succeeds by dint of hard work and self-sacrifice is an exception to the rule that pervasive white racism precludes the possibility of black progress.

Remarkably, we think that the mere announcement of the small number of blacks who attain a certain achievement constitutes an indictment of society, and not of ourselves. We practice an *exhibitionism of nonachievement*, hurrying to advertise every instance of our underrepresentation, not recognizing that in doing so we are only announcing our own failure. For it is an axiom of this credo of racial loyalty that when blacks do not succeed, it is whites who have failed. We display the false security of those who, having been violated historically, think they can do no wrong—that right must inexorably be on their side. Demagogues can run among us spewing hatred and venom, and we express the barest annoyance, reasoning that these haters are but the natural result of that ever-present, ultimately cleansing, oh-so-convenient hate we call white racism.

Lest the reader think the foregoing too extreme, consider some of the enormities that have driven me to this despairing conclusion. Between the summers of 1979 and 1981 there occurred a series of approximately two dozen child killings in Atlanta, plunging the city into a state of fear. All of the victims of these crimes were black. The black mayor, black police chief, and substantially black police force threw themselves into the hunt for the killer, calling on the FBI for assistance. In due course a suspect, Wayne Williams, was arrested, tried (before a black judge) for two of the murders—though evidence suggested his involvement in others—and convicted of the crimes. One might think this would be cause for rejoicing among Atlanta's blacks, but one would be wrong.

The fact that the convicted killer turned out to be a black man greatly disappointed many blacks in Atlanta and across the country. For months some had been insisting that the Ku Klux Klan was behind the child disappearances, and they continued to assert this despite the overwhelming evidence to the contrary presented at the trial. Others agreed with popular black activist Dick Gregory that the Centers for Disease Control in Atlanta were kidnapping and murdering young black boys for an exotic cancer-fighting drug to be found in the tips of their sex organs. The (largely black) jury's verdict is rejected by many blacks to this day.

It could hardly be otherwise, given the extent to which prominent blacks had used the killings to exemplify the fact that blacks continue to suffer the ravages of racism. Indeed, in 1981, before the Williams trial, Jesse Jackson had said of the killings: "It is open season on black people. . . . These murders can only be understood in the context of affirmative action and Ronald Reagan's conservative politics."

One victim's mother, derisively referring to Atlanta mayor Maynard Jackson as "that fat boy," led a campaign against the middle-class black Atlanta establishment, accusing it (in collaboration with the white "powers that be") of having found in Williams a convenient scapegoat. Rather than celebrate the cessation of a murder spree, the victims of which were black children, many chose instead to absolve the apparent perpetrator and use the case as a platform for expressing their discontent with American society. (This approach was taken to an extreme by James Baldwin in his 1985 meditation on the Atlanta child killings, *The Evidence of Things Not Seen.*) Evidently, no act of a black man, however willful and depraved, is unfit for exploitation in this manner. For the "sophisticated" observer, one seeing beneath the surface to the "true" nature of racial oppression, the formula injustice (a black man on trial for murder in white America is by definition a victim) proved more politically salient than the reality of mass killing being finally brought to a halt. This is a kind of collective madness. Are we so obsessed with our victimization by whites that we have lost the capacity to make moral judgments about other blacks, even the pathologically violent who prey on our children?

Consider how Charles Rangel, a black Democratic congressman from New York City, responded to the efforts of prominent New Yorkers to get him to condemn the speaking appearance of Louis Farrakhan at Madison Square Garden in October 1985. The Muslim minister's speech on that occasion, greeted by wild cheers, was described in one eyewitness account as follows:

> "The scriptures charge your people [the Jews] with killing the prophets of God." Farrakhan contended that God had not made the Jewish people pay for such deeds. However, if something happens to him, then God will make the Jews pay for all the prophets killed from biblical times to the present. "You cannot say 'never again' to God, because when God puts you in the oven, 'never again' don't mean a thing. If you fool with me, you court death itself. I will not run from you; I will run to you!" Farrakhan reserved a little of his hatred for black political leaders, telling the audience that "when a leader sells out the people, he should pay a price for that. Should a leader sell out the people and live?"

Not only did Representative Rangel refuse to issue a statement condemning this event, he went so far as to suggest that the pressure for him to do so constituted yet another example of white racism. In a public statement published in the *Washington Post* days after the speech, Rangel decried the "most objectionable assumption that I and other elected leaders who happen to be black have a special obligation to issue denunciations of Farrakhan on demand." He likened efforts to get him to make a statement to a requirement that he carry a "South African–like pass book stamped with issued denunciations" of the Muslim leader.

Rangel further suggested that "to renounce Farrakhan prior to his scheduled appearance at Madison Square Garden" would somehow have interfered with the minister's constitutional rights. He urged that we "differentiate between . . . the anti-Semitic garbage and the advocacy of discipline, self-help, and black pride" in Farrakhan's message, explaining that the real problem here is "the despair in the black community, the frustration and rage over America's failure to come to terms with its racism."

It is a measure of the great pressure this member of the U.S. House of Representatives was under that he would resort to such a transparently faulty attempt to evade his responsibilities as the principal national political spokesman for the blacks of Harlem. How would the public expression of his opinion regarding Farrakhan have limited the latter's right to speak? Why should it matter that "black pride" is also touted by one who preaches that no "leader [should] sell out the people and live?" While there were many thousands of Rangel's constituents in that auditorium cheering on Mr. Farrakhan, many thousands more reject that hate-filled message. To whom else ought concerned observers have gone to ascertain whether the sentiments that were expressed there represented the views of the majority of black New Yorkers? Were Rangel the black representative of a farm district in Iowa, one might take more seriously his cry of "South African–like" racism when asked to respond. As it is, his talk of politicians who just "happen to be black" seems disingenuous at best. He would, after all, be among the first to insist that blackness is a primary qualification for one who would occupy the seat once held by Adam Clayton Powell.

There is a stunning moral insensitivity here, born of being too long in the habitual status of victim. Rangel ends up absolving Farrakhan's supporters of their anti-Semitic bigotry with his reference to "America's failure"; yet no white politician could similarly dismiss the expression of antiblack sentiments among his constituents, however impoverished.

In December 1984, Bernhard Goetz, the so-called subway vigilante, shot four black youths who, he claimed, were about to accost him on a New York subway. He instantly became a folk hero among many urban dwellers, black and white, who live in fear of victimization. In the ensuing public discussion of the problem of urban crime, Kenneth Clark, perhaps the most eminent living black social scientist, offered the theory that in today's big cities it is not poor young men but "society" that is the "real mugger." Writing in the *New York Times*, Clark condemned the unseemly vigilante sentiments evoked by the Goetz case, and he ascribed to "society" responsibility for the criminal acts of urban muggers. Those committing most street crimes, he asserted, have been mugged themselves: they are the victims of "pervasive community, economic, and educational muggings" perpetrated by a "hypocritical society," at the hands of which "their humanity is being systematically destroyed." The theft and violence that many city dwellers fear are, for Clark, but "the inevitable criminality that comes out of the degradation of human beings."

This is a remarkable argument, not only for its questionable sociology—some impoverished urban minority populations (the Chinese in San Francisco, for example) have very low crime rates—but more significantly for what it reveals about Dr. Clark's view of the values and capacities of the inner-city poor. Quite simply, he is willing to avoid judgments about the behavioral differences among blacks in the interest of portraying the problems of the community as due to racism. Yet it is factually inaccurate and morally disturbing to say of poor black persons generally that their economic deprivation has destroyed their humanity. Even in the harshest slums the vast majority of residents do not brutalize their neighbors; they can hardly be taken as aberrant exceptions to some sociological law requiring the unemployed to become, in Clark's words, "mindlessly anti-social."

Moreover, even the black poor who are violent must be held responsible for their conduct. Are they not made poorer still when they are not accorded the respect inherent in the equal application of the obligations and expectations of citizenship? What is most dangerous about Clark's social-muggings analogy is that it invites both blacks and whites to see the black poor as morally different, socially distorted human beings. What such a construction (which is but a restatement of the old blaming-the-victim argument) may "achieve" by way of fostering guilt and pity among the population at large would seem to be more than offset by the extent to which it directly undermines the dignity of these persons.

I will offer one final example. In January 1986 CBS aired a documentary, moderated by Bill Moyers, called "The Vanishing Black Family." It sensitively described the lives of three young families in Newark, New Jersey—the unwed mothers and their children struggling to survive on the meager public provisions available to them, and the unemployed fathers and their desultory lives in the ghetto subculture. One of the most striking figures was a young man named Timothy, the attractive, articulate father of the three children in one of the families. Timothy, having fathered a total of six children by four different women, expressed no regret about the fact that he supported none of them. He proudly bragged about his sexual prowess. When asked about his obligation to the women who bore his children, he said, "That's on them. . . . I ain't gonna let no woman stand in the way of my pleasures." He explained that he would like to marry the mother of three of his children, but only when he could afford "a big wedding . . . with all the trimmings." He seemed not even to be trying to provide financial help to his children, explaining, "What I don't do, the government does." Evidently a bright and artistically talented young man, Timothy spent his time "on the streets," with no visible means of support. He took great pride in his children, though, noting that if they were to accomplish great things in their lives, he would experience a vicarious feeling of achievement.

For many viewers, black and white, Timothy symbolized a great problem in the black ghettos—male irresponsibility toward their progeny. His attitude, and not simply the fact of his unemployment, seemed to be part of the problem. Indeed, the mother of Timothy's children openly complained to Moyers about his lack of support. Nevertheless, a number of influential blacks came to his defense and denounced Moyers for projecting false and damaging images of black family life.

Nationally syndicated columnist Carl Rowan was typical of these. Referring to the Moyers program as "just more slander of the black family," he declared himself "tired of seeing the black family analyzed" and worried that such analyses would only be used as an excuse for mean-spirited social policies. Rowan unabashedly defended Timothy as a victim, saying that he was "just this side of slavery," comparing his circumstance to that of a handicapped child and suggesting that he deserved our compassionate understanding rather than our condemnation. Rowan, caught up in the ostentatious exhibition of his finely honed moral outrage concerning American racism, found himself without the capacity to *judge* Timothy's behavior. Being a "loyal" black, he could thus only apologize for it. He seemed not even to notice how his line of apologia implicitly devalued the efforts and sacrifices of those many black young men and women who have faced the same hardship as Timothy, but who have married, worked when they could, and struggled against the odds to give their children a better life. By taking Timothy's behavior as beyond his control, as the necessary consequence of being born in the Newark ghetto, Rowan was dishonoring the accomplishments of millions of working-class black Americans and contributing to the intellectual malaise in which we blacks now find ourselves.

These examples serve to illustrate the contemporary crisis in black intellectual and political leadership. I have had quite enough of the timidity, wrongheadedness and moral relativism that characterizes so much of the commentary of contemporary black elites on the racial issues of our day. The time has come to break ranks with them. These elites are caught in a "loyalty trap." They are fearful of engaging in a candid, critical appraisal of the condition of our people because they do not want to appear to be disloyal to the race. But this rhetorical reticence has serious negative consequences for the ability of blacks as a group to grapple with the real problems that confront us. Moreover, it represents a failure of nerve in the face of adversity that may be more accurately characterized as intellectual treason than racial fealty. After all, what more important obligation can the privileged class of black elites have than to tell the truth to their own people?

For most people, loyalty is a highly prized trait. We expect it of our friends, demand it of our kin, and look down on those of our fellow citizens who evidence disloyalty to their nation. Yet it is not always so easy to say what really constitutes loyalty in any particular case. Was Elliot Richardson being disloyal when he refused to obey Richard Nixon's order to fire special prosecutor Archibald Cox? Or was he remaining true to a higher authority? Similarly, were those who protested the Vietnam War being disloyal Americans? Or were they showing us just what genuine loyalty is all about?

These questions are of particular importance to black Americans who may choose to depart from group consensus in order to stand up for what they believe. To criticize the civil rights leadership openly for their ineffective response to the social dissolution of much of black America is to invite being called a traitor, an Uncle Tom, or even a racist. To fail to jump for joy at the prospect that Jesse Jackson might become president of the United States is to be labeled, by the many self-appointed guardians of racial virtue who roam the landscape, as being either brain-dead or morally corrupt. The examples of intolerance for critical discourse by black American intellectuals at variance with the racial party line are legion.

Consider that Martin Luther King's much-honored widow, Coretta Scott King, and his former lieutenant, Andrew Young, were actually booed by the black supporters of Rev. Jesse Jackson at the Democratic National Convention in 1984 because they supported the Mondale campaign during the primaries. Political scientist Adolph Reed has observed that such intolerance has roots deep in the history of protest movements among blacks. In his book *The Jesse Jackson Phenomenon* he wrote: "The long-standing anti-participatory style of organic spokesmen has been reproduced among elective leadership, and as a result the entrenched elites have been able with impunity to identify collective racial interest with an exceedingly narrow class agenda. The main focus for practical political activity within the black community in this context must be breaking down the illusion of a single racial opinion."

When, in the 1970s, law professor Derrick Bell began to question the efficacy of busing as the primary remedy sought by civil rights advocates in school desegregation cases, he became *persona non grata* among those advocates. When economist Thomas Sowell began his sustained intellectual assault on the assumptions underlying the development of civil rights advocacy in the 1970s, pointing out that discrimination alone could not account for observed economic differences between racial groups, he was denounced in terms so vitriolic that one would have thought "Uncle" had become his first name. When sociologist William Julius Wilson published *The Declining Significance of Race*, a book with the principal argument that poor blacks suffered more because of their class status than their race, he was denounced as a tool of conservatives, in league with those who would reenslave America's black population.

Recent history demonstrates that we are entitled to question the conception of loyalty implicit in these denunciations, and to decry the limited debate to which it has led. The issue here is not whether the individuals subject to such attack have been treated unfairly, though it is arguable that they have. "The real issue," as Sowell has pointed out, "is whether the new McCarthyism creates an atmosphere in which only a handful of people dare to question publicly the prevailing vision. If it succeeds in discrediting ideas and facts it cannot answer, in intimidating others into silence, then the whole attempt to resolve urgent social issues will have to be abandoned to those with fashionable clichés and political cant."

Blacks confront economic, social, and political problems of staggering magnitude. Yet we have a leadership and intellectual class mired in a vision of racial advocacy more suited to the 1950s and 1960s than to the 1990s and beyond. Our professional racial advocacy organizations seem unable or unwilling to address these profound problems in an effectual way. While these conditions are clearly beyond the direct control of anyone in the black community, it is entirely appropriate to assess the quality of leadership by its response to this circumstance. Judged by this standard, the traditional civil rights leadership leaves much to be desired. In the face of a pervasive social pathology in the inner-city ghettos of this country, these spokesmen have found little else to do but repeat the litany of charges about slavery, racism, discrimination, and the callous policies of Republican administrations.

While they busy themselves with making excuses for failure, poor and working-class blacks live with its consequences. Murder is now the leading cause of death among black males under twenty-five, and more than 90 percent of the victims are killed by other blacks. Inner-city black women are more than twice as likely as urban white women to be rape victims, mostly at the hands of black men. Rampant drug use destroys the chances for many to find a way out. Irresponsible sexuality, with children produced without any provision being made for their support, makes it almost impossible for individuals to take advantage of the opportunities now widely available to black Americans.

It is now clear that protest marches, civil rights lawsuits, or affirmative action for millionaire black businessmen cannot be expected to bring about change for those living in the ghettos. It is obvious that racism—though continuing to exist—cannot be blamed for all that ails the black community. Yet the civil rights leadership continues to talk as if it were 1965. They have not noticed that most white Americans have long since stopped listening. In light of the failure of the policies and programs that these leaders have chosen to emphasize, it is vital that there occur a discourse among blacks regarding how things might be improved. Effective leadership for blacks requires creating an environment where critical intellectual exchange can occur without it undermining the basis for cooperative association among members of the group. Those who demand of all blacks blind loyalty to the agenda of the NAACP make this more difficult to achieve. Their natural distrust of the "heretics" must be suspended long enough for there to occur a serious reflection on whether the traditional positions of the racial advocacy groups continues to serve blacks' best interests.

We blacks who express deviant opinions risk ostracism and denunciation. This is no surprise; it is the price one pays for intellectual integrity. It is to be expected that most people will defend tradition, even when tradition is wrong. There should be a high threshold of resistance to change in long-standing, deeply held beliefs.

Throughout history, though, it has often been the case that profound change has come from those who are considered outsiders. There is also a noble tradition of courageous dissent from racial orthodoxy by black Americans. At the turn of the twentieth century W. E. B. Du Bois spoke out against the-then dominant views of Booker T. Washington, who was urging that blacks moderate civil rights claims and seek accommodation with whites, despite the spread of lynchings and the enactment of Jim Crow laws. Du Bois objected, urging blacks to fight for all of their rights and going on to help found the NAACP. Though Du Bois paid a heavy price for this apostasy at the time, history has shown that his position had merit, and black people have been the beneficiaries of his courage and integrity.

Martin Luther King, Jr., also emphasized the crucial importance of open, critical discourse among blacks about our most serious problems. In the last book he published during his lifetime, *Where Do We Go from Here: Chaos or Community*, he wrote the following:

> *It is not a sign of weakness, but a sign of high maturity, to rise to the level of self-criticism.* Through group unity we must convey to one another that our women must be respected, and that life is too precious to be destroyed in a Saturday night brawl, or a gang execution. Through community agencies and religious institutions we must develop a positive program through which Negro youth can become adjusted to urban living and improve their general level of behavior.[1]

Were King at the helm of the civil rights movement today, I believe it is in this direction that he would be taking us.

10

Second Thoughts and First Principles

My fellow racialists, it is a pleasure to be able to address you on this occasion.

Franklin Delano Roosevelt once began a speech to the Daughters of the American Revolution with the salutation "My fellow immigrants . . . ," making the point that we are *all* immigrants here in the Western Hemisphere—a point that the DAR had conveniently forgotten. In like fashion, the late philosopher Allan Bloom, author of *The Closing of the American Mind* (1987), began a lecture at Harvard with the greeting "Fellow elitists . . . ," confronting a radically egalitarian audience with the irony that its institutional existence depends upon the most thoroughgoing intellectual elitism imaginable. Similarly, my opening is intended to expose as a dangerous hypocrisy the view that, in America, there is some neutral ground from which to address the race question.

When David Horowitz invited me to give this luncheon address at a conference entitled "Second Thoughts on Race," my initial response was: "I don't have any. I am a black man, and I intend to stay that way. That is one part of my 1960s heritage I see no need to go back on." And I *am* a product of Chicago's South Side; a veteran in spirit of the civil rights revolution. I am a partisan on behalf

195

of the inner-city poor. I agonize at the extraordinary waste of human potential that the despair of ghetto America represents. I cannot help but lament, deeply and personally, how little progress we have made in relieving the suffering that goes on there. It is not enough, far from being enough, for me to fault liberals for much that has gone wrong. This is not, for me, a mere contest of ideologies, or a competition for electoral votes. So, whatever "second thoughts" I may have about the enthusiasms of my youth, I hold certain primary commitments that are not open to renegotiation.

Indeed, even if I wanted to escape the implications of my race and social origins, it would be impossible. We Americans, black and white, all have to confront the saliency, the power, the inescapability of race. There is a sense in which this society *is* fundamentally racialist. (I avoid the more condemnatory, and less informative term "racist.") After all, intermarriage rates are not that high. Segregated residential communities remain widely to be observed. Our definitions of personal identities, and our choices of intimate association, reveal the racial distinctions that we make routinely, daily, in terms of whom we befriend, whom we embrace. We are never unaware of the race of a person with whom we interact; ambiguity on this question makes us nervous, and we seek to resolve it as quickly as tact and circumstances permit.

We Americans are stuck with the race question. We will be confronting it for years to come. We are the heirs of an ambiguous legacy—the idea of free self-government bequeathed us by the Founding Fathers, now the envy and goal of all the world; but also the legacy of a slave society. In our midst, among us here, standing before you now, are the descendants of people who were held forcibly as chattel. This fact has, of course, been abused. "Four hundred years of slavery" is the typical formulation, the touchstone of the complaint industry, of the "professional black," of the guilt monger. Yet it is good to start with this historical fact. We do well to reflect upon it. We ought not try to escape from it. For this legacy of slavery and the incompleteness even today of the process begun with the emancipation, this continuing struggle to create a common civic life for all Americans, is what brings us together here. This legacy makes black Americans unique among minority claimants. This history of subjugation, violence, dehumanization, alienation, and the efforts to legitimize and rationalize it, is where racialism—that ubiquitous consciousness of and obsession with racial identity in this society—is born.

We are all racialists now. Convened here as we are, having our "second thoughts about race," we do well to remember that no one in America can afford to be truly color-blind. The very fact that I stand here before you, defined as a black neoconservative, being praised and honored for the courage to "do the right (wing) thing," even as I am branded a traitor by many blacks, reveals the power of race in our political lives today. And you former radicals, now engaged in rethinking old racial truths in light of the intervening failures, excesses, and disappointments, would have it no other way!

My racial identity is useful to you; it is an important part of what commends me to your attention. My breaking ranks confirms you in your own apostasy. It helps you to see your deviation from the "progressive" ranks as valid and nonracist because here I am, a prominent black, agreeing with you. If by some magic I were suddenly to become white, my brilliant, perceptive, and courageous insights would just as suddenly be reduced to pedestrian, commonplace complaints, of little political or personal comfort to you.

That being the case, it is incumbent upon me to remind you that, while we are having and must have some second and third thoughts about race, while we must think hard and be honest and truthful and try to analyze what has gone wrong and figure out where to go from here, we must also not lose sight of the fact that there were and there remain reasons for a thrust toward racial reform. There were and remain good grounds for a *movement whose goal is the attainment of racial justice.* The objective then and now ought not be to get beyond racial justice, but rather to consider how we might deliver it, what we might do about it.

The so-called underclass is the key racial problem of our time. It constitutes a fundamental moral challenge to us. It represents the major unfinished business of the struggle for racial justice. True enough, this problem is shamelessly exploited by opportunistic charlatans whose programs of reform relate little to the genuine malady; who, in a self-promoting fashion and in ever more aggressive ways, offer nonsolutions; who then seek credit for being more "concerned about the plight of America's disadvantaged" than their political opponents. Certainly demagogues use this problem as grist for their mills. It is indeed the case that politicians posture, spout rhetoric, and seek to garner for themselves some moral bona fides by virtue of having a progressive position on this issue, when in fact they have accomplished virtually nothing after two decades of such antics. All of this is true, but this does not relieve us of the responsibility to be actively engaged with the problem ourselves.

We are not off the hook because *they* are crazy. We have to get beyond a recitation of the litany of their wrongs and begin to find constructive and positive things to say, and to do, about the problems of racial justice around us. For we are becoming two Americas now. I know that you do not expect to hear this from me. You do not expect me to decry the terrible homelessness that exists. But it is, after all, pretty bad in some places. You do not expect to hear from me about how a black kid born in a certain social context has poorer chances of succeeding in life than a white kid born in another context. But in fact so many black kids' chances, actual life chances, are so miserable that fundamental questions of justice—racial justice—are raised.

The infant mortality rate in black urban America is a problem. Let me by all means acknowledge that the high infant mortality rate is not due to racism. Yet having observed that, and having noted that the crack epidemic and the violence that accompanies it are not due to racism of the sort remediable by a civil rights bill, may we then have a conversation about what *we* are going to *do* about the infant mortality problem and the crack epidemic? These are complex problems affecting our cities, and they are inescapably racial problems as well. These problems cannot be solved simply by spending money, yet the issue of spending this or that many millions of dollars on infant mortality really ought not to delay us very long, if as people who seek justice we are appropriately motivated by our sense of outrage at the condition. I am assuming that a neoconservative can still be outraged by conditions of awful deprivation. I certainly hope this is so.

Can we not learn how to keep two or three ideas in our heads at the same time? That the demagogues on the left have gotten it wrong is one idea. That a part of America is going to hell in a handbasket is another idea, and there is absolutely no doubt about it. We sit here now, comfortably waxing eloquent, just a couple of miles from it. We must not lose sight of that. We have a moral responsibility to be doing something about it, no matter what our political persuasion. So this afternoon, while you are decrying how the glorious civil rights movement of our youth was taken over by the "crazies," I hope you will occasionally reflect on that truth.

Of course, the plight of the inner-city poor is not our only racial problem. Race is salient on the campus as well. I was lecturing at Vassar College not long ago. It was, for me, a standard situation. I had been invited by the "conservative" students, who turned out not to be conservative at all. One of them had campaigned in high school for a Martin Luther King Day celebration, which helped her get admitted to Vassar. Another saw Fay Wattleton of Planned Parenthood as a great heroine. A third argued with me that the welfare state should be dramatically expanded, and so forth. What made them "conservatives" at Vassar was their willingness, indeed eagerness, to speak out against the politically correct line on racial issues. That they were prepared to disagree publicly with the outspoken black students on campus set them apart.

I gave my talk to a segregated audience—self-segregated. The whites sat to one side and the blacks to the other. When I said blacks must affirm universal ideals, rely upon self-help, and stop whining and start building, cheers rang out—from the white part of the audience. Meanwhile the blacks seethed, shifting uncomfortably in their seats, waiting for their turn. During the question-and-answer period they let me have it. They did not even try to conceal their hostility, their outrage, their hatred of my ideas. I was taken to task—corrected, as it were—for my errors. The interesting thing is that, while administering their chastisement, they were not so much talking *to* me as talking *through* me to their white peers. What seemed to be important was that the whites be reminded of the "authentic" black stance.

I had dared to use the first person plural to refer to the body of people who constitute the citizenry of the United States: "we," "our," "us." "Don't you know that we were not there at the Constitutional Convention, and that we were valued as three-fifths of a man?" yelled out one angry young man, triumphantly, to wild applause. Because the framers of the Constitution had reached a compromise *limiting* the influence of Southern states by counting, for the purpose of determining representation in Congress, three-fifths of their slave populations, this middle-class young American in the plush auditorium of an elite university at the end of the twentieth century was prepared to chastise me for uttering the phrase "we Americans." Of course, this was not an original thought on his part. We know that the late Supreme Court justice Thurgood Marshall agreed. Tenured law professors can be found to affirm his view.[1]

Shortly after that the name of Yusef Hawkins, the young black man who had recently been shot dead by a white in Bensonhurst, began to ring out in almost literally a chant: "Yusef, Yusef, Yusef . . ." For I had dared to say that you can do anything in America. I had asked people to try to place some kind of historical perspective on what exactly it meant to be an undergraduate at Vassar College in 1990. Anything is possible; we black Americans are the most privileged, empowered people of African descent anywhere on the globe, I had said. All things lie within our grasp. We must not take on this self-limiting mantle, saying, "I'm just a black and I'm oppressed."

Because I said this to the young people, they started chanting Yusef Hawkins's name. Didn't I know that Yusef Hawkins, having been shot down in Bensonhurst, canceled out everything? That fact, they were saying, made it impossible for them to see American society as open to them. But what of the many more Yusefs who are gunned down in Harlem or Bedford-Stuyvesant? And how did the isolated event in Bensonhurst limit the objective opportunities open to them as college-educated black Americans?

The students did not have good answers for these questions, nor did they seem to feel they needed any. They had made their point, to me and to their real audience, so it was time for them to march out en masse, showing their contempt for the "collaborator." After this performance a white professor of Chinese studies, who had recently become embroiled on the wrong (that is, the right-wing) side of some multicultural issue, approached me, earnestly shook my hand, commended me for my "courage," solicited my opinion of the controversy in which he had become entangled, and asked, "Do you know Tom Sowell?" (As I said, we are all racialists!) This professor, wanting desperately not to be condemned as a racist but agreeing with everything that I had said and that had so enraged the black students on his campus, looked to me for deliverance. In me he saw personified before him courage, and license. I would make everything all right for him; Tom Sowell and I would come riding in, battle scarred, to say to this erstwhile liberal who has had enough of the campus nonsense that all is well, that he does not have to go along with the latest, outrageous demands of "those people." Sowell and I would tell the runny-nosed black kids who have been tyrannizing these white liberals to go to hell.

During this visit at Vassar I learned of the experience of a black student who was driven off the campus by the administration, had financial aid canceled at the last minute just before finals, and received a letter telling him that four thousand dollars (which his folks could not pay) was due in tuition—all because he had dared to join the conservative club and start showing up at campus events wearing a suit and bow tie. (You know how those conservatives dress!) While he was wearing this get-up to some function another black came up to him, grabbed his arm, and began to rub his skin, saying, "I'm sure it's going to rub off and we'll find a white man underneath." When the "conservative" black student complained about this, the response of the administration was to declare that he had provoked the incident by being part of that club and dressing in the way that he did. One complaint led to another, and in the end (so I'm told by the other "conservative" students), this fellow was driven out.

I thought of all these things as I traveled back to the relative tranquility of my Cambridge office, the chant of Yusef Hawkins's name still ringing in my ears. An elite young black who thinks, or believes that others think, that he is three-fifths of a person. "Conservative" whites cheering, and liberal blacks seething, every time I say something unconventional but arguably true about race, something that really does need to be said but seldom is. Ingratiating liberal professors prepared to canonize me for talking back to the "mob." A young black student literally ruined by a college administration for the crime of provoking racial discord by espousing conservative views. I thought to myself, "Man, this race thing is deep." I wondered how I got myself into the habit of standing before such audiences—after all, I am trained in economic theory, not conflict resolution! "What the hell was I doing there?" I asked myself out loud. How did I get to this point of brokerage, and why am I standing astride this cultural/racial fault line?

I am not sure I know the answer to those questions. Perhaps after a decade in analysis I would be better able to say. It seems clear, though, that the saliency and the power and the depth of race, in our society and in my own life, have compelled me to take up these matters such as I have. To some extent, I am trapped; I simply cannot ignore racial issues. As a society we are trapped, too; there is no easy way out. There is no talking our way out; no "ideologizing" our way out. The great temptation that we Americans must all resist is the belief that we can escape the dilemmas and discomforts of race by embracing some great transcendent truth, some fundamental principle. We become advocates of a color-blind society: if only people would not emphasize color so much, everything would be fine. Or we discover that all our efforts to help simply made things worse, so there is no point in trying anything else. Or we conclude that "white racism" causes all our troubles, and progress is impossible until white people own up to their ongoing crimes.

But we are not going to get free of this "race thing" by finding an idea, whatever it may be—a libertarian or an ultramarxist lens—through which the world suddenly looks simple. No system of thought will adequately encompass our racial experience. No incantation of a slogan can free us of the tensions and conflicts. We are in this thing together, caught up in a historical dynamic that goes back centuries. We are going to have to *work* our way out of it. And in order to do that we are going to have to talk candidly with each other about it. We have to create the possibility of mutual honesty, without having to pay obeisance to the politically correct line every time we speak—without having to look over our shoulders, running scared at the prospect that we might be called racists.

This will require courage from many people and institutions. I was dismayed to read a *New York Times* editorial recently, after a black city councilman in Milwaukee had called openly for urban guerrilla warfare unless his demands were met. I was astounded; I could not believe it. That editorial said, in effect, that we must understand how the conditions in Milwaukee's black ghetto could provoke such a statement. Those conditions are very bad, and I have already said that we must address them. But the fact of the matter is that if an elected public official calls for urban guerrilla warfare, he deserves to be condemned.

When the *Times* takes the easy way out, saying in effect, "Oh, well, we must not offend sensibilities," in the face of a clear affront to common values worthy of defense, it either exhibits a lack of respect for those values, or it shows its racism by virtue of regarding the councilman as insufficiently worthy of attention and concern to be confronted with a genuine judgment of his behavior. (The *Times,* by contrast, wastes no time denouncing white racism and incivility wherever it raises its ugly head. Do they perhaps think that, whereas whites warrant criticism because they are capable of reform, blacks do not, because they are not capable?)

As a member of Harvard University's faculty, I know something about this phenomenon. I know how people posture; how they see what is going on, despise it, and yet sit quietly and wait for me—a man of courage—to do their work. Well, I'm tired of doing y'all's work.

11

Professors and the Poor
Discussion at a Poverty Conference

It is both my privilege and my burden to respond to the papers of Charles Murray and Christopher Jencks. It is a privilege for the obvious reasons—two distinguished social scientists, an assemblage of important persons, a topic of crucial importance to the nation; it is gratifying to have been asked to offer one's views. But it is also a burden, because frankly, I am weary of attending conferences about poverty. I have been at too many of these gatherings in the last decade. I have reluctantly concluded after many such experiences that the solutions to the problems of poverty are not going to be found inside conference rooms. Rather, solutions, if any are to be had, must be sought out in the communities, in the lives of the individuals who are subject to some of the forces and conditions discussed in these academic gatherings.

I confess to being pessimistic about the prospects that social science analyses can ultimately contribute very much here. This is not to say that the effort to evaluate the effects of programs, or to do research on the causes of unemployment, teenage motherhood, drug addiction, and the like should be abandoned. Billions have been spent on such work since the advent of the Great Society, which, among other things, created a huge demand for the services of academic economists, statisticians, sociologists, and others to chronicle and analyze the effects of government efforts to help the poor. We have learned much, though we remain ignorant about even more. But my point is not to disparage the often ingenious efforts of analysts to fathom the intricacies of human motivations, of bureaucratic machinations, or of structural transformations. Rather, I question whether the prospect of real improvement in the conditions under which the poor are living depends much at all on the answers to the kinds of questions that social scientists are inclined to pose.

In the two papers at hand we have typical examples of the scholarship of the right and left, respectively, among social scientists addressing poverty issues. In essence, these two scholars are arguing about whether the core of the problem is that people do not know how to live, as Murray maintains, or that they simply do not have enough money, as Jencks urges. A commonsense observation of the world around us suggests that both are true. I cannot agree with Murray when he states, "We must reach a state of affairs in which the dialogue begins from a common agreement that everyone in the country can if they behave with a modicum of sense have enough material resources to live a decent existence." Translation: The poverty problem is entirely driven by the behavioral failings of poor people.

Why must we all sign off on this rather extreme view before useful dialogue can begin? How will our assent to this proposition lead to a solution to the problem of poverty? Suppose one grants, for the sake of argument, that Murray's assertion is valid. What exactly are its policy implications—to do nothing, and wait for people to reform themselves? This kind of ideological posturing is not helpful. Murray complains in his paper that the strictures of "political correctness" prevent candid discussion of the real bases for the problems of the poor. This has sometimes been true, though that is increasingly less the case. In any event, the flaw in his passage quoted above is not that it is politically incorrect, but rather that it is most likely just plain wrong and leads nowhere.

On the other hand, Jencks seem determined to ignore entirely the behavioral element—the extent to which many of the poor are implicated, through their own freely chosen acts, in their condition and that of their children. There is no mention of these factors in his paper. His analysis is essentially a counting exercise: how much money does it appear that a mother living alone with two children needs to live "decently" in urban America, compared to how much she might be expected to earn in a minimum-wage job? He notes that the numbers do not add up. She cannot earn enough, net of the costs of child care, transportation, and so forth, to live reasonably well. So Jencks concludes that it is unreasonable to expect welfare reform to reach the point of demanding self-sufficiency from its recipients after a short period of time (say, two years) without a massive and quite expensive program to supplement the earnings of all of the working poor.

Here I agree that we should ask Murray's implicit questions: if it is indeed impossible for an unskilled young woman without a husband to support herself and her children decently in our society, why does she choose to bear these children under such conditions? Is it the responsibility of society to provide her with an adequate provision without regard to whether or not she evidences a willingness to meet her own responsibilities? How shall we communicate to those prospective mothers and fathers the awesome consequences of their behavioral choices in such a way that they choose differently?

Jencks seems to have no taste, or stomach, for these questions; but they must be asked and answered. It is not acceptable that the behavioral underpinnings of the conditions in which many poor families are living be placed out of bounds, and kept out of the discussion of policy. But being willing to entertain these questions is not the same thing as having answers to them. Moreover, social scientists are not necessarily the best people to provide answers. These are not, in the main, technical questions with answers to be derived from a thorough knowledge of statistical data. These problems will not be solved by retiring to a computer laboratory for the analysis of the latest reports of the Census Bureau.

The issues raised by behavioral dysfunction, and the questions of who bears what responsibility in the face of that dysfunction, are inherently political and moral questions for which our nation, as a political and moral community, must produce answers. To find these answers we must have the will to examine ourselves, how we live and what we value—and this self-examination must involve not just the poor, but all of us. As a number of social critics have recently emphasized, there is a relationship between the behavioral problems of the poor and the cultural crisis affecting the middle and upper classes in America, as evidenced by rising divorce rates, the spread of venereal diseases, the problems of our education system, increases in teen suicide, alcohol and drug abuse, our problems with international competitiveness, and the like.

At issue here is our capacity as a political and moral community to engage in an effective discourse about values and ways of living, and to convey normative judgments that arise out of that discourse. I am dubious, for example, that it will ever again be possible for the federal government of the United States, through the Congress or the executive branch, to put the force of its enormous power behind the simple normative proposition that children ought not be born to parents prior to marriage. In the last quarter century it has become increasingly more difficult for a public figure to give voice to this belief, one that not so long ago would have been universally regarded as appropriate. Consider the contempt with which elite opinion received the promotion of "family values" by Dan Quayle during the 1992 presidential campaign.

This is a curious situation. National campaigns have been aimed at some aspects of behavior, with positive results. Smoking, for example, has been successfully inveighed against over the last generation with both public and private efforts. Our national consciousness of environmental issues has been raised in recent decades, in part through the use of public rhetoric and exhortation. But efforts to shape private values about sexuality, marriage, and childbearing are far more contentious, raising ideological conflicts with feminist and gay rights advocates. And the tools available to policymakers to influence behavior in this area—taxes and transfer programs, mainly—seem to have little effect. We have seen a huge growth among blacks and whites in the incidence of teenage pregnancy and births out of wedlock over the last thirty years, but however one reads the evidence, it is difficult to attribute much of the change to the marginal incentives of tax and transfer programs. There is talk about increasing the tax exemption for families with children, but I know of no data to suggest that this would have any substantial impact on divorce or illegitimate-birth rates.

Despite being an economist, a believer in the power of incentives to shape human behavior in the marketplace, I do not find this at all surprising. For people do not construct their basic understandings of what is important in their lives by considering whether they will receive a few thousand dollars more if they embrace one way of life as opposed to another.

Professor David Hayes-Bautista presented some powerful data during his discussion that underscores precisely what I am saying here. His charts demonstrated convincingly that the low-income Latino population of California cannot be accurately characterized as an "underclass" population. On one indicator of "behavioral pathology" after another, Latinos seemed to be doing as well if not better than Anglos. However, those very same charts showed dramatic variation across ethnic groups within the California population—blacks, whites, Asians, and Latinos—on the very same indicators of pathology which Hayes-Bautista was using to show that Latinos are not doing too badly. There are huge differences between these population subgroups with respect to measures of mortality, labor force participation, drug use, and violence. Blacks fared much worse than did Latinos or Asians. Of course, no one believes that race per se is important here, but cultural differences that vary with race may be. The local culture that socializes an individual through childhood and adolescence into adulthood may have more impact on whether that person will perpetrate a drive-by shooting or end up addicted to crack cocaine than would any policy activity undertaken by a mayor, governor, or the president.

Stated directly and without benefit of euphemism, the conditions under which many people live today in poor black communities like South-Central Los Angeles reveal as much about the disintegration of urban black society as they do about the indifference, hostility, or racism of white society. Institutional barriers to black participation in American life still exist, but they have come down considerably, and everybody knows it. Everybody also knows that other barriers have grown up within the urban black milieu (and not only there) in these last decades that are profoundly debilitating. These effects are most clearly manifest in patterns of behavior among young men and women in these communities—involving criminal offending, early unwed childbearing, low academic achievement, drug use, gratuitous violence, and guns—that destroy a person's ability to seize existing opportunity. These behaviors have to be changed if broadly gauged progress is to come.

Here our social scientists, and our politicians, have failed us. For the longest time, as Charles Murray reminds us, it *was* forbidden to speak of the unraveling social fabric of ghetto life. This has changed in the last decade, with the discovery of the so-called black underclass, but the former conspiracy of silence has not been replaced with a meaningful discourse on how this broken world will be mended. Liberals like Christopher Jencks have now acknowledged that behavioral problems are fundamental, but insist that these problems derive ultimately from the lack of economic opportunities and will abate once "good jobs at good wages" are at hand. Conservatives, like Murray, see the tragic developments in the inner cities as the unintended legacy of a misconceived welfare state. If the government would stop underwriting irresponsible behavior with its various transfer programs, they argue, poor people would be forced to discover the virtues of self-restraint.

These polar positions have something very important in common. They both implicitly assume that economic factors lie behind the behavioral problems, even behaviors involving sexuality, marriage, childbearing, and parenting, which reflect people's basic understandings of what gives their lives meaning. Both points of view suggest that behavioral problems in the ghetto, or anywhere else for that matter, can be cured from without by changing government policy, by getting the incentives right. Both smack of a mechanistic determinism wherein the mysteries of human motivation are susceptible to calculated intervention. Both have difficulty explaining why some poor minority communities show a much lower incidence of these behavioral problems than others, and are apparently less influenced by the same objective economic forces.

Moreover, these economic determinists' views of social disorder in the inner city lend themselves easily to the favored lines of political argument about social policy. Those who favor expanded government can argue that we either pay now for social "investment" programs, or pay later for welfare, prisons, and the like.

Those who want the federal budget to shrink can cite the worsening conditions of the ghetto in the face of the growth in social spending over the last generation as evidence that the Great Society failed. Those who seek a middle way—the welfare "reformers"—can split the difference by talking about how the receipt of benefits must be accompanied by an acceptance of responsibility on the part of the poor, though the government must provide services that help the poor to accept their responsibilities.

These debates over policy on social spending are no doubt important, but there is something sterile and superficial about them. Ultimately, they fail to engage questions of personal morality, of character and values, and of moral leadership in the public sphere. Politicians and social scientists have had little to say in public about what is wrong with the ways people in a particular community are living, and what ways of life are better for them and their children. The view seems to be that in a pluralistic democracy such discussions from public officials are inappropriate. Nor do we teach in our public schools that a specific way of living is virtuous, in part because we do not agree among ourselves about such matters. We give only muted public voice to the judgments that it is wrong to use drugs, to be sexually promiscuous, to be indolent and without discipline, to be disrespectful of legitimate authority, to be unreliable, untruthful, or unfaithful. We no longer teach values to children but offer them "values clarification" instead, elevating process (how does one discover his or her own values?) over substance (what are the values that a "decent" person should embrace?).

The advocacy of a particularistic conception of virtuous living has vanished from American public discourse, and it is unthinkable that it would be evoked in the context of a discussion of race and social policy. Marriage as an institution is virtually dead in inner-city black communities. The vast majority of poor black children are now raised by a mother alone. But who will say that black men and women *should* get together and stay together more than they now do, for the sake of their children? Who will say that young people of any race should abstain from sexual intimacy until their relationships have been consecrated by marriage? These are, in our secular age, not matters for public policy. Most Americans believe that 1.5 million abortions a year is too many, constituting a moral problem for our society, but the public discourse on this issue is dominated by the question of a woman's right to choose this morally problematic course. Nearly all of us would prefer, on moral as well as pragmatic grounds, that our fifteen-year-olds not be sexually active, but to urge such a stance publicly in response to an epidemic of sexually transmitted disease among young people is to invite ridicule. Government, it would appear, must confine itself to dealing with the consequences of these matters not having been taken up elsewhere.

Evidently we are going to have to look to the nongovernmental agencies of moral and cultural development in particular communities to take on some of the burden of promoting positive behavioral change. In every community there are agencies of moral and cultural development that seek to shape the ways in which individuals conceive of their duties to themselves, their obligations to each other, and their responsibilities before God. The family and the church are primary among these. These are the natural sources of legitimate moral teaching—indeed, the only sources. If these institutions are not restored, the behavioral problems of the ghetto will not be overcome. Such a restoration obviously cannot be the object of programmatic intervention by public agencies. Rather, it must be led from within the communities in question, by the moral and political leaders of those communities. However, the "bully pulpit" of public leadership *can* be used to encourage, rather than disparage, these private efforts at the inculcation of specific moral codes.

The mention of God may seem quaint or vaguely inappropriate at such an august academic gathering, but it is clear that the behavioral problems of the ghetto (and not only there) involve spiritual issues. A man's spiritual commitments influence his understanding of his parental responsibilities. No economist has yet to devise an incentive scheme for eliciting parental involvement in a child's development that is as effective as the motivations of conscience deriving from the parents' understanding that they are God's stewards in the lives of their children. The effective teaching of sexual abstinence, or of the eschewal of violence, is most naturally based on an appeal to spiritual concepts. The most effective substance abuse recovery programs are built around spiritual principles. The reports of successful efforts at reconstruction in ghetto communities invariably reveal a religious institution, or set of devout believers, at the center of the effort.

Although public policy should not be reflective of particular religious doctrines under our form of government, this is no reason to keep an understanding of the importance of spirituality out of public discussions of poverty. Everything worth talking about in public need not issue from a government program or a federal statute! We should recognize the importance of the efforts, ongoing in many communities, to reconstruct systems of beliefs and values from which individuals derive meaning, and around which people can organize their lives. From such conceptions of ultimate meaning do people derive their understanding of their fundamental responsibilities, and their sense of their own worthiness.

III

A Critical Look at the Field
(Selected Reviews)

12

Preaching to the Converted

Race Matters
by Cornel West

No one would likely dispute the claim that coming to grips with racial matters is fundamental to understanding American politics, history, or culture. But an argument is certain to arise if one ventures to be more specific. There is no common definition of the problem, no consensus historical narrative explaining how we have come to this juncture, no agreement about what should now be done. Perhaps most importantly, Americans lack a common vision for the future of our racial relations. We lack a common understanding of what we are trying to achieve—with our laws, through our politics, in our classrooms, from our pulpits—as we struggle with the legacy of African slavery. Indeed, Americans of all races seem to be confused about who "we" are.

In *Race Matters* Cornel West, professor of religion and director of Afro-American studies at Princeton, tries to bring order to our collective intellectual chaos on this vexing question. Sadly for all of us, he does not succeed. A philosopher, theologian, and social activist, Cornel West has emerged in the last decade as an important critical voice on the left of American public life. Though it

217

may be an exaggeration to say, as one admirer boasts, that he is "the preeminent African-American intellectual of our generation," there is no arguing that he is a thoughtful, articulate, and quite influential social critic. His analyses of our "American dilemma" are studied in universities and seminaries across the country. His opinions on social and cultural policy were solicited by Bill Clinton in the wake of his 1992 presidential election victory. And shortly after his installment at Princeton, West acquired official academic celebrity status when he was profiled in the *New York Times Magazine*.

This new book is a collection of eight short essays that, taken together, sketch the outlines of an interesting, if problematic vision of race in America. West offers a stunning array of propositions about our economy, politics, and culture—each one elegant and provocative, and some possibly true. But because West writes more in the manner of the prophet than in that of the analyst, he never stays long enough with any one point to convince us that he has gotten it right.

West believes that public discourse about race matters in this society is pathetically impoverished. In this he is surely right. But his explanation is a good deal more controversial: the absence of an effective dialogue on the race question, he believes, derives from the fact that not all Americans are seen as equal members of the national community. This is a failure for which he holds both liberals and conservatives responsible. Both mistakenly define the "racial dilemma" in terms of the problems that black people pose for white people. Liberals see poor blacks as the historical victims of American racism, needful of government assistance, while conservatives see in the behavior of the black poor the need for moral reform. Both, however, look upon lower-class urban blacks as a people different in some elemental way from themselves. The problem for both is how to transform "them" so they will be more like "us." This, West believes, tragically misconstrues the problem:

> To engage in a serious discussion of race in America, we must begin not with the problems of black people but with the flaws of American society—flaws rooted in historic inequalities and longstanding cultural stereotypes. How we set up the terms for discussing racial issues shapes our perception and response to these issues. As long as black

people are viewed as "them," the burden falls on blacks to do all the "cultural" and "moral" work necessary for healthy race relations. The implication is that only certain Americans can define what it means to be American—and the rest must simply "fit in." (p. 3)

West is talking here about hegemony, though (thankfully) he avoids the word. He has in mind the historical fact and ongoing reality of the oppression of black folk—our separation from mainstream American life for generations, even after the end of slavery, as well as the horrible conditions under which many blacks continue to live. The "cultural stereotypes" he mentions are negative ideas about the beauty, intelligence, moral worth, and even the humanity of Africans that, given the need to rationalize slavery in a putatively Christian democracy, evolved over the early years of the American experiment into an ugly antiblack ideology. He is asserting that we can get nowhere in our discussions of race until we unburden ourselves of the remnant of this ideological legacy. It is a superficially appealing position. But is it right?

Is it true that racial progress depends upon a more ecumenical, less judgmental approach to the question of which ways of life embraced by various groups of American citizens are worthy of tolerance and respect? Is it entirely obvious that certain Americans have no right to say to others that inclusion—if not in terms of legal rights, then in social, cultural, and moral terms—is contingent upon "fitting in" (that is, upon adopting values more or less universally agreed upon)? Surely this was what we said to segregationists during the civil rights movement. Should it not also be our message today to an Afrocentric spokesman who insists on the moral superiority of blacks ("sun people") over whites ("ice people"); or to a black city councilman who states that, unless the needs of his constituents are met, urban guerrilla war will be waged against the white establishment; or to the black mayor of a drug-ridden metropolis who, when caught in the act of illegal drug use, declares himself a victim of racism in law enforcement?

Criticism of offenses such as these—offenses not simply against whites' sensibilities but against what should constitute core American values—are hard to find in *Race Matters*. This, in no small part, is due to the fact that West is usually preaching to the choir. His words collected here serve an emblematic function; they con-

stitute for his like-minded readers banners of progressive sentiment. Few among the students and teachers of the humanities at
the many universities where this book will be on the reading lists
will need to be persuaded of the correctness of West's views. Not
many of the black activists and intellectuals who will be energized
by West's rhetoric are concerned about affirming core American
values as a starting point for productive interracial dialogue. But
out in the "real" America—the blue-collar districts of the industrial states that elected Bill Clinton last November; the suburban
rings around the core cities where whites (and blacks) have fled
from the problems of urban decay; in the South, where interracial
coalitions must still be built—few doubts will be dispelled or souls
converted to the cause by these essays. Yet without the engagement of these people in these places, true progress on racial problems is unlikely to be achieved. My concern is that these essays fail
in their task of persuasion because they are too politically correct;
they are so imbued with the peculiar ethos of the contemporary
academy that they cannot provide a healing vision for our racial
problems.

West does not deal evenhandedly with the conflicts of value and
differences of perception that lie behind much of the racial tension
in our country. A fitting metaphor for this split is the war of words
that has raged over what to call the 1992 civil unrest in Los Angeles: "riot," or "rebellion"? This verbal struggle is really about the
assignment of responsibility: Did we fail the minority poor of
South-Central Los Angeles, or did they fail us? A respectable case
can be made that both are true, but West primarily credits the former. He does not acknowledge that the fear, anger, and contempt
felt by many whites in the face of urban violence perpetrated by
blacks and Latinos are legitimate reactions. Nor does he consider
the poisonous effect on race relations caused by the antisocial
behavior of some among the urban poor.

It is not enough to note, as West does, that such behavior is the
fruit of hopelessness and despair now rampant among poor blacks.
Bridging the racial gap requires the affirmation by minority advocates of the legitimacy of those social norms that the hopeless and
desperate are wont to violate. West mentions, for example, the
"xenophobic" attacks directed at Korean-owned business during

the Los Angeles disturbance, saying that this shows the extent of "powerlessness" felt by the poor. Yet blacks assaulting Koreans reveal something else—envy and resentment of the material success of hardworking people, success that stands as an indictment of the claim that the country affords little opportunity for nonwhites to advance. This disparity between groups in their interpretations of and responses to the opportunity structure of American society may require us to make judgments about which viewpoint is the more reasonable. But this means challenging the progressive orthodoxy, something West is apparently reluctant to do.

One instance where West does challenge the conventional progressive wisdom, however, is in his discussion of the spiritual condition of the urban underclass. His willingness to confront this phenomenon head on, and to place it at the center of the crisis of urban black life, is admirable. He dares to peer into the vast emptiness and nihilism of the spirit that characterizes life at the bottom of our society, where one youth can kill another over a pair of sneakers or a disrespectful gaze, where children give birth to children amid multigenerational poverty and dependency, where the alienation is radical, the violence random, and the despair rampant. West understands that these conditions announce the arrival of "post-modern poverty," a truly new phenomenon on the American scene.

But what he has to say about the causes and the cures of these problems makes very little sense to me. The spiritual problems of the black poor, it turns out, are due to the predation of market capitalism. They have been infested—as have we all, West says—with a materialistic acquisitiveness fueled by profit-seeking manufacturers, distributors, and marketers of consumer goods. The poor have gotten the worst of this capitalistic onslaught on cultural stability because their civil institutions, churches, families, and community structures are too weak to provide a counterweight to the dictates of television advertising. West dismisses without an argument the possibility that the explosion of teen pregnancy, violent crime, family dissolution, and drug use among the poor might have something to do with the sexual revolution and subsequent liberalization of moral norms in American society that began in the 1960s and was (and still is) championed by liberal elites. Nor does he promote the restoration of "traditional values" as an antidote for the spiritual malaise. He simply asserts, without any support for the claim, that the root cause of the problem is the market.

One cannot dismiss this claim out of hand. There is a respectable tradition, on both the left and the right, that is skeptical about the cultural results of capitalism. But it is far from clear, given the historically unprecedented severity of the problems that have emerged in urban black society during the last three decades, that West's explanation explains enough. After all, a television commercial may lead a youngster to desire a pair of sneakers, but only a pathological deprivation of moral sensibility will allow him to kill for them. In any event, placing responsibility on "market-driven corporate enterprises" tells us nothing about what must be done to reverse the decay.

West's answer to the underclass problem is rather to advocate an all-too-predictable "progressive" policy agenda: more money from the government for schools, investment in infrastructure, the creation of good jobs at good wages, the continuation of affirmative action, and so on. But there is no serious inquiry into why such efforts, which have been tried repeatedly, have had so little impact on the deteriorating condition of the urban black poor. To counter this decline, West proposes that spiritual renewal can be achieved through a "politics of conversion." As I understand it, he is implying a kind of communitarian democratic socialism, built from the grass roots. Through a collective effort to influence the economic structures affecting their lives, this "politics of conversion" would foster a "love ethic" among the downtrodden and promote their sense of agency. In advocating this new politics West seems to argue that spiritual emptiness can be vanquished through political struggle, if only that struggle is undertaken in a way that encourages self-respect among the poor: "Nihilism . . . is tamed by a turning of one's soul. This turning is done through one's own affirmation of one's worth—an affirmation fueled by the concern of others."

Yet one cannot help but observe that this vision, from a professor of religion and sometime preacher of the gospel, oddly makes no reference to the role of religious faith. The spiritual malaise is to be transcended not by a vertical relationship with the Almighty but through horizontal relationships with fellow combatants in the struggle against white supremacy and corporate greed. This sounds just a bit romantic. West offers little useful advice about how to put this new politics into effect, even as he ignores the ongoing ministries in the inner cities who are managing to "turn the souls" of some of those at the bottom.

About some of the more difficult questions that must be asked and answered if real change is to occur, West has even less to say. Why are the relations between black men and women so difficult, and why is the institution of marriage literally disappearing among African Americans? Why does black academic performance lag so in comparison with other students, even recent immigrants, and not just among the poor but at all levels of the income hierarchy? How can effective engagement in the lives of the alienated urban poor be promoted and achieved by middle-class Americans of any race, when the poor are seemingly so divorced from the social and political commonweal? And what practical political program, implementable in the here and now of American public life, can secure enough consensus to support concerted action on these problems?

Questions such as these cannot be answered by sloganeering, or with the clever deconstruction of our "patriarchal society" whose "machismo identity is expected and even exalted—as with Rambo and Reagan." It is no political program to call for the emergence of a "jazz freedom fighter" who will "attempt to galvanize and ener- gize world-weary people into forms of organization with account- able leadership that promote critical exchange and broad reflection." It is an insufficient defense of affirmative action, which must be sustained by courts and electoral majorities, to invoke the need for an "affirmation of black humanity, especially among black people themselves . . . [that] speaks to the existential issues of what it means to be a degraded African (man, woman, gay, lesbian, child) in a racist society." This may be the rhetoric prescribed in the mul- ticulturalists' handbook, but it is a rhetoric, I fear, that is largely irrelevant to the serious racial problems that continue to beset American society.

West talks about transcending race as, he asserts, blacks should have done when instead we rallied in large numbers behind the nomination of Clarence Thomas for the Supreme Court. Yet he mires himself in an essentially racialist vision that makes it difficult to see how such a transcendence can be achieved. Why, one wonders, does he find it necessary to equate the violence-promoting lyrics of rap performer Ice-T with the public statements of former Los Angeles police chief Daryl Gates? More disturbingly, how can a man whose claim on our attention here rests upon the morality of his denunciations of racism speak of "visible Jewish resistance to affirmative action and government spending on social programs" as "assaults on black livelihood," as if the fact that some American Jews hold some ideas is an offense properly ascribed to the entire group? This is the language of collective guilt. West would certainly, and rightly, be offended by a similar-sounding charge that blacks as a group should be judged as engaged in an "assault on Jewish survival" because some criminals who are black have murdered some victims who are Jews. He spends no time apologizing for "black criminality" in these pages. Why should Jews be held to account for what he regards as the intellectually indefensible writings of some of their ethnic fellows?

In the end, the moral authority of Cornel West's voice in these pages cannot be derived from the substance of his argument; it must be supplied by the reader. If you come as a true believer, you will be entertained and energized by the eloquence and commitment of this "preeminent black intellectual of our generation." As for the rest of us, perhaps we should take our lead from the current fashion in literary criticism and read this text not for what it seems to be arguing directly, but rather for what it can be understood to say about the curious disposition of power and authority in the contemporary American academy.

13

Liberal Racism

Two Nations
by Andrew Hacker

The shockingly violent reaction to the verdicts in the police beating of Rodney King, destined to be remembered as the great Los Angeles riots of 1992, has provoked more intense discussion among the American public about the nation's perennial problems of race relations and urban affairs than at any time since the "long hot summers" of the 1960s. Sadly, the heat of this greater scrutiny has not often yielded the light of insight or wisdom. Instead, in the aftermath of this tragedy we have been repeatedly subjected to the hysterical ravings of political and academic demagogues who seek to build their careers by exploiting the alienation of the urban black masses, and the gullibility of liberal white elites. This demagoguery has taken many forms, but it is perhaps most dangerous when disguised as "analysis" and offered up by a respected social scientist. Andrew Hacker's book *Two Nations: Black and White, Separate, Hostile, Unequal* (1991) provides an instructive illustration of the mischief now afoot in the land.

Though not written in reaction to the Los Angeles riots, this volume was nevertheless catapulted onto the best-seller lists, and

225

widely cited as a prescient foretelling of the coming "rebellion," in the aftermath of the disturbance. As the title suggests, and as the author repeatedly emphasized during numerous interviews (some given while the looting and arson were ongoing), it is Hacker's view that the events in Los Angeles were entirely predictable, and indeed inevitable. From his perspective, what we observed there was the well-deserved consequence of the systematic neglect by "white America" of the basic human needs of blacks. According to Hacker, the racial gulf now stands wider than ever in American life, despite a growing black middle class, increasing numbers of black elected officials, and the continuing political clout of the civil rights lobby. He advances one reason only for this sorry state of affairs: the persistent racism of white America, a racism that has evolved from its historical "no blacks need apply" character into a more subtle, covert, institutionalized form. According to Hacker, "racial tensions serve too many important purposes to be easily ameliorated." And while "there are things that should be done . . . there is scant evidence that the majority of white Americans are ready to invest in redistributive programs, let alone give them- selves in more exacting ways."

Hacker takes as his mission to lay bare the true nature of covert white racism in contemporary American life. The irony is that he succeeds in powerfully revealing the face of a new strand of Ameri- can racism, but not the one he thinks he sees. This book can be most profitably read not for what it discloses about the racism of the avowed enemies of black aspirations, but rather for its inadver- tent revelation of the deep racism of some liberal whites who, like Hacker, think themselves to be friends of the black cause. He man- ages in the course of this book to convey a profound contempt for blacks and whites alike, offering sweeping generalizations about the behaviors and attitudes of groups of people based on nothing more than racial identities.

He employs throughout an insipid, matter-of-fact prose style, affecting the attitude of a disinterested observer and giving the impression that he is oblivious to the possibility that he has given offense. But Hacker intends to offend whites, the better to shock them from their racial complacency, and he wants desperately to placate blacks, the better to show that he understands their plight.

Thus we learn, in an opening chapter called "Dividing American Society," that the root cause of our racial woes is a fundamental asymmetry of power between blacks and whites, not as individual persons, but as racial collectives. This asymmetry is discernible to Hacker in the very definition of racial categories, for whites have determined to consign all persons with any visible Negro ancestry to the degraded status of being black, while welcoming European immigrants, however swarthy, into the privileged club associated with whiteness. For Hacker, being black is to be degraded from birth in America, while being white is to know that you are inherently superior to anyone with darker skin than your own.

Hacker combines simplistic anthropomorphic thinking with a flair for the conspiracy theory, writing as if a single actor that he calls "white America" sat down to decide upon the linguistic rules of the racial identity game, with the explicit objective of creating a racial bipolarity:

> Hence "mestizo" and "mulatto" have disappeared from our parlance, as have "creole" and "quadroon." Nor has this country retained the generic term "colored" for people whose ancestries are obviously mixed. . . . It has been far from accidental that this country has chosen to reject the idea of a graduated spectrum, and has instead fashioned a rigid bifurcation. . . . Had white America really believed in its egalitarian declarations, it would have welcomed former slaves into its midst at the close of the civil war. Indeed, had that happened, America would not be two racial nations today.

Of course, this country has abandoned the term "colored" because, in the first instance, Negroes regarded the term as undignified. And whatever Hacker may intend by suggesting that "white America" ought to have "welcomed former slaves into its midst," the failure to engage in wholesale intermarriage across racial lines is hardly a test of the extent to which egalitarian political ideals are genuinely held. Indeed, his suggestion to the contrary displays breathtaking ignorance of American political history. Admittedly, Abraham Lincoln was decidedly not in favor of wholesale social intercourse between blacks and whites. But this does not mean that his differences with Judge Stephen Douglas and Chief Justice Roger Taney (author of the infamous *Dred Scott* decision) over the meaning of the founders' "egalitarian declarations" were inconsequential, or reflective of nothing but Lincoln's hypocrisy. Yet, for Hacker such differences amount to nothing at all, given his determination to paint "white America" as a place of implacable racial prejudice.

But it is pointless to argue with the belief system evident in this book, for as Hacker states explicitly, these are not matters subject to resolution through the dispassionate review of historical fact. This becomes painfully obvious when we consider Hacker's account of how blacks think and feel about their position and possibilities in American society. It is here that his own racism becomes most evident, for he writes as if, when he looks upon today's black Americans, he sees as a confused, defeated, and disturbed collection of people, obsessed with what whites have done to them and incapable of doing anything for themselves. He seems to think of blacks as though they are children whose failures can best be explained by reference to the inadequate tutelage of their betters.

His is the clearest, most candid statement that I have yet seen of the new liberal racism—a patronizing attitude that conveys contempt by means of apology, explaining every black failure or foible as the result of something white people have or have not done. Of course, Hacker would deny this vehemently, but his words speak for themselves. Thus, if you have sought to understand why "black men and women [find it hard] to assimilate into the American mainstream," here is Hacker's answer:

> The 'Africa' in African-American contrasts with much of the European structure of technology and science, of administrative systems based on linear modes of reasoning. . . . [For if] the European heritage imposes the regimen of standardized tests, the African dream inspires discursive story telling celebrating the soul and the spirit.

If you were puzzled by the persistent deficit in performance on standardized tests which blacks suffer relative to whites, here is Hacker's explanation:

> [The reason] why even better-off blacks tend to do less well than whites on tests used by schools and employers . . . [is that] since blacks

of all classes are more likely to be raised in segregated surroundings, they grow up with less exposure to the kinds of reasoning that standardized examinations expect. . . . One outcome of this isolation is that black Americans have less sustained exposure to the "modern" world than have many members of immigrant groups.

And if you were wondering how to account for the low percentage of blacks in certain occupations, you now have the following Hackerism at your disposal:

Perhaps most revealing of all is the small number of dental hygienists (2.5% of the total in 1990). While white patients seem willing to be cared for by black nurses (31% of nursing aides and orderlies were black in 1990), they apparently draw the line at having black fingers in their mouths.

In Andrew Hacker's America, blacks are responsible for little that affects their lives, and they can achieve nothing unless whites reform themselves. The African sensibility, unlike the Asian, he seems to say, is incompatible with the intellectual rigors of "the modern world," though it is possessed of a superior spirituality. Unless whites choose to integrate with blacks, thereby sharing some of the former's natural affinity to the things of modernity, we ought not be surprised that blacks achieve little. The small numbers of black optometrists, actuaries, or physicists is due to racism, not the choices and efforts of blacks themselves. Blacks are not even capable of racism on their own; acts of hatred when emanating from blacks do not have the same moral significance of those same acts undertaken by whites, for "racism should be attributed only to those who have the power to cause suffering," and blacks, being "an oppressed people," purportedly lack such power. (This will come as news to Reginald Denny or the Central Park jogger.)

Hacker's stubborn refusal to take blacks seriously, as morally responsible agents capable of shaping their lives according to their will, leads him to perverse and dangerous conclusions. When he writes of family structure and relations between parents and children, he reports that 56.2 percent of black and 17.3 percent of white households were headed by women in 1990. But Hacker, stressing that the ratio of the two percentages has not changed over the last forty years, concludes that the apparent disparity is in fact the consequence of "concurrent adaptations to common cultural trends" on the part of blacks and whites alike.

But this reasoning is specious. Why would a social scientist focus on the ratio of percentages as the measure of racial difference, when the scale of the phenomenon of single parenthood is obviously so much vaster among blacks than whites? True enough, the proportion of single-parent households has more than tripled among both races since 1950, but this means something quite different for whites (where the change has been from one of every twenty households to one in six) than it does for blacks (where the change has been from one of every six households to better than one in two).

Were it the case that the majority of American children, and not just black American children, had come to be raised without a father present, I doubt that even Andrew Hacker could ignore the tragic implications for our country of the collapse of the traditional family. But when that collapse is already well advanced among blacks he manages to overlook the tragedy, seeing only the working out of "common cultural trends" that have no racial significance. That is, the meaning to Hacker of these deeply disturbing events among blacks is to be found not in what they tell us about how black men, women, and children are living together, but rather in what they show us about the shortcomings of white society. Blacks will improve their family lives when and if whites manage to improve theirs, Hacker argues. Blacks are not agents who can shape their cultural and behavioral patterns, but instead mere bellwethers of developments among whites.

————————

In his discussion of racial differences in criminal offending and victimization, Hacker continues his apparently unwitting assault on the dignity and moral integrity of black people. Noting that black men commit the crime of rape at three to four times the rate of whites, and that one quarter of their victims are white women, Hacker sees in this disparity the stuff of political protest:

> Certainly, the conditions black men face in the United States generate
> far more anger and rage than is ever experienced by white men . . . If

black men vent their frustrations on women, it is partly because the women are more available as targets, compared with the real centers of power, which remain so inchoate and remote.

And a black rapist choosing a white victim is especially significant, for he "compounds defiance with the thrill of danger. . . . Each such act brings further demoralization of the dominant race, exposing its inability to protect its own women from the worst kind of depredation."

Robbery, in Hacker's view, is a crime particularly rich with opportunities for freelance racial justice, as white victims surely know:

> For white victims caught in interracial robberies the loss of cash or valuables is seldom their chief concern. Rather, the racial character of the encounter defines the experience. In the social scheme of things, the tables have been turned. For the present, a black man has the upper hand. Hence the added dread that your assailant will not be satisfied simply with your money, but may take another moment to inflict retribution for the injustices done to his race.

Hacker is all too ready to understand why some young black men terrorize the cities and towns in which they live, but is adamantly unwilling to judge or condemn their behavior. He reserves his considerable capacity for outrage for a condemnation of Bernhard Goetz's "vigilantism," and of police officers whom Hacker contends, without offering a shred of evidence, give "scant attention" to black crime victims. "Underlying this official unconcern," he says, is the belief that "less is lost when a black person dies, whether they are slain by the police or a criminal." Just who believes this, and how Hacker knows that they do, he does not bother to tell us here.

Nor is this all. In an amazing feat, Hacker manages to sustain this tone of condescension toward blacks and unctuous moral self-righteousness toward whites for more than two hundred pages. Commenting on the use of quotas to promote black police officers to the rank of sergeant in New York City, he criticizes the exam (passed by more than 10 percent of the white officers taking it but less than 2 percent of the blacks) as racially biased because it required test takers to know the meanings of words like "relevant," "disposition," "unsubstantiated," and "tactfully." Hacker, presuming to know the fears of whites and the hurts and angers of blacks, is quick to set down his general presumptions with the authority, if not the care, of a social scientist. "Not surprisingly," he tells us, "white people seem to do most of the worrying about this apparent harm [of racial preferences] to black self-esteem." Just how would Hacker know that to be the case? "The experience of being black in America cannot help but stir suspicions that in most cases you were never given a fair chance," he writes blithely, despite having no evidence to support the claim.

What of the blacks who have risen from humble origins to the tops of their chosen fields of endeavor, who know that being black in America (as opposed to just about any other country on the globe), together with their own hard work, is what has made their achievements possible? What of the millions of blacks of West Indian descent, whose immigrant forebears came here seeking freedom and opportunity, and finding it? How dare Andrew Hacker characterize the sentiments of 30 million people toward their country based on nothing but the color of their skin and a presumed racial enmity that he seems required to impute to them by his own ideological commitments? Did it ever occur to him that for many blacks it is far more infuriating to be told by a white liberal what they "cannot help but" feel than to deal with the less insidious, more direct racism of everyday life in this country? Must blacks' participation in the national enterprise be made hostage to the anachronistic need of Hacker and his ilk for a victim class whose inevitable alienation proves the bankruptcy of American ideals?

Hacker smugly dismisses white complaints about affirmative action in admissions at the University of California at Berkeley, which had reduced white representation in the entering class from two-thirds to two-fifths over a period of seven years, with the retort: "it was not easy for white Californians to complain, since their overall scholastic records were not very auspicious." He means that 16 percent of whites, compared to 33 percent of Asians, had high school records making them eligible for admission at Berkeley in 1988. But then, the fact that only 5 percent of black and Hispanic high school students were eligible does not occasion from Hacker any comparable qualification of the legitimacy of their claims. Indeed, I have calculated from his numbers that an eligible black student was ten times more likely to be admitted to the entering class at Berkeley in 1988 than an eligible white, and an eligible Asian student was four times more likely to be admitted than an eligible white. You might think this would lead Hacker to reflect upon the legitimacy of discriminating against white students at Berkeley, but you would be wrong.

The same data imply that for the entering class of 1983 a black student had about half the chance of a white or Asian to have graduated five years after admission. Furthermore, the vast disparity in qualification between admitted students of various races proved to be easily observable in the classroom after admission. Hacker reports, without comment, that at Berkeley "it is almost as if two dissimilar colleges were sharing the same campus. Indeed, [a] . . . study of freshmen calculus courses found that whereas only 5 percent of the Asian students failed, half of the black students did." Might such occurrences have anything to do with racial tensions on campuses around the country? Hacker does not say. Does this information suggest that affirmative action is a poorly conceived policy at UC Berkeley? Apparently Hacker does not think so. Instead he gloats that at Smith College, which has only 3.2 percent black enrollment, "the paucity of black faces [is] . . . a cause for shame" among many students and professors. He discards the suggestion (made by the late Supreme Court justice William O. Douglas, among others) that affirmative action in college admissions be based on class, not race. Why? Because "low-income whites and Asians would end up with all the 'race blind' awards." The awards cannot be genuinely "race blind" for Hacker unless they result in the requisite number of "black faces" on campus; we can worry later about how many graduate or pass calculus.

This book clearly illustrates one little-examined reason why our nation is so deeply divided along racial lines. Hacker's singular failure to be able to criticize constructively the sacred cows of politically correct thought on racial issues is a common problem, not limited to him, and undoubtedly shared by many of the readers who made this work a best-seller. The problem is that in an effort to avoid the accusation of being a racist, with the good intention of "understanding" the rage, incivility, and incapacity of their black neighbors, students, and friends, these people abandon their responsibility to treat blacks with the seriousness that they reserves for whites.

For Hacker, and for much of liberal white opinion in our time, a history of victimization has made black people disappear insofar as being accountable moral agents capable of shaping their own destinies. The patronizing tone of his discussion of blacks is unrelenting. Hacker's whites are powerful, his blacks pitiable. Whites warrant being condemned because they can choose to do better, to stop being racists, to become more generous and compassionate. Blacks do not warrant critical exhortation because they are without choices; their misery and mediocrity are inevitable, and their racial hatreds derivative from the primary moral failings of whites. Never does Hacker allow that, despite the bad hand blacks have been dealt, they need not react with violence; instead he rushes to note that whites have been violent, too. Never does he suggest that even black policemen who grew up in segregated neighborhoods might be capable of and expected to learn the meaning of words like "tactfully"; instead he endorses quotas for those who cannot, and he castigates whites who might dare to be offended by the policy. Never does he worry that black parents could be letting their children down by not marrying at a higher rate; instead he relishes the "explanation" that whites are marrying less frequently as well.

In his headlong rush to condemn white America, Hacker so reduces black Americans that, by the end of his book, even the murderous drug gangs who kill innocents with automatic weapons during drive-by shootings are not seen as responsible for their acts. They are, paraphrasing Ralph Ellison, "morally invisible men" to Hacker. Concerning these murderers he writes:

> These would certainly seem to be acts for which the perpetrators should be held strictly responsible. . . . Yet it may also be asked *why* so many young men are engaging in what amounts to a self-inflicted genocide. While in one sense these are "free" acts, performed of personal volition, when they become so widespread, they must also be seen as expressing a despair that suffuses much of their race. . . . No other race

is wounding itself so fatally. Nor can it be said that black Americans chose this path for themselves.

So in allocating responsibility, the response should be clear. It is white America that has made being black so disconsolate an estate. Legal slavery may be in the past, but segregation and subordination have been allowed to persist. Even today, America imposes a stigma on every black child at birth.

This, then, is the brave new vision of the liberal racist. I am outraged at the specter of a white academic apologist invoking the purported generalized despair of my race as excuse for the venal acts of a handful of murderers, and this to the broad acclaim of the liberal political elites of my country. What of the millions of young men similarly situated who do not maim and kill? Must the nobility of their choices be ignored in the haste of blaming "white America" for the crimes of a few thousand? Cannot Mr. Hacker and those who share his views see the damage their rationalizations are doing to the dignity of my people?

14

Dilemmas of a Black Intellectual

Reflections of an Affirmative Action Baby
by Stephen L. Carter

In 1989 Stephen Carter attracted wide attention with an essay on the subject of affirmative action that appeared in *Reconstruction,* a journal of ideas relating to African American public life. Carter, a black professor at the Yale Law School, offered a disarmingly frank personal account of how affirmative action in the academic world had affected his life. Neither attacking nor defending the policy as such, he sought instead to analyze its consequences, drawing on his own experience as an object of racial preference in law school admissions.

Two years later Carter extended his arguments in the book *Reflections of an Affirmative Action Baby.* His approach remained highly personal, even autobiographical, though he expanded his subject to include many of the most pressing issues of African American intellectual life. Appearing at a time of significant ferment among black intellectuals—with related works by Shelby Steele, Stanley Crouch, Julius Lester, and Patricia Williams having recently been published—Carter's work was widely read and discussed by students of American race relations.

Carter grapples in his book with many themes now ascendant in black social commentary: the subtle racism of liberal whites, the ambiguous blessing of racial preference, conflicting identities, self-doubt, anxiety over the status of the black poor, and tension between racial loyalty and intellectual independence. A certain dualism of perspective pervades the text. Carter is on the one hand a legal scholar offering abstract arguments for his various theses, and on the other hand a young black man who, having lived smack in the middle of the affirmative action turmoil over the past two decades, draws freely on his experiences. This admixture of analysis and autobiographical reflection makes for an important contribution to the public conversation about race and social policy, and it deserves our careful attention.

Carter's core argument about affirmative action is this: racial preference necessarily creates doubts about the abilities of its beneficiaries who, by definition, have not been judged with the same standard as others. It is pointless and counterproductive to deny this. But preference is justified in many situations, and the concomitant doubt need not be debilitating or permanent. What blacks should do is what Carter himself has done—get on with the unavoidable task of proving themselves by seizing the opportunity that preference has afforded. Moreover, whites should endeavor to examine the individual qualities of black people to form judgments about their merit, and not rely on the crutch of racial stereotype.

Doubt is a key player in Carter's drama. Blacks wonder, "Do I really deserve to be here?" Whites wonder, "Is this one among the best, or merely among 'the best blacks'?" Carter has an answer for both. He reminds blacks that doubts unacknowledged, or merely railed against, cannot be overcome. He implies that by accepting preferential admission, a black student incurs the responsibility to prove himself. But he also insists that a white's suspicion about what is in some black's admission folder is a very thin basis for making a personal assessment. Blacks are not all alike, and they are more than the sum of their test scores. (Besides, some blacks like himself have high test scores!) He indicts the lazy habit of thought that leads a white onlooker to see in each black face a projection of his own racial anxieties and generalizations. Such stereotyping can make life miserable for blacks, denying them an elemental personal dignity that no degree of preference should be allowed to undermine.

This argument has two significant conservative implications. First, since blacks have something to prove, they have a great stake in the maintenance of objective measures of professional performance in their chosen fields. It is by meeting these accepted criteria of excellence, not by arguing about them, that beneficiaries of affirmative action can silence the voice of doubt, whether from without or from within. Carter offers himself as a case in point. Having amassed a scholarly record sufficiently distinguished to warrant tenure at Yale, he now answers those who raise the preference issue with the quip, "Yeah, I got into law school on affirmative action. So what?" One finds this triumphalist undertone throughout the book. But it is a triumphalism premised on his acceptance of currently prevailing standards of judgment as to what constitutes excellence in legal scholarship. He counsels that blacks act to dispel, not dismiss, the doubts of whites and themselves—a distinction of profound importance.

The second, related implication is that since whites are urged to see blacks as individuals, blacks should see themselves that way, too. They should reject the notion that there is a "black" way to be, to argue, to think; in other words, that there is a black sensibility to which whites cannot gain access. Carter distinguishes between affirmative action intended merely to increase the number of blacks with access to elite educational opportunities and that rationalized by the belief that blacks will bring an otherwise unrepresented view of the world to the institutions they join. He rejects the latter as wrong and pernicious, arguing that it shades all too easily into a demand for conformity among blacks that is hostile to the individual's right and obligation to think for himself and to express himself freely.

These arguments are, to my mind, compelling, and they are artfully advanced. As a black intellectual who has spent the last twenty years in elite academic environments, I understand the impetus that compels Carter to some of his conclusions. The academic politics of race creates agonizing conflicts of identity and authenticity for many blacks, whether students or faculty. Our struggles and compromises in the face of these conflicts can be quite painful to witness and to experience. The choice of a roommate, a dining hall table, an intramural sport, a date, a professional peer group, a subject of study, or a set of ideas to embrace can mark a scholar among his racial peers as, somehow, not "really" black. Carter is trying, by sheer force of argument, to carve out space for black intellectuals (not least himself) to explore all the possibilities of the life of the mind, to go where their interests, aptitudes, and moral sensibilities lead them, unfettered by conformist pressures from other blacks or by the condescension of whites.

Yet I must regretfully conclude that despite his noble intent and adroit argumentation, Carter does not fully succeed with this book. The problem he defines is not only an intellectual one; it has crucial political and psychological dimensions as well. Carter never fully faces these complications.

The fact is that there is real power to be had in our universities by exploiting exclusive racial claim to certain experiences and sensitivities. It pays to play the "race card" in academia. Why should blacks willingly relinquish that power? Could it be that the intellectual integrity and the surefooted confidence to be gained by succeeding according to extant standards in one's profession dominate the tenuous gains associated with becoming the voice of black alienation at Harvard or Yale? One suspects this is Carter's position, but he never says so.

Flight from the anxiety of racial doubt can be an overpowering psychological drive. Many blacks in these elite educational environments have not had the special competitive training that Carter brought with him to Stanford and Yale. Many of them are intimidated by these places. One way effectively to banish the question "Am I really good enough to be here?" is to embrace the conviction that "these people will/can never judge me fairly, for they see the world differently than I do." Carter seems hopelessly naive about these psychological dynamics, failing to detect them even when they operate within himself.

The power issue is illustrated by Carter's analysis of the problem with old-boy networks: professors make favorites out of those students who affect the conventional signs of being smart—those who are glib, quick, aggressive in seminars, and self-confident to a fault. This tends to favor white males over women and blacks. Some of the latter are smart, too, but they are frozen out of the inner sanctum by gatekeepers who can or will not see their promise. What is needed, Carter seems to say, is reform that gives all students an equal opportunity to show their smarts. He takes the elitism of the basic structure as given, questioning only the biased way in which it operates.

But might not a student from the impoverished black community surrounding Professor Carter's law school in New Haven be inclined to demand more of Yale than an equal chance to gain access, as an individual, to its ivory tower? And what means of leverage will be available to this student to bring about such change? Will rational argument alone suffice, or might not the authority and authenticity that come from the life experience of such a person be appropriated to advance the end of fundamental reform? Is it really true that the only means of persuasion we have in the academy are our arguments? And what about those who simply do not know their way around an argument as well as does Professor Carter? The reader is left unclear as to what he intends for the thousands of economically and intellectually marginal affirmative action admittees for whom the so-what retort is either an empty bluff or a distant dream.

My own view is that law school is no place for this lad from New Haven to try to solve the world's problems, that he should be judged by the quality of his arguments alone, that he can basically rely on receiving a fair hearing on the merits regarding his abilities, and that if he cannot fashion arguments then he should not be there. But then, they call me a black conservative.

Carter wants very much to avoid that pejorative label. As a result, he conducts a discourse that strikes one blow after another at the most cherished prerogatives of those making academic livings as self-styled "authentic blacks," without ever taking political responsibility for the implications of his position. He makes a sustained argument bolstering conservative reaction against the excesses of the "politically correct" but then takes pains to point out that on some issues, like capital punishment, he really does hold the correct views. (He says he likes being unpredictable; I think he just likes being liked.) How can a brief for the preservation of the status quo disposition of authority and control in the academy, which this book in large part surely is, not be conservative? Carter even bandies about talk about "standards of excellence" being essential for the maintenance of "civilization," and so forth. But through all of this he asks us to see him as simply "an observer willing and able to use rational faculties to distinguish wisdom from folly." He is not taking sides, you understand, just dispensing enlightenment!

But such "enlightenment" will not dispel all darkness. It certainly offers no succor for those blacks who doubt where they stand among their academic peers, and who are ill equipped to command the respect of these peers through the kind of brilliance to which Carter lays claim. Indeed, so subtle are the psychological dimensions of race in the academy that they are even illustrated by Carter's attitude toward his own work in this book. He makes sure the reader is aware that this writing on racial topics is just a part-time pursuit, that his real academic work focuses on constitutional law and intellectual property issues. Why? He says these are just some things about race that he wants to get off his chest, that's all. But if he is giving us cogent arguments (which he is), and if he is contributing to understanding on the most important domestic ill of our democracy (which he also is), why would he feel the need to explain taking time away from work on patent law to write this book?

Two observations are irresistible: first, he regards (or believes his professional peers regard) the racial stuff as somehow not as respectable or challenging an area of inquiry. Second, though he holds a named chair at an Ivy League law school, a fact that should leave little doubt that he is an intellectual heavyweight, he wants not to be seen as one of those black professors (of whom there are many) making a living by writing about race. It as if Carter has been looking over his shoulder for so long, fearing his white competitors would somehow overtake him, that he is unable to relax—even after having so obviously made it into the clear.

Of course, this kind of armchair psychoanalysis is unfair to Carter, but he invites it. His autobiographical voice, used at times with great effect, combined with a pose of disinterested intellectual objectivity that is advertised through much of the discussion, forces a reader to occasionally ask himself, "What's up with this guy? What is he really saying here?" He seems to be ambivalent, wanting to draw on his experience as an "affirmative action baby" to lend authority to his arguments and to vouchsafe his innocuous intent in making them. But he also wants to think of himself as a freewheeling intellectual, calling the facts as he sees them, beholden only to his own standards of rigor in the process. He wants to be an iconoclast without owning up to the fact that he is smashing some sacred symbols of the race-conscious brigade. As a self-professed—and self-conscious—black intellectual, he stands with "his people," yet insists he must sometimes go his own route. I am not persuaded by this book that he can have it both ways.

15

Demanding More of Blacks Than Whites

The Content of Our Character
by Shelby Steele

The appearance in 1990 of Shelby Steele's collection of essays *The Content of Our Character* was a major event in the field of race relations. This critically acclaimed book was read widely and discussed avidly in scholarly and popular circles. In my experience, there was a discernible difference in the response of blacks and whites to Steele's arguments. Many whites but fewer blacks were persuaded of the core proposition that connects these several essays and gives them coherence: Racial conflict in our time is essentially a struggle for innocence, with blacks and whites engaged in a contest over the assignment of collective guilt for past and ongoing racial violation. Blacks seek acknowledgment of their victimization, while whites seek exculpation from the accusation of bigotry that is implicit in much public discourse on racial matters.

It is easy to see why this argument would evoke a sympathetic response from many whites (both liberals and conservatives), while enraging many blacks. For, having posed this opposition between white innocence and black victimization, Steele goes on quite naturally to suggest the invalidity of both extremes. Blacks are not

just, or even mainly, victims of white racism, and seeing themselves in that way is profoundly debilitating of self-esteem and the
impetus to seize such opportunities as are at hand. And whites in
twentieth-century America, given our nation's history and the
ongoing racial problems we face, cannot be let totally off the hook
regarding responsibility for racial conflict. Their desire to be
relieved of such responsibility blinds some whites to the reality of
continuing racial insensitivity and discrimination.

Most whites with whom I have discussed Steele's work accept
both sides of this coin, agreeing that blacks cling overly much to
victim status, and that whites too often and too quickly look to
avoid entanglement in and responsibility for the problems of
which blacks complain. Of course, it costs them very little to make
this concession, since the operational implications for them of
acknowledging some responsibility are quite unclear. At most, it
seems to me, Steele is asking whites to look on America's racial
scene with greater empathy and subtlety than is required by the
search for innocence in which so many seem to be engaged.

In contrast, many blacks have a huge investment in seeing
through a lens of victimization. Their identities are intimately
interwoven with a recognition of their condition as past and potential victim of some injury, large or small, based on their race. For
them, acceptance of Steele's argument demands a great deal more
than most have been willing to cede. The fact that some whites
may be saying, "Come on, I'll meet you halfway," makes this concession all the more difficult to grant. The implication of Steele's
arguments for blacks are graphically clear and profoundly threatening: he is asking them to let go of the security blanket of racial
accusation, to perform without a net, to stop bellyaching and get
on with it. Small wonder then that blacks have rejected and
denounced his book throughout the land, labeling him variously
(and quite unfairly) as a reactionary, a turncoat, and an ignoramus.
The viciousness of these attacks suggest how much is at stake here,
and just how raw is the nerve upon which Shelby Steele has tread.

Of course it is only natural that Steele, a black man who writes
(at least in part) so as to work through and record his own views
about racial identity and responsibility, would pose an argument
demanding more of blacks than of whites. In effect, he demands of

his black readers no more than that which he has already given—critical self-evaluation. One of the virtues of this book for teaching on race relations is that it can be used to provoke discussion of the nature and far-reaching implications of race-conscious behavior in students' everyday lives. These discussions are inevitably personal and painful, but when undertaken with candor, they can be very productive. In my experience a few black students have benefited greatly from these conversations, which continued privately, because they were led for the first time to realize the extent to which certain dysfunctional aspects of their own racial identities had blocked the attainment of their full human potential.

Contrary to the much publicized reports of a "new racism" on college campuses, a much more serious threat to the successful matriculation of black students at elite colleges today is that they may fail to engage these institutions fully and avail themselves of the unparalleled opportunities for growth and development that they afford. Often there is a self-imposed limitation on the extent to which the student will open himself or herself to the intellectual, cultural, and social influences of the university and its cosmopolitan milieu. Choices that students must make—including about friends and associates, fields of study, extracurricular activities, books to read, music to listen to, sports to play, museums to visit, political associations, how much time to spend studying, which dorm to live in, what to do with one's summers, and more—are influenced by prevailing notions among these middle-class black Americans of what it means to be truly and authentically "black."

It is inevitable and fitting that to some degree this should be so. But the nature of the influence too often induces a narrow, parochial, and unchallenging set of choices to be made. A central task of any college student is the development of self-knowledge and the refinement of personal identity. This is a vastly different undertaking from the development of racial awareness; Steele's essays underscore the difference. This distinction has been a theme in some of the finest literature coming out of the ethnic experience. In *Portrait of the Artist as a Young Man* Joyce's character Stephen Daedalus objects to the limitations on the development of his artistic sensibility induced by the blind celebration of

Irish ethnicity so popular with his peers. Echoing this theme, Ellison's protagonist in *Invisible Man* evokes the memory of Joyce
when struggling with his own existential dilemma of choosing
between his personal development and the furtherance of collective racial objectives.

Toward the end of chapter 16 of *Invisible Man,* Ellison's hero
recalls a lecture on Joyce that he heard while in college at
Tuskegee, in which the teacher argues about Stephen Daedalus as
follows:

> Stephen's problem, like ours, was not actually one of creating the
> uncreated conscience of his race, but of creating the uncreated features
> of his face. Our task is that of making ourselves individuals. The con-
> science of a race is the gift of its individuals who see, evaluate, record.
> . . . We create the race by creating ourselves and then to our great
> astonishment we will have created a culture. Why waste time creating
> a conscience for something which doesn't exist? For you see, blood and
> skin do not think!

It is nothing short of tragic that so many young blacks, with
unbounded talent and opportunity, define their task as creating the
conscience of their race, rather than the features of their own face.

Naturally this judgment will be controversial; not everyone will
accept it. But no one can deny that vast expanses of intellectual
and cultural terrain at our leading universities are virtually devoid
of a black presence, even though due to affirmative action, black
representation in the student bodies of these institutions is substantial (if not entirely adequate). It would be silly to say that
racism and discrimination are unrelated to this absence, but it
would also be inane to assert that choices of black students have no
bearing on this situation. A simple question should be posed to all
with responsibility for elite higher education: is the precious
resource of talent and human potential among these very bright
black youngsters being developed to its maximal extent? This
question should be posed as well in a personal fashion to each and
every such student embarking on the voyage of self-discovery and
development that the pursuit of higher education ideally ought to
be.

Shelby Steele has made a contribution through his effective and
cogent prose, by leading some of us to face this question in our

own careers and lives. Toward the end of his book he writes, "I have . . . come to realize that in this . . . society, I have been more in charge of my fate than I always wanted to believe, and that though I have been limited by many things, my race was not foremost among them." The challenge in this observation to other blacks who, like Steele, have not been mired in poverty or prisons but rather have enjoyed the opportunities of middle-class life opened fully to blacks only in the last generation, is obvious. It is a difficult challenge to face—as difficult as it is necessary. Much of the wrath directed against Steele by the thought police of African American intellectual authenticity derives from the fact that they would simply rather not be bothered with facing up to this challenge.

But history will not wait for politically correct black voices to see the true nature of the problems confronting our people. "Guilt is the essence of white anxiety, just as inferiority is the essence of black anxiety," Steele writes. Here again we see the asymmetry between black and white that makes Steele's argument weigh so much more heavily on blacks. For anxiety about guilt does not lead whites to make choices that squander their potential and reinforce their limited status, nor, to the extent that it is present, is it so difficult to acknowledge. But anxiety about inferiority means rationalizing failure instead of learning from it; it means avoiding hard but necessary tasks instead of facing up to them; and it means, even in the face of success, living with an inchoate but disquieting sense that there is something fraudulent and undeserved about one's status, that one is at any moment about to be unmasked as "not good enough." Acknowledging anxiety about inferiority is an extremely difficult psychological problem, perhaps the most problematic of the bombshells Steele drops with his disquieting argument.

The reality of our contemporary racial history is one of ambiguity insofar as black performance in the post–civil rights era is concerned. The loudest voices of African American authenticity attempt to bluff their way past this ambiguity, but it can never be overcome until it is honestly faced. Nothing significant is going to happen with respect to black faculty representation at the leading universities until there are more distinguished black academics. Cajoling and chastising whites who express fear and resentment about crime and violence in urban centers will not make those fears and resentments go away; only an improvement in the objective behaviors of the perpetrators will do so. Calling the view that affirmative action sometimes leads to less qualified people getting promoted a canard cannot eradicate the observations in myriad settings of mediocre performance by blacks who boast of having been helped by affirmative action. At best this bluffing strategy, playing as it does upon whites' recognition of the vital psychological importance to blacks of their unchallenged position as America's victim and upon whites' anxiety about being accused of racism, drives discussion of the performance question underground. There it flourishes.

Republican politicians and radical black nationalists have been mining this vein of resentment, dishonesty, and obfuscation for twenty years now. Steele—an English professor, not a social scientist—only hints at the powerful political implications of his thesis with his discussion of how Reagan played on whites' desire for racial innocence, and of Jesse Jackson's defiant efforts to deny whites any such comfort. But the matter goes much deeper than that. There is now an open question of whether blacks are capable of gaining equal status, given equality of opportunity, and it is a question in the minds of blacks as well as whites. Let me state unequivocally my personal belief that blacks are, indeed, so capable. But the point is that this assertion is a *hypothesis* not obviously supported by the facts. Blacks have something to prove both to themselves and to white onlookers, many of whom may appear not to be particularly sympathetic. This is not fair; it is not right; but it is the way things are.

Some conservatives are not above signaling, in more or less overt ways, their belief that blacks can never pass this test, and that there is little point in the rest of society bearing guilt for blacks' failures. Some radical black nationalists are not above saying, increasingly more openly now, that blacks can never make it in "white America"—and so we should stop trying, go our own way, and maybe burn a few things down in the process. At bottom these two parties agree that the magnitude of the challenge facing blacks in this post–civil rights environment is beyond our capacities. What Shelby Steele and others (myself included) have been saying is that blacks can and must meet this challenge. In proving our capacity to do so we deserve the support of our fellow citizens, but petitioning for it cannot be the highest order of business for us when we are confronted by the more urgent task of developing ourselves, our families, and our communities in this new era of opportunity. It is for saying this that the barons of righteous social thought on racial matters, black and white, have condemned writers such as Steele. But, to reiterate, this condemnation changes nothing.

The essential truth of which Shelby Steele reminds blacks is that it is primarily the human condition, not our racial condition, that we must learn to cope with. What the apostle Paul wrote to the Corinthians many centuries ago remains true today: "No temptation has seized you except what is common to man; but God is faithful, He will not allow you to be tempted beyond your ability, but when you are tempted He will provide a way out so that you can bear it." The Greek word for "temptation" can also be translated as "trial" or "test." Black Americans must now bear up under the weight of a great trial. Our choice is to confront and dispel the difficulties, or to deny and avoid them. *The Content of Our Character* is aptly titled, for the response that we choose to the current difficulties will reveal more about our own character than about the moral culpability of whites. One can only hope that, away from the bluster, some young blacks are doing with Steele's essays what a few whom I have encountered have done—reading them closely while asking themselves some painful but necessary questions.

16

The Family, the Nation, and Senator Moynihan

Family and Nation
by Daniel P. Moynihan

In the spring of 1985, Daniel Patrick Moynihan—the Democratic senior senator from New York, former U.S. Ambassador to India and to the United Nations, and once professor at Harvard University—returned to Cambridge to deliver the prestigious Godkin Lectures at Harvard's Kennedy School of Government. His return to Cambridge involved a return as well to discussing issues of the family, a topic on which his ideas had generated great controversy two decades earlier, when he was serving as assistant secretary of Labor in the Johnson administration. Indeed, Moynihan devotes the first part of *Family and Nation*,[1] the published version of his Godkin Lectures, to a review of the events surrounding the release and subsequent denunciation of the 1965 policy paper he prepared, "The Negro Family: The Case for National Action."

In this paper, later dubbed simply the Moynihan Report, he advanced two arguments. The first was that the debilitating effects of slavery and the long years of racial oppression had so undermined the position of the black male within the family that a "matri-focal family structure" had emerged in this group and seemed likely to persist. The second was that the attainment of full racial equality was so threatened by this reality that, despite the recently enacted civil rights statutes, substantial economic disparity between the races also seemed likely to continue. On both points, what was necessary by way of response was a national policy aimed at changing family behavior among blacks.

To explain the diminution of the black male's family role during slavery and its aftermath, Moynihan borrowed virtually intact an analysis that had been made more than a quarter century before by the black sociologist E. Franklin Frazier. Subsequent historical research, though, has demonstrated that this analysis is almost certainly wrong. The racial differences in family structure that so alarmed Moynihan are a post–World War II phenomenon, not to be found in the earlier historical record, and they cannot be explained by reference to the experience of black slavery. Examination of census forms for individual cities and counties in the late nineteenth and early twentieth centuries has shown that for blacks and whites alike, most women heading families were widows; that even among the very poor, a substantial majority of families was intact; and that the association between broken family structure and lower social class derived mainly from the higher mortality rate among poor men. The evidence also shows that in the early twentieth century the intact family was the norm among black migrant communities in the urban North. Historian Herbert Gutman has found that 85 percent of black families living in Harlem in 1925 were intact, and that the teenage mother raising her children alone was virtually unknown; he found similarly stable families among blacks in Buffalo in 1910. As late as the 1940 census, when 10.1 percent of white families were headed by females, only 14.9 percent of black families were so headed.

But Moynihan did not have the benefit of this research when writing his report, and at the time Frazier's explanation for the growth of out-of-wedlock births and female-headed households among blacks seemed as plausible as any. What Moynihan did have was the hunch that without some concerted effort aimed at reversing this now-critical pattern, the civil rights revolution alone would be inadequate to secure the equalitarian expectations it had released:

Nothing was done in response to Frazier's argument. Matters were left to take care of themselves, and as matters will, grew worse not better. The problem is now more serious, the obstacles greater. There is, however, a profound change for the better in one respect. The President has committed the nation to an all-out effort to eliminate poverty wherever it exists, among whites or Negroes, and a militant, organized, and responsible Negro movement exists to join in that effort. Such a national effort could be stated thus: the policy of the United States is to bring the Negro American to full and equal sharing in the responsibilities and rewards of citizenship. To this end, the programs of the federal government bearing on this objective shall be designed to have the effect, directly or indirectly, of enhancing the stability and resources of the Negro American family.

This was, Moynihan now acknowledges, an extraordinary proposition. He could not be sure he was correct in all particulars. Still, the matter was sufficiently urgent and the mood of the administration in domestic policy matters sufficiently adventuresome that he chose to seize the moment, with fateful consequences.

———

Within a month of the receipt of his report at the White House, Moynihan's ideas became the basis for a historic speech by President Johnson, given at Howard University in June 1965. (Johnson called it "the greatest civil rights speech of my life.") In it the President committed his administration to move beyond equality of opportunity for black Americans and to seek "not just equality as a right and a theory, but equality as a fact and as a result."

One aspect of this effort, for which Johnson's speech is most often remembered and quoted today, was to be the promulgation of Executive Order 11246, the legal basis of affirmative action requirements for federal contractors. But looming just as large in Johnson's initial conception of how "equality as a fact and as a result" could be achieved was the family: "So unless we work to strengthen the family, to create conditions under which most parents will stay together, the rest—schools and playgrounds, public assistance and private concern—will never be enough to cut completely the circle of despair and deprivation." He announced his intention to convene a White House conference of experts, black leaders, and government officials to explore how this might be done.

Initial reaction to Johnson's speech was positive. In the *New York Times*, Tom Wicker likened it to the Supreme Court's 1954 school desegregation decision, noting that Johnson had extended the "separate is inherently unequal" principle into the area of family life, where the races were quite separate indeed. In doing so, Wicker wrote, Johnson had "face[d] squarely what must be ranked as the most difficult problem in American life." Another liberal columnist, Mary McGrory, reported that the speech had been cleared with Roy Wilkins, then head of the NAACP, and with Martin Luther King, Jr., both of whom were "in enthusiastic accord."

But it was clear even in the first days after its delivery that Johnson's speech had created serious problems for black leaders. For the conception put forth there implied that blacks would have to be involved actively in remedying the social disorganization of the ghetto. As McGrory noted at the time: "The first Southern President in a hundred years . . . told the Negroes that in compassion and concern he would not be outdone. Now to be constructive, he must have their help." This, it soon emerged, would not be forthcoming. Associates of civil rights leader James Farmer were cited by McGrory as saying that Farmer "has been prevented from speaking out for fear that a call to improve Negro community life might be misinterpreted as a slow down to integration. In the past Negroes who have advocated the 'bootstrap' approach of Booker T. Washington have run the risk of being called 'Uncle Tom.'"

There were few willing to take this risk in 1965, or for many years thereafter. By the fall of the year it was already clear that the President's foray into this sensitive area had failed. At a planning session for the full White House conference, amid the political echoes of the rioting in the Watts section of Los Angeles in August, one black leader after another downplayed the importance of the family issue, insisting that only a massive infusion of federal dollars into the ghettos could begin to address the crisis. High on their agenda was the $100 billion (in 1965 dollars!) "freedom budget" of A. Philip Randolph and Bayard Rustin. Floyd McKissick insisted that the plight of poor blacks could only be remedied by a change in "the capitalistic system." Moynihan's report was bitterly attacked; the need for greater family stability was dismissed without debate. When the White House conference itself finally convened in June 1966, the subject of the family had been stricken from the agenda. As one White House aide put it: "The family is not an action topic for a can-do conference."

———————

By daring to suggest that dysfunctional family behavior among poor blacks constituted an insuperable barrier to economic equality, Moynihan had elicited an emotional, ideologically charged response that permanently altered racial discourse in America. The now-familiar indictment of "blaming the victim," which is still invoked whenever anyone suggests that failings of values and character might somehow be connected with an individual's poor economic condition, was literally invented in reaction to Moynihan's argument (by psychologist William Ryan in an article in *The Nation*).

Moynihan's *Family and Nation* is at its best in these passages of political memoir. Particularly striking is the author's description of the effect on President Johnson of the collapse of the family initiative: "From being buoyantly open to ideas and enterprises, he became near contemptuous of civil-rights leaders who he now believed cared only for symbols." A precious moment had been lost; from that point forward, a cynical president would manage the race problem rather than attempt to solve it—certainly not if solving it required getting out front and leading. Soon enough he became absorbed by other matters. Those committed to the silencing of Moynihan, and to the banishment of the topic of behavioral pathology in the ghetto from public discussion, managed to have their way.

A dear price was paid for this indulgence, although it was not paid by those responsible for it. The years immediately following saw a deepened radicalization of the civil rights community, a turn northward that culminated in the "poor people's campaign" of 1968 and a sweeping expansion of the Supreme Court's desegregation decrees into the ethnic enclaves of the urban Northeast and Midwest. Then came the advent of the era of racial preference, accompanied by the invention by intellectuals, both black and white, of ever more elaborate constructs to rationalize the brutal facts of inner-city life as the inevitable consequence of a bankrupt society. In the meantime, the social disruption that so alarmed Moynihan continued, and in fact it has grown much worse in the intervening decades.

In his recapitulation of this course of events Moynihan is as gracious as could be expected of one who, having been vilified as a racist, has lived to see history prove him right. He notes approvingly the modest movement among black leaders and intellectuals in the 1980s toward facing squarely and at long last the problem of family disorganization in the black community. By way of an I-told-you-so, he allows himself no more than to note that "controversy is never resolved among those who begin it. Rather, a succeeding generation comes along that accepts one of the competing views, and that is that."

Alas, if only it were so. The intellectual rubble of that earlier period has yet to be fully cleared. To invoke such terms as "values," "character," or "social pathology" in speaking about the poor (black or otherwise) is still to invite the charge of blaming the victim or, if the speaker is black, of being an Uncle Tom. Remarkably, one still encounters the same line that was used to dismiss Moynihan thirty years ago—namely, that acknowledging a behavioral basis to economic deprivation feeds stereotypes about blacks and provides grist for the racists' mill. It is as if the facts about inner-city life, staggeringly evident to anyone with eyes to see, could be blunted by simply banning any discussion of them from polite society.

———

In any event, if Moynihan is on the whole pleased at the greater readiness among many to discuss the issue of family disorganization in the ghetto, there is another development in the arena of social policy that troubles him deeply: the increasing influence, as he sees it, of conservative ideas. In the latter part of his book he sets himself the task of refuting these ideas, and here he becomes much less convincing.

From this point forward *Family and Nation* turns into a brief for three propositions: (1) the massive expansion of the social programs associated with the Great Society has been of enormous benefit in reducing poverty, especially among the elderly; (2) this success, along with demographic developments and shifting sexual mores, has created the historically aberrant and morally disturbing circumstance that poverty is now much more pronounced among young children than among older persons; and (3) some common ground might be found on which sensible liberals and conservatives can construct a national policy aimed at increasing the welfare of the American family, but only if we first abandon the idea that government efforts to help may have sometimes made matters worse.

I do not take issue with either the first or the second of these propositions. The reduction in poverty among the elderly resulting from the growth in the real value of Social Security benefits and the advent of Medicare represents an achievement of historic proportions. And there is something disturbing in the cumulative effects, noticed by Moynihan, of an ever more generous provision to the elderly combined with the erosion (due to inflation) of real levels of assistance to families with dependent children (AFDC) down by nearly one-fourth since the early 1970s. A reexamination of priorities seems warranted.

That the poor have come increasingly to consist of young women and their children living without a husband and father is a matter of great significance. But the Moynihan of 1986 believes that we can meet this problem simply by summoning up the will to do for the young what we have managed to do for the old, and that in so doing we need not concern ourselves with the question of whether our efforts might not exacerbate the proliferating social pathology he has documented.

Thus Moynihan seems intent upon negating the political effect of Charles Murray's influential book *Losing Ground* (1984) and especially the "thought experiment" Murray conducted to determine what would happen if we did away with all federal assistance to working-aged persons. So preoccupied is he with this analytic exercise—which no one, not even Murray, takes seriously as a realistic proposal—that he dismisses without proper consideration some of Murray's most trenchant ideas. And as for his own ideas, these are so vaguely stated that one arrives at the last page of this book without ever having been given an indication of the specific features of family life that Moynihan would seek to promote through his "family policy." In his wandering and discursive narrative one is often entertained, and occasionally informed, but mostly left longing for the Moynihan who in 1965 could write the following:

> From the wild Irish slums of the 19th-century Eastern seaboard, to the riot-torn suburbs of Los Angeles, there is one unmistakable lesson in American history: a community that allows a large number of young men to grow up in broken families, dominated by women, never acquiring any stable relationship to male authority, never acquiring any set of rational expectations about the future—that community asks for and gets chaos. Crime, violence, unrest, disorder—most particularly the furious, unrestrained lashing out at the whole social structure—that is not only to be expected; it is very near to inevitable. And it is richly deserved.

One knew where the Moynihan who wrote that statement stood. He admired the nuclear family and thought its preservation essential, especially among the poor. He had a healthy respect for the central role of male authority in the child-rearing process. He understood how the norms and values characteristic of an entire community could work to induce individuals to act in ways destructive of their own possibilities for advancement. He saw a role to be played by political leadership in publicly affirming the old-fashioned virtues and in promulgating policies that encouraged them. For all one knows, he may still believe these things, but the reader of *Family and Nation* cannot so conclude with confidence. Instead, the reader will find here the idea that a healthy family policy for the nation would consist simply in increasing the financial resources in the hands of heads of households in which children happen to be raised.

———

But it hardly constitutes a sufficient formulation of social policy toward the family to say that its objective should be to make children better off. As Moynihan notes, the problem of family instability is no longer confined to poor blacks; much of the American population is now affected, with teenage pregnancy and unwed motherhood reaching alarming proportions. What should we do about this? Is it enough to put more cash in the hands of those responsible for the care of children? Should public policy attempt, as well, to encourage the avoidance of births before marriage? Should it consciously attempt to strengthen the male role within the family? Should the increasing frequency of divorce engender any policy response? Should dependent minor parents be abetted or discouraged in their efforts to receive assistance directly, without involving their parents? Is homosexual adoption a good idea? On these matters, we receive no useful guidance.

Though Moynihan argues strongly that poverty and family structure are intimately intertwined, he seems unwilling to consider how policy might, directly or indirectly, promote any specific type of family structure in the interest of ameliorating poverty. He urges at one point that social policy be based on social values, not on social science, yet he relies entirely on social science to defend his few proposals to increase the resources of households containing children. He never refers in this discussion to the social values motivating these proposals (other than the imperative that a decent provision be made for the poor), just as he fails to consider their potential effects on the values and the behavior of their beneficiaries.

To judge from *Family and Nation* itself, one reason for this would seem to be Moynihan's diffidence before the internal politics of the modern Democratic party. He recalls how President Carter, early in his administration, naively proclaimed his intention to hold a White House conference on the family; bickering over matters of definition delayed the event until 1979, when a much watered-down conference on "Families" finally took place. (Indeed, the divorced black mother who had been slated to chair that conference later wrote proudly of her principled resignation when the White House urged upon her a married white male vice chairman. How dared they suggest that a husband and wife raising children together were preferable to a mother doing the job alone!) In the 1990s the growing influence within the Democratic party of feminist and homosexual-rights constituencies would probably render such a conference altogether out of the question.

Shortly after his 1965 experience, Moynihan wrote: "The time when white men, whatever their motives, could tell Negroes what was or was not good for them, is now definitely and decidedly over.

An era of bad manners is almost certainly begun." Today's version of this wisdom would appear to be as follows: the time when public officials (whatever their motives) could intimate to citizens (whatever their race) what manner of family life was or was not good for them is now definitely and decidedly over. This is tantamount to saying that the time for leadership itself has passed—yet how, one may ask, will pathological social trends so broadly based and pervasive as those underlying the "feminization of poverty" be reversed without such leadership? Does Moynihan perhaps really believe they are not to be reversed, but institutionalized instead? On this, as on so much else, he leaves us in the dark.

It is certainly true that an effort to lead public opinion on this matter would entail serious political risks. But would those risks not be outweighed by the potential benefit to be derived from stemming the tide of early out-of-wedlock births? It can be seen in retrospect that the black community has paid an enormous price for delaying by three decades a concerted effort to grapple with the problem that Moynihan identified in 1965. Surely the nation as a whole will suffer grievously if we refrain further from any effort to shape our citizens' values on these matters.

Consider, for example, the great debate that raged in New York City during 1984 over the local board of education's proposed course of instruction in "Family Living Including Sex Education for Grades K–12." The planned course avoided any judgment concerning the relative merits of different family structures, a matter that caused concern to some local clergy. The *New York Times*, however, editorialized at the time that one could not teach that intact families are preferable to broken families without offending great numbers of students; public health statistics showed that some 79 percent of the children born in central Harlem had mothers who were not married. But is this simply a fact about the world that public instruction must accommodate through a studied neutrality? Or does it call for a concerted effort to teach the values of the traditional family even (or perhaps especially) to those children least likely to see them confirmed in their private lives at home? Can there be an effective family policy that takes no position on such an issue?

I am reminded here of a distinction introduced by economist Albert Hirschman between tastes (defined as individual preferences about which we do not argue, such as whether we like apples or pears), and values (defined as preferences over which we do argue, both with ourselves and with others). We do not treat a preference for discrimination against blacks or women as a taste to be accommodated. Rather, we attempt to persuade, cajole, or compel our fellows to make "progress" in such areas, and we insist that our educational institutions instill in our young the proper views concerning them. Values, in other words, are personal preferences so central to our collective lives that as a political community we cannot properly be neutral about them. As Hirschman has noted, "A principal purpose of publicly proclaimed laws and regulations is to stigmatize antisocial behavior and thereby to influence citizens' values and behavior codes."

Senator Moynihan seems to have implicitly accepted the notion that preferences concerning household living arrangements and childbearing outside of marriage ought to be regarded as tastes rather than as values. One might, however, argue—just as it was argued regarding racial discrimination—that these are instead issues on which we can and must establish a commitment. After all, the well-being of our children is at stake.

Participants on both sides of the great contemporary debate over "traditional values" understand this very well. Radical feminists and gay rights activists want the nuclear family dethroned from its position as the presumptive ideal type. Fundamentalist Christians consciously seek its preservation. At issue here is something far weightier than a demographic projection showing how household living arrangements have changed since the 1950s. The central question must be whether we view that change with indifference or with alarm, and the way we answer that question as a nation will depend in turn upon our answer to the even more fundamental query: what kind of people are we? The senior Senator from New York seems to think he can lead a search for a national policy on the family while standing on the sidelines of these questions. In truth, he cannot.

———

That is why I am skeptical, to say the least, of Moynihan's notion that liberals and conservatives might yet find some common ground on which to build a national family policy. Conservatives, much influenced by Charles Murray's argument, are concerned about the possibly detrimental effects of public assistance on the behavior of young adults. Liberals answer (correctly) that there simply is no proof that variations across states or over time in the level of AFDC payments are significantly associated with comparable variations in the extent of unwed pregnancy and female-headed families. But this hardly exhausts the matter.

Public policies affecting the poor range far beyond direct cash assistance to dependent children. A systematic study has yet to be undertaken of the effect on family structure of the full package of benefits, which includes food stamps and medical and housing subsidies. Murray has also documented changes in educational and criminal justice practices—the increasing difficulty of getting unruly youngsters out of public school classrooms so that others might learn, and the declining likelihood of arrest and punishment for remunerative criminal activities—that have had the effect of reducing the perceived return to "good behavior" on the part of the very poor. He argues as well that the growth and increased liberalization of the "welfare complex" have undermined the old ethos of working-class communities that one can achieve a position of respect among one's peers by staying with a low-wage job, marrying and supporting the mother of one's children, and avoiding trouble with the law. The fact is that we do not know the extent to which trying to help the very poor, in the specific ways characteristic of the late 1960s and early 1970s, may have abetted the growth of dysfunctional behavior. But Murray and others have shown that we have good reason to be concerned.

Moynihan's principal criticism of *Losing Ground* is that Murray cannot prove with data that his speculations are correct. This is fair enough—until we recall that neither could Moynihan in 1965 "prove" his hunch that, unless drastic action were taken to improve family stability among blacks, the opening up of economic opportunity would be inadequate to the task of achieving racial equality. As he himself notes, public policy-makers often have to act on their hunches without the benefit of a "definitive" study.

Among the major hunches of liberals in the 1990s is the notion that, were federally provided jobs available to the many unemployed ghetto youths, we would see a substantial reduction in the number of single-parent families, since women would have a greater incentive to marry the (now gainfully employed) fathers of their children. The senator shares this hunch, and it sounds plausible enough, but he cannot prove it. For one thing, the lack-of-jobs hypothesis does not account for why the pregnancies occurred in the first place. One might, indeed, argue with equal plausibility that it is the failure or refusal to assume responsibility for a family that accounts for the lack of initiative among young fathers to find and keep such low-wage employment as does exist. This latter hypothesis would also explain why welfare mothers in one employment training experiment (Supported Work) showed more favorable results than did ex-criminal offenders or male high school dropouts: the mothers had to go home and look their children in the face every day, realizing that the responsibility for these youngsters lay on their shoulders alone.[2]

On these issues Moynihan sometimes speaks with disturbing confidence: "Government did not transform the behavior of those in greatest difficulty; it pretty much left them be. Behavior that was already self-destructive simply went forward, with the consequences growing more pronounced—which is the normal progression of self-destructive behavior." But we must ask the senator, as he asks Charles Murray: how does he know? Who says so? The "community women" employed in Harlem to advise teenage mothers in Project Redirection (a two-year program aimed at preventing a second unwed pregnancy among poor young single mothers) seem to have come to different conclusions concerning the effect of government aid on behavior. According to the evaluation report of the project, done by the respected Manpower Development Research Corporation, these women

> initially took an activist stance in their efforts to intercede with the welfare system on behalf of participants. This pattern changed, however, when [certain] behavior patterns were beginning to emerge. It seemed that many were beginning to view getting their own welfare grants as the next stage in their careers. . . . It became apparent that some participants' requests for separate grants and independent households were too often a sign of manipulation by boyfriends, in whose interest it was to have a girlfriend on welfare with an apartment of her own. . . . Staff realized that these attitudes and behaviors were . . . counterproductive to the . . . goal of promoting self-sufficiency.[3]

True, these firsthand observers cannot prove their hunches, either. Should we nevertheless listen to them, or does their testimony perhaps lend too much support to the "conservative" side of the debate?

When it comes to the effect of intricate, interacting social policies on complex individual behaviors, there is an irreducible level of uncertainty attached to our knowledge. This does not mean we should be agnostic on such matters; it does mean we should be pragmatic, and ready to acknowledge the truths that come from experience. Senator Moynihan, no stranger to these virtues, might find more scope for their application were he less concerned with defending a liberal policy edifice against both the promptings of experience and the encroaching judgment of the American electorate.

17

A Crisis Grows in Brooklyn

Canarsie
by Jonathan Rieder

In his book *Canarsie: The Jews and Italians of Brooklyn Against Liberalism,* Jonathan Rieder provides an insider's account of white ethnic reaction to the pressures of urban change.[1] This community of working- and middle-class Jews and Italians attracted national attention in the late 1960s and early 1970s when some of the ugliest conflicts in the country over the issues of residential integration, busing, and urban crime erupted in its midst. When ten thousand students were kept from school during a white antibusing boycott in the fall of 1972, the *New York Times* wrote in an editorial that "the shameful situation in Canarsie illustrates the forces of unreason sweeping over the city and nation," and hoped that "the arrival of new [black] pupils can be turned into a friendly occasion rather than a shameful blocking of the schoolhouse door à la Little Rock." Rieder presents an anatomy of racism and bitter reaction, fear and anger, and doubt and resignation. Canarsie's residents come vividly to life in this superb ethnography as Rieder, who lived in Brooklyn during nearly two years of field research for the book, renders their voices in readable prose.

There is evidence for all of the clichés of the conventional (dare I say elite?) wisdom concerning the "silent majority" here. An Italian plumber sees nobility in his forebears' struggle against poverty, but only depravity in the desperate lives of the contemporary black poor. The Catholic wife of a municipal employee complains that "the blacks have ten kids to a family," seeing "their overpopulation" as the problem. An Orthodox Jewish man laments what has become "a degenerate society" in which criminals "kill people like they would kill a fly." In response to the airing of "Roots," a woman declares, "If they keep shoving that stuff down our throats there's never going to be peace. . . . I expect this summer the blacks will be out there on the streets with axes to cut off white feet."

We learn of an organization among Italian youths called SPONGE (Society for the Prevention of Niggers Getting Everything), of the systematic intimidation of neighbors who consider selling their homes to blacks, and of firebombs thrown at the homes of those black families brave enough to challenge the community's ethnic purity. A Jewish member of a backlash group explains, "Well, I'm against violence, but they are jeopardizing my home and my children, and I will bomb to protect them." We enter the world of antibusing activism, the epitome of Canarsie's collective resistance to the advancing liberal reforms. Rieder recalls the genesis of the "Canarsie Schools for Canarsie Children" boycott campaign and provides frightfully detailed accounts of "howling," "fiendish," and "ghoulish" mobs of white parents, determined to let the black students and the rest of the world know of their displeasure at "forced busing." We are not spared the violent, bloody details, nor the zeal with which young Canarsie residents carried out their assignments. One young Italian tough laughingly announces, "I hate niggers. I've been fighting them all my life. I enjoy it."

While Rieder skillfully depicts the bigotry, ignorance, and prejudice of this troubled neighborhood, he is equally adroit at capturing the palpable fear, acute sense of injustice, and moral ambivalence that plague many Canarsie whites. A trucker tells of having defecated in his pants when accosted by knife-wielding black youths. Neighbors, gathered to discuss street crime, "occasionally tried to best each other in duels of grotesque incidents" that they had witnessed, one of which involved the burning alive of a subway token clerk. Elderly residents tell of feeling imprisoned in their own homes. Devout Jews recount being beaten on their way to synagogue when muggers found that, for religious reasons, they never carried money on their person. An undercover police-man whose job it is to pose as a likely mugging victim recalls that of the more than one hundred incidents in which he has been involved, only one of the perpetrators was white.

Those who had moved to Canarsie after watching their former neighborhoods in the New York area succumb to racial integration and subsequent decay explain that they have nowhere else to run, that it is here in Canarsie that they must make their stand. Hard-working people of limited means and proud, family-oriented tradi-tions look on the massive welfare dependency of fatherless black families with bewilderment and disdain. Italian workers of quite modest incomes—and a precarious toehold in the American mid-dle class—vent their sense of outrage at being lumped together with slaveholding whites of the previous century as racist victimiz-ers of blacks. One man explains: "They made us dig the [subway] tunnels. When the earth caved in, it was always one of the Italians who died, nobody of consequence! We were slaves."

Rieder discusses white outrage at a government-mandated "eth-nic" census that made no distinction among European nationality groups: "The HEW form seemed to relegate all whites to a resid-ual category of otherness and to reserve the dignity of a name for groups officially designated as deprived." One ethnically conscious man exclaims, "What the hell does 'white' mean?" It becomes clear why demands for bilingual education, public recognition of black culture, quotas, reparations, open enrollment, and leniency for urban rioters so deeply offended these people's sense of justice. With similar, though clearly not identical, grievances they had no standing to make comparable claims, and were denounced as racists if they balked at paying (with their homes and children, as they saw it) for the claims being ever more aggressively pressed by blacks.

What emerges is a complex, nuanced picture of northern urban racial reaction among the Canarsie ethnics. Some of the residents, especially those conservative Italians among whom Joe McCarthy remains a hero, are without doubt unreconstructed racists using the perils of the ghetto as an excuse for their bigotry. But others, especially those liberal Jews with backgrounds in radical politics and the civil rights movement, are greatly troubled by the reaction that circumstance has forced upon them. Many search for a vocabulary in which to express their legitimate concerns without running afoul of their deeply ingrained sense of social justice, or their antagonism to stereotypes and racial prejudice.

Rieder argues that the better educated are more likely to succeed at the delicate task of voicing concern about the behavior of "bad" blacks, while continuing to convey a willingness to live in peace with "good" blacks. Yet this distinction is only of theoretical value in those situations where it is impossible to know what "kind" of black one is dealing with. Similarly, it does blacks who encounter the bitter reaction of some white Canarsie residents little good to know that others want desperately to be able to live harmoniously with decent neighbors, regardless of race. Among people who resist school integration and open housing, often vociferously and violently, it is hard to distinguish unreconstructed racists from merely anguished victims of circumstance. For blacks experiencing Canarsie's rage, the distinction between "good" and "bad" whites—between whites whose fears deserve to be taken seriously in the interest of living together in peace, and those who would resist integration no matter what—is also of little practical value.

This touches on the principal problem with Rieder's book: the absence of any serious effort to treat the black side of this great divide. The central characters of the racial drama remain offstage; we see them only through the eyes of Rieder's whites. Because of his decision to focus exclusively on white perceptions, values, and fears, he misses a crucial point—the extent to which each group's anticipation of the "bad" behavior of the other creates self-fulfilling prophecies. In the close quarters of urban living, where peoples of vastly different cultures and norms are brought cheek by jowl, peaceful cohabitation depends upon the willingness of each group to afford a modicum of deference and respect to the different traditions of the others. As Rieder makes clear (though this is not his purpose), it is precisely because of such mutual respect and deference that the Jewish and Italian cohabitants of white Canarsie are able to live together despite vast differences of tradition between the two communities.

But the willingness to defer to the sensibilities of others is a reciprocal and delicate balance, likely to be destroyed if either party loses faith in the cooperation of the other. Rieder describes well the sense of violation felt by whites who encounter in their shared public spaces the loud radios and foul language of black and Hispanic youths. He touches not at all, though, on the anger evoked in the young black at being called "nigger," an anger that makes him less likely to respect the sensitivities of those whom he, not implausibly, presumes to be racists. As a result, Rieder fails to convey a full sense of the *tragedy* of urban race relations in places like Canarsie. Whites are hardened in their resistance to integration by the offensive behavior of blacks, while blacks perceive the fierce resistance to integration as indication that, no matter what they do, the racist whites will never accept them. Add to this drama of mutually reinforcing negative perceptions the fact that there really were some irreducibly hostile blacks and irremediably racist whites on either side of the chasm, and one begins to understand how intractable this conflict is.

Yet, of course, it is not simply perceptions but also the stark realities of the ghetto that cause Canarsie residents to view blacks with suspicion. White racism, however virulent and unreasoning, cannot plausibly be held accountable for the drug addiction, street prostitution, family breakdown, and criminality that confronted the people of Canarsie daily. As Rieder puts it, "The seamy aspects of ghetto life were so vivid that they overwhelmed the ability of whites to note all other aspects that did not conform to the stereotypes." Nor can one dismiss the affront to white ethnics' sense of morality that was caused by the apparent unwillingness of those in authority to condemn what seemed to them to be inexcusable behavior.

To people who had tried to live by the rules as they understood them, it seemed unfair that blacks could breach those rules without sanction. A housewife complains: "You see, we did what we had to. We worked hard and lived right. It's not right that they think they can do what they want to." Rieder, lamenting the fact that Canarsians, themselves descended from poor minorities, had so little empathy for their black neighbors, notes, "Unfortunately, physical closeness to blacks widened the moral and social chasm between them. The legendary sacrifices of Jewish and Italian immigrants nourished contempt for poor blacks, who seemingly failed to bust their chops as had the forebears of the whites."

But where life among ghetto blacks evoked contempt from many whites of Canarsie, it evoked sympathy and pity from the liberal establishment of the Democratic party. As Rieder amply demonstrates, Canarsians felt that liberals, epitomized by the Lindsay mayoral administration locally and the McGovern presidential candidacy nationally, had sided with the blacks. On issues like school desegregation, affirmative action, law and order, and social welfare policy it seemed to them that liberal Democrats no longer represented their views. Indeed, they were made to feel that it was illegitimate to hold these views. Increasingly, those identifying themselves with the forces of conscience in American political life came to give less credence to the values and concerns of white working-class ethnics in places like Canarsie. In many "progressive" minds these people were lumped together with southern segregationists as reactionaries who stood in the way of the attainment of racial justice.

Yet the fears and the anxieties of the Canarsians rested on much sounder moral ground than did those of Southern whites resistant to change. When the civil rights movement turned northward in the mid-1960s, it encountered a kind of resistance that should have been usefully distinguished from that which had just been overcome in the South. But neither the leaders of the movement nor their liberal white allies within the Democratic party were capable of making such distinctions. This, it can be fairly said in retrospect, was a monumental error. The result, Rieder suggests, was a permanent alienation from the party of this vital component of the New Deal coalition, an alienation that, as Thomas and Mary Edsall document in their book *Chain Reaction*, continues to haunt the Democrats in the 1990s.[2]

18
Other Reviews, 1992–1994

Doing Well by Doing Good

The Death of an American Jewish Community

by Hillel Levine and Lawrence Harmon (The Free Press, 1992)

In September 1971 the Subcommittee on Antitrust and Monopoly of the Senate Judiciary Committee held hearings in Boston to investigate the activities of a consortium of Boston banks. A little more than three years earlier, twenty-two of the city's leading financial institutions, through a coalition called the Boston Banks Urban Renewal Group (B-BURG), had initiated a program of mortgage lending to low and moderate income minority families seeking to buy homes in the Boston area. Responding to a growing concern among the city's business and political leadership that there might be violent disturbances if a substantive response to demands from black activists for expanded housing opportunities was not forthcoming, and hoping to "do well by doing good," the banks had pledged to make $50 million in mortgage monies available to borrowers whose loans would be guaranteed by the Federal Housing Authority.

Why then the Senate investigation, if this was simply a case of socially conscious capitalism exploiting a federal program to earn a profit while helping the disadvantaged? The remarkable truth about the B-BURG program was that these bankers were willing to make loans to black home buyers—for which repayment was guaranteed by the federal government and on which a higher interest rate was charged in order to defer administrative costs— only if the buyers purchased within a designated geographical area. They were unwilling to lend to blacks seeking a place to live, even (as the hearings revealed) to the widow of a decorated veteran who was entitled to Veterans Administration mortgage benefits, if the property sought lay only a few blocks outside their approved zone. At a meeting of the participating bankers prior to initiation of their efforts to help the disadvantaged, lines had actually been drawn in red pen on a map of the city to mark off where the money could be spent.

Disturbed by this practice, Barney Frank, then an aide to Boston Mayor Kevin White, ordered a review of the B-BURG program to determine why the consortium refused to make loans outside a narrowly circumscribed area of the city. The review determined that the bankers had strenuously resisted requests from city officials that borrowers be permitted to buy homes outside the designated areas. Indeed, in an August 1968 memo, prominent Boston banker Joseph Bacheller, chairman of B-BURG, had responded to one such request by declaring, "you have been advised on at least three or four occasions that we are not willing to process applications for relocatees outside of the area which the Group is prepared to serve" (Levine and Harmon, p. 271).

It happened that the area into which this special lending activity was "redlined," parts of the neighborhoods known as Dorchester and Mattapan, lay in the heart of Boston's Jewish community. This was not an accident. The bankers needed to have some purchases in white areas; otherwise it would appear that segregation was being encouraged. Other Boston communities, those where Italian and Irish ethnics resided, could have been predicted to react violently to a massive influx of new black neighbors. And despite Barney Frank's urging expansion of the program to suburban areas, the bankers would have none of that. You see, they were concerned about the quality of their existing loan portfolios. They were heavily invested in the suburbs and did not want to undermine the value of the collateral securing loans already outstanding by encouraging blacks to move into these communities.

In *The Death of an American Jewish Community* Hillel Levine and Lawrence Harmon tell the sordid story of how the "good intentions" of these and other powerful Boston elites led inexorably to the total destruction of a Jewish community in this city. They liken the B-BURG housing program to the disastrous court-ordered school desegregation efforts. In both cases the results were far different from those reformers had anticipated. Ultimately the blacks involved gained little and the working/middle-class whites lost much. Moreover, in both cases the reform efforts were pushed by upper-middle-class, suburban do-gooders who did not have to live with the consequences of their action or pay the price of their moralizing.

This is not a pretty tale. The bitterness, anger, and fear experienced by residents who perceived their community to be under siege are made palpable. The tremendous sense of loss felt by many Jews who, like Harmon, had grown up there is also clearly articulated. Today one can drive south through the city along Blue Hill Avenue, once the busy center of a rich Jewish community life, and see not a thriving and prosperous black community but instead one that is in decay. One can visit the former cite of Temple Mishkan Tefila, a once beautiful building overlooking the Franklin Park Zoo which was turned over to an African American arts group for one dollar a quarter century ago. It now stands boarded and unkempt, amid weeds, like a ruin from some long-lost civilization. One can walk through the halls of the Solomon Lewenberg junior high school on Wellington Hill in Mattapan, which once served as a center of academic striving and excellence, sending many of its students on to the prestigious Boston Latin academy. It no longer does so; black parents living in the area who want a good education for their children now seek other alternatives.

All of this change was not brought on solely by the B-BURG program. The Jewish community in Boston had been under pressure from the growing numbers of lower-class blacks on their borders for years before the program started. Many young Jewish families had been moving out to the suburbs south and west of town. Left behind was an increasingly aged population of people too poor or too settled or too devout to leave the old neighborhood that held their friends and their synagogues, that embodied their way of life. These people became increasingly subject to criminal victimization. Their children were assaulted on their way home from school. Their elderly were robbed in the streets. They were afraid, and many felt trapped. The authors tell of a visit to Boston in 1969 by Rabbi Meir Kahane, shortly after he founded the Jewish Defense League. A pathetic audience, few younger than sixty, turned out for his exhortations of self-defense.

But while this program of loans to black home buyers exclusively redlined into a Jewish area did not create the problems and pressures of inner-city life for the area's long-time residents, it greatly aggravated them and dramatically hastened the demise of the former community. It is not certain that the outcome would have been any different. But it is beyond doubt that the forces set in motion by the banks' lending practices made any other outcome impossible to imagine. A panic atmosphere was created on which unscrupulous realtors fed. Blockbusting practices seen in many cities during the 1950s and 1960s came to Dorchester and Mattapan with a vengeance. "For Sale" signs sprouted like weeds on the front lawns. Neighbors moved out in the dead of night to avoid having to face those they had left behind. Fantastic claims were advanced by brokers who stood to profit from turnover: that housing prices were falling at $1,000 per month, for example. Some realtors even arranged for house break-ins, the better to encourage an especially recalcitrant family that *now* really was an appropriate time to sell.

Blacks, too, were victimized by these practices. People were overcharged for the properties they bought. Normal screening practices were abandoned. Appraisers and inspectors were bribed to overlook serious problems. Houses were sold with essentially no down payments to people who often could not afford them. Within six years, the authors report, fully one-half of the purchasers under this program had defaulted. City services, trash collection and street cleaning for example, diminished in proportion to the increase of black

residency in these communities. Blacks seeking an integrated neighborhood, able and willing to live in harmony with their new neighbors, found themselves instead having bought into what turned out
to be an extension of the ghettos from which they had come.

Levine and Harmon are not blaming the blacks for what
occurred. Though there is a sharpness in their reports of the violent crime that seemed to accompany greater black presence in
these neighborhoods, they say it is understandable. Mainly they
see blacks and Jews as having been victims of external machinations by parties who had no intention of being personally involved
in the consequences of their actions. They acknowledge that blacks
were getting a raw deal in the housing market through restrictive
lending practices and because of mismanaged Model Cities and
urban renewal efforts. They make it clear that something had to be
done to assist blacks with expanded housing opportunities. But
they insist that Jews were made to bear an unfair burden as a
result of a willful disregard for their interests and well-being. They
make a very persuasive case.

Miracles Are Still Happening

Upon This Rock: The Miracles of a Black Church

by Samuel G. Freedman (HarperCollins, 1993)

The Manhattan Institute, a conservative public policy organization
with a particular focus on issues affecting New York City, has since
1987 sponsored an annual lecture named in honor of financier Wal-
ter Wriston. A black tie affair attracting leaders from the worlds of
politics, business, academia, and the arts, the Wriston Lecture has
become a noteworthy event in the city's cultural life. In recent
years the institute has offered its podium to the likes of Tom Wolfe,
Milton Friedman, V. S. Naipaul, and Rupert Murdoch. But the
1992 Wriston Lecturer was a comparatively unknown figure—the
Reverend Johnny Ray Youngblood, pastor of St. Paul Community
Baptist Church in East Brooklyn.

Reverend Youngblood's ministry among the predominantly black residents of a troubled New York City neighborhood is the subject of Samuel Freedman's book *Upon This Rock,* an account of a year spent observing closely the various undertakings of the church and its pastor. Freedman provides a sympathetic and occasionally quite moving portrait of the moral and cultural universe created and sustained by black American Christians in the midst of the maelstrom that contemporary inner-city life has become. His book should be read, not so much for its prose, which is adequate to his task though seldom more than that, but rather for the window Freedman opens onto a world little known to outsiders.

Upon This Rock takes the reader on an unforgettable journey into the heart of black civil society—a society which, from the time of slavery, has been dominated by the church. It reveals the depth and power of the personal commitments held by a legion of believers from every social background, to their God, of course, but also to their fellow human beings of all races. In so doing it makes clear why it is possible to hope that revival, physical and spiritual, may yet come to our blighted urban communities.

Reverend Youngblood's Wriston Lecture, presented just days after the 1992 elections, was entitled "Where the Hope Is." The irony of the situation that evening was lost neither on the speaker nor on his audience: Here was a black Baptist minister, a product of a New Orleans ghetto, a child of fundamentalist church upbringing. Here was an African American keen to affirm the dignity and integrity of the black cultural heritage, a man whose political instincts owed much to the biblical example of Amos, who issued prophetic denunciations of injustice. Yet he spoke in a secular forum to an audience of elite power brokers, representatives of "the system," at the behest of an avowedly conservative organization. And this took place just days after the election of a Democratic president, who entered office with a mandate to address the central domestic ills of our society. How could the speaker be true to his deepest convictions—political, racial, and spiritual—while making constructive use of the occasion? What forces had conspired to bring about such an event?

The irony extended beyond the personal. If Reverend Youngblood had never imagined he would one day be speaking before such an audience, it is also likely that many in the audience would not, until quite recently, have been particularly interested in hearing from him. Indeed, ten years ago Freedman's account of life inside a black Baptist church would have interested mainly those with a special interest in the sociology or theology of black religious life. But the profound problems of urban social decay and the failure of programmatic efforts to fix what ails our inner cities have forced all but those with an unshakable faith in the power of government to look in unusual places for hope.

For blacks, too, the cultural politics of the 1990s have made for strange bedfellows. As political analyst Michael Barone has noted, whereas feminists set the dominant tone at the 1992 Democratic convention, the sentiments of religious traditionalists prevailed at the Republican gathering. In view of the indisputable cultural fact that vast numbers of black Americans see the Bible as the inerrant word of God, and believe Jesus of Nazareth was crucified, buried, then literally raised from the dead so that they personally might have eternal life, a reflexive support by spiritual leaders like Reverend Youngblood for the liberal political agenda has become increasingly difficult to justify.

The resulting tension between cultural politics on the one hand and the desperate need to find mechanisms of revival in the black ghettos on the other has created consternation among some early reviewers of *Upon This Rock*. For many liberals, blacks in their victimized state have been the archetypal emblems of the need for a more "progressive" politics in American public life. But what is a good liberal to do if these very same victims, when acting as subjects of their own renewal rather than as objects of state-sanctioned relief, create institutions that embody culturally conservative principles, like the legitimacy of male governance of the church or the righteousness of the age-old sanction of homosexuality?

When the principal implication of black religiosity to reach the public forum was the social gospel of Martin Luther King, Jr., liberals could take comfort in the authority being thus lent to the forward march of political reform. But when blacks, faced with the implications of astronomical out-of-wedlock birth rates and the virtual disappearance of male figures from positions of authority in the home, reject feminism for a more traditional perspective, then some liberals see it as their duty to decry that people of good intentions should have stumbled upon such reactionary means to address their problems.

Thus the writer Anthony Heilbut panned Freedman's book in the *New York Times Book Review,* seeing Reverend Youngblood's concern with the standing of men in his community as a disturbing "obsession." Heilbut belittled the pastor's opposition to abortion, found his sexual politics to be "disquieting," and claimed, hysterically, that his efforts to salvage black fathers were taking place "at the expense of their wives and gay sons." Similarly, the generally favorable reviewer of Freedman's book in the *Washington Post Book World* worried that Freedman was insufficiently critical of male dominance among the governing councils of St. Paul Community Baptist Church.

The point here is not that Youngblood or Freedman is above criticism. But against the backdrop of what is being accomplished at St. Paul, the concerns of these reviewers seem bizarre. The black male as an endangered species is a perennial topic these days at liberal conference gatherings; how then can one reject as sexist a ministry that is successfully resurrecting precisely this endangered species. One listens in vain to hear the wives and children of these reclaimed husbands and fathers complain that the methods of reclamation employed by Youngblood and other Christian practitioners engaged in similar efforts around the country are offensive to *them.* At the very least, apostles of "tolerance" owe inner-city black congregations respect, not derision, for the autonomous cultural choices they make.

Nor, it should be stipulated, does Youngblood's position in this area make him a political conservative: No one attending his Manhattan Institute lecture or reading Freedman's book could be confused on that point. Youngblood is an agitator; he is a critic of a system that has ignored God's mandate that we be in relationship with those at the bottom of society. He uses the first person plural when talking of such people, savagely defending their dignity and their right to the presumption of an equal humanity from the predations of elitists of all political persuasions. In his sermons, some quite eloquently and artfully captured by Freedman's eyewitness account, he offers sharp criticisms of conservative political neglect.

At the same time, he stuns a group of white seminarians with an unapologetic indictment of their abstract, philosophical stance of solidarity with the poor, when there are so many opportunities to genuinely serve these same poor which are going unexploited.

But Youngblood recognizes that respect from the larger political community for inner-city blacks will not come about as a result of legislative initiatives or increased program budgets. To a former drug addict, habitual felon, or prostitute, politics cannot bring the sense of fulfillment and personal worth that is to be had through the hard and dedicated work of redemption and reconstruction. "Why do we rebuild?" Youngblood rhetorically asked his audience last fall. His answer: "We rebuild 'that we no more be a reproach.' We rebuild for our own dignity."

The deepest scars of the victims of racism and oppression are worn, Youngblood understands, on the inside; the problems in their lives are often as much the manifestations of a spiritual vacancy as the evidence of a societal failing. He recognizes that to say this out loud is to risk being misunderstood by whites who are only looking for an excuse to be rid of their social responsibilities. At the same time, he sees a Faustian bargain in the seductive temptation to remain silent.

As Freedman paints him, Youngblood is a model of spiritual and moral leadership. Perhaps this is why some observers find it so hard to accept the message that flows out of his success and that of his congregants. For the ultimate irony here is that this success, achieved by deeply convinced believers in the face of the worst devastation our society seems capable of producing, may just point the way toward recovery not only of the ghettos but of the entire country.

Teen pregnancy has risen astronomically among whites as well as blacks. The ravages of drugs know no racial or sociological barriers. The problems of our schools and our seeming inability to meet effectively the challenges of foreign economic competition are warning signs that all is not well with the American soul. Could it be that, in defiance of the dictates of political correctness and postmodern relativism, the struggle for survival and dignity among America's traditional outcasts might yet point the way toward an ecumenical, multicultural salvation?

Spiritual Politics

The Culture of Disbelief

by Stephen L. Carter (Basic Books, 1993)

Stephen Carter, the Cromwell Professor of Law at Yale University, is one of the more interesting new voices in the legal academy. In a stream of articles, essays, and reviews that have appeared over the last decade, Mr. Carter has addressed with insight and verve a number of fundamental issues in constitutional jurisprudence. The breadth of his inquiries and the quality of his intellect are genuinely impressive.

His politics are liberal, though not reliably so. Thus his first book, *Reflections of an Affirmative Action Baby* (1991), caused a stir when he provided only qualified support for that controversial policy while critically appraising its impact on blacks who, like himself, have been its beneficiaries. Now comes *The Culture of Disbelief*, an ambitious and courageous commentary on the legal and political status of religion in American life. With this latest offering Mr. Carter walks straight into the fire storm of controversy over cultural issues that has raged so fiercely in our politics for the past quarter century. It is doubtful that he can emerge with his liberal credentials intact, notwithstanding some heroic efforts at preserving them.

Of course, Mr. Carter is a nominal dissenter from most conservative positions in the cultural wars. He is against prayer in the schools, is moderately pro-choice, supports greater social welfare spending, and as a member of the Episcopal church, has favored the ordination of women. But he also takes issue with those liberals who denounce the Christian Right *because* it is Christian and who see religious activism in politics as a threat to the American Way. Indeed, Mr. Carter is alarmed at the open animosity that many liberals feel free to direct toward those religious persons who would participate in our public life. Among the many examples of this animus that he cites is the comment of Florence Kennedy, a member of the board of the National Organization of Women who, in the wake of Clarence Thomas's nomination, declared that there were too many

Catholics on the Supreme Court. (In a rather clumsy effort at damage control, he hurries to inform us in a footnote that he did not support the Thomas nomination and even that he is a believer of Anita Hill's story—views of no relevance to his substantive argument.)

The most interesting and persuasive aspect of his argument that conservative Christians should be received as legitimate (if, to his mind, mistaken) participants in political debates is his recollection of an earlier movement of religious activists with political ambitions—a movement marching under the banner of civil rights. When Christians and Jews openly invoked the Almighty in their effort to overturn segregation, they enjoyed enthusiastic support on the Left. They were not criticized for seeking to impose on the country a moral vision grounded in their particular interpretation of Scripture, though that is clearly what many of them sought to do. Mr. Carter asks why, if Martin Luther King, Jr., could legitimately call on God's name and His word when addressing matters political, should not Pat Robertson also be able to do so?

Mr. Carter's criticism of Pat Robertson and company is subtle, no doubt too subtle for many of his readers. He objects not to the fact that Robertson invokes the word of God, but to the way in which he interprets it. This, of course, is an argument only a believer would make, and Mr. Carter confesses his faith throughout the book. He is saying, in effect, that the alignment in American public life of strong religious conviction with a right-of-center political position is a recent and dangerous trend, and that liberals have wrongly responded to this trend by attempting to discredit as presumptively intolerant any public discourse rooted in religious belief. He does not fear conservatives who bring their God talk into the public square because, having read his own Bible, he is prepared to answer them in kind.

Here, then, we have that rarity, a liberal lawyer inclined to counter religious conservatives on theological rather than procedural grounds. Thus his problem with the "political preaching" at the Republicans' 1992 convention was that these speakers trivialized the role of religion. He faults them for acting so as to make religion *less* politically influential. His reasoning is that because the will of God is not predictable, those who genuinely seek His guidance on matters political, through prayer and meditation, should occasionally be surprised by what they hear. When they are not, when it turns out that religious reflection always supports one side of the partisan political divide, then one suspects that their religion is in the service of their politics and not the other way around. That the Christian Right is so predictable therefore undermines the credibility of their religious witness.

This argument applies with equal force to political preachers on the left. Unfortunately Mr. Carter does not fully develop this theme. For example, the vaguely religious rhetoric of Jesse Jackson—exemplified by his speech at the 1992 Democratic Convention in which he likened Dan Quayle to King Herod, and evoked the abortion issue in the context of Mary giving birth to Jesus—certainly devalued the currency of public religious argument. And although Mr. Carter disapproves of how the national media often overlook the extent and the conservatism of religious belief among black Americans, he has nothing to say about how black political leaders—many drawn from the pulpit—give only muted public voice to the social conservatism of their own religious tradition. Neither does he remark upon the plain fact that success within the Democratic party requires a politician either to mute his religious voice or to put it in the service of the liberal cultural agenda. Arguably this abdication of the exercise of independent moral judgment by believers within the Democratic party (with some noteworthy exceptions, of course) is more damaging to the authority of religion in our politics than is, say, the inflexible pro-life stance of conservative Christians in the Republican camp.

In any case, Mr. Carter seems not fully to appreciate the implications of his position. For even as he rejects the political content of the public interventions favored by religious conservatives, he ends up giving tacit support to their cultural position: a deep dissatisfaction with the dominance of secular ideas among our policy elites. He writes with an admirable sympathy for those with whom he disagrees. At one point he declares: "The truth—an awkward one for the guardians of the public square—is that tens of millions of Americans rely on their religious traditions for the moral knowledge that tells them how to conduct their lives, including their political lives."

He sees this not as a cause for despair but rather as a reason for hope. One can almost hear the cries of "Amen" echoing across the

Bible Belt, mixed with audible sighs of disappointment issuing from the Ivy League colleagues. At stake here is a conflict over the legitimacy of a public discourse rooted in explicitly religious values. By urging the appropriateness of such a discourse, Mr. Carter cedes substantial leverage to the political right. When the issue was nuclear weapons or socialism in Latin America, invoking the Bible did no harm to the liberal cause. But when the issues are homosexuality and abortion, can there be any doubt that the net effect of conducting public debates in religious terms is to favor the conservative position? The exegetical skills of Mr. Carter or of his fellow Episcopalian, the Reverend Peter Gomes (Plummer Professor of Christian Morals and Pastor of Memorial Church at Harvard who now openly professes his homosexuality), may carry the day in New Haven or Cambridge, but they are unlikely to persuade those "tens of millions" of devout Americans who keep busy that legion of religious broadcasters now active across the nation.

It is naive to think that the symbolic vocabulary of public discourse can be divorced from the substance of policy formulation. The framing of political discussion is crucial. The more that spiritual themes and religious values are brought openly into the public square, the weaker will appear all those liberal arguments to the effect that people must be able to pursue any life-style that suits them without the discomfort of being judged for making what many Americans regard as an immoral choice. If the culture war is fought within the terms of a religious discourse—both sides starting with the same Bible, but defending different conclusions—then the Left will certainly lose it. This is, in my view, why liberals are seen so often to attack the authority and the relevance of religious traditionalism whenever its exponents—Pope John II in Denver in summer 1993, for example—critically discuss questions of sexuality.

Mr. Carter thinks the current alignment of religious activism with conservatism derives from the politics of abortion. He suggests that because the pro-choice position is now so fundamental to liberal politics, and because pro-life activism is driven largely by religious conviction, it has become necessary for liberals to impugn the legitimacy of their opponents' religious *motives,* not simply to reject their political position. Mr. Carter thinks this attack on motives is unsound. But he must proceed cautiously. He begins by declaring that, "like most Americans," he supports a woman's right to choose. The phrase "like most Americans" is revealing. By suggesting that the relative popularity of the pro-choice position is a justification for it, he seems to undermine his argument for the propriety of basing political judgments on religious conscience. Evidently this is a price he is willing to pay to put some distance between himself and the pro-life folk, whom he goes on to defend against the antireligion sentiments of many in the pro-choice camp.

He recalls how when Cardinal O'Connor suggested that some Catholic politicians might risk excommunication if they continued to support abortion, a howl of protest arose from the usual suspects, denouncing the cardinal's intervention as inappropriate and coercive. Yet some three decades earlier, a number of Southern Catholics actually were excommunicated for their opposition to integration, an action that has drawn no protest from civil libertarians then or since. We may not agree with the pro-life activists, he says to liberals, and we may not approve of their methods, but we must not base our rejection of their public claims on the fact that they are religious people. It is a telling commentary on our times that this obvious observation will be controversial in some quarters.

Mr. Carter's discussion of abortion becomes especially interesting when he defends the validity of basing a pro-life stance on a religious belief that the fetus is a human person. He concludes that any intellectually defensible case for abortion must be "based on an approach that allows abortion *even if the fetus is human.*" He notes that nothing in the Constitution requires the government to punish, or to punish equally, every taking of human life. He implies that the goal of sex equality for women is of such sufficient import as to warrant the overriding of the fetus's claim to life, were we to acknowledge its personhood. One can admire the candor and intellectual consistency of this position, even while doubting, were the political debate to be framed in these terms, that the pro-choice argument could possibly prevail.

Although Mr. Carter is on solid ground when defending the legitimacy of pro-lifers' motives, his explanation of the origins of the liberal antagonism toward religion in politics leaves much to be desired. The secularization of American public life predates the advent of the abortion issue by decades. The rise of radical feminism, gay activism, and cultural relativism surely has something to do with the diminished respect that intellectuals are willing to accord to the religious beliefs of ordinary people. Also, Mr. Carter says far too little about the class dimensions of this development. He focuses on elite opinion and thereby fails to appreciate the extent to which a modest conservative revival among Christians and Jews is taking place throughout the country, even as Washington, New York, and Hollywood continue in their respective ways to trivialize religious faith. And while mainline Protestant denominations are losing members, the Pentecostal and charismatic movements are going strong. He also says too little about two developments of the 1960s, the countercultural assault on authority and the sexual revolution, which certainly bear on the growing contempt shown toward traditional religious views by "progressive" political activists. It well may be that the deep conflict in our public life over the issue of abortion is more effect than it is cause of the secularization of liberal political discourse.

At the more general level, Mr. Carter makes a two-pronged argument for his case that religious citizens deserve respect (if not a> vays support) when taking political positions rooted in their faith. First, he notes that religiously motivated political activity enhances liberty in a democracy by fostering resistance to state power. "A religion is, at its heart, a way for denying the authority of the rest of the world," he observes. Such civil disobedience, whether on behalf of the antisegregation cause a generation ago or the antiabortion cause today, may of course lead to excesses Mr. Carter would not defend. Still, overall he judges that we are better for the presence among us of deeply committed believers prepared to act on their convictions against impositions of state power and to accept responsibility for their actions.

Second, he suggests that because religious belief is so fundamental an aspect of personal identity, to discourage citizens from citing religious reasons for their political positions is to "force the religiously devout to bracket their religious selves before they may enter into politics." This, he urges, we must never do. Insisting on strictly secular arguments in public life in effect forces the religious among us to pass as secularists, that is, to affect a false identity, when acting as citizens. A religious worldview ought not be regarded as a forbidden epistemology in public discourse. We must not privilege secular ways of understanding the world in public debates, he argues, if we are to show tolerance for our nation's spiritual diversity.

These last arguments raise difficult philosophical questions that, in my view, Mr. Carter handles poorly. Indeed, though he cites a range of academic sources on these philosophical issues, his treatment of them seems the least satisfactory part of his argument. He writes in defense of religion in general, but in fact there is no generalized religious sensibility. There is only the cacophony of religious voices whose very discordant inconsistency ought to deny to any one of them a claim to *public* authority. (Their private authority for the believer is another matter.)

Thus he worries that the deprogramming of cult members denies their religious freedom, even when the cult is as offensive in its practices as the unfortunate Branch Davidians who met their end in Waco. He rejects the claims to equal time in the classroom of the creation science movement, but only because it deals poorly with some purely scientific questions (such as methods of dating the age of the earth). That creation science begins with an account of the development of the earth and the origin of the species based in Christian religious doctrine is not disqualifying for him. His discussion of this topic leaves the reader unclear how or whether he would limit the intrusion of the mythologies of all manner of rival religious world views (those of various Native American tribes, for example) into the nation's science classrooms.

Indeed, Mr. Carter's desire to avoid privileging secular epistemologies is deeply problematic when one considers the pluralism of religious belief. We reject the Christian Scientists' claim to be able to withhold medical treatment from their children precisely because we do privilege the epistemic view of medical science over that of faith healing. (Which is not to say that God cannot heal the sick, but only to acknowledge that one way in which He has chosen to do so is through the increased knowledge the human race has been able to obtain about the functioning of our bodies!) Moreover, any argument *in favor of* the Christian Scientist position that parents should be free to deal with their children's medical ailments via strictly spiritual means will inevitably be advanced in secular terms (by, for example, citing the *evidence* that prayer really works and not the relevant scriptural passages).

At no point in this book does the author, a devout Christian, defend a legal position by reference to religious authority. His motives for taking one or another position on this or that legal question may draw on his religious convictions, but the reasons he offers to others as to why we should agree with his conclusions are invariably framed in secular terms. I think Mr. Carter does a valuable service by arguing so cogently for the position that people motivated by religious belief deserve respect when they forcefully display their values in public debate. Yet as his argument for this very position implies, to insist on the acceptance of a particular set of religious values (or on the rejection of all religious values) as a precondition for having influence over policy shows disrespect for the autonomy of those who believe otherwise.

Therefore no particular set of religious beliefs, no single religious epistemology, can be the standard for the adjudication of conflicting public claims. This seems to imply that when we seek to persuade others of the rightness of state action that would enforce a common position on everyone, we should be prepared to give secular justifications for any such program. Our *motives* may rightly be religious, but the *reasons* urged upon our fellow citizens should, at least in those matters of greatest significance and broadest impact, be secular. This position does not force believers to deny their truest selves when acting as citizens, for the expression of their religious motives is in no way forbidden by my argument. I simply say that such expression is, and should be, inadequate to the task of public persuasion about the exercise of state power in a pluralistic democracy.

Permanently Alienated

Faces at the Bottom of the Well: The Permanence of Racism

by Derrick Bell (Basic Books, 1992)

Derrick Bell is not optimistic about the future of race relations in our country. He doubts that any meaningful change in the position of American blacks has occurred since the 1954 *Brown* decision ushered in a new legal dispensation by outlawing *de jure* segrega-

tion and overturning the doctrine of "separate but equal." Moreover, he is skeptical that any real progress is possible, given the
unwillingness of whites to relinquish their privileged position atop
the racial/caste hierarchy that, in his view, constitutes our permanent social order. This grim outlook is evident on every page of his
book *Faces at the Bottom of the Well*, the entire purpose of which
seems to be to persuade the reader that all efforts at racial reform
are doomed to failure, short of massive and enforced psychother-
apy for the scores of millions of irredeemably racist whites now living in abject denial.

A veteran civil rights lawyer, long-time law professor, and former
law school dean, Bell has been an important figure in American
legal scholarship for more than twenty years. After becoming the
first black American to be made a tenured professor at Harvard
Law School, he left to become dean of the law school at the University of Oregon, subsequently returning to Harvard in the early
1980s. He has been active in civil rights causes throughout his
career, formerly as a litigator and recently as a fierce advocate of
racial diversity in the elite faculties and journals of the legal profession. In the spring of 1990 he declared, amid much public fanfare,
that he would boycott the Harvard Law School by taking an
unpaid leave from his teaching duties there until the faculty hired
a tenured black woman. Harvard has not made such an appointment, but the university has recently indicated that Bell's "strike"
amounts to a *de facto* resignation, given its firm rule that faculty
members cannot be on leave for more than two years consecutively
without relinquishing their tenure. Bell is now teaching at NYU
Law School and giving public lectures on his ideas throughout the
country. It seems clear that his strike has resulted in no diminution
of his standard of living.

Faces at the Bottom of the Well elaborates further on a mode of
discourse Bell introduced in his earlier and widely read *And We
Are Not Saved: The Elusive Quest for Racial Justice*. Both works
use an allegorical technique to illustrate what Bell regards as basic
truths about the nature of race, racism, and the law in America.
The allegories envision fantastic scenarios and then tell stories of
how important actors in our society might be imagined to react to
these circumstances. In the course of considering the stories, we

are led to reexamine our basic assumptions about race relations, or so in any case Bell intends.

In what is probably the most important chapter of *Faces at the Bottom of the Well,* Bell offers the allegory of the Space Traders, a group of aliens from outer space who descend upon the United States, speaking perfect English in the mechanically reproduced voice of Ronald Reagan and promising America wealth beyond its dreams if only it would surrender every black American for transport back to the aliens' home planet. The account Bell gives of the ensuing debate over whether to accept the aliens' offer supposedly shows the deep and various motives for racial antagonism—economic, social, and psychological— that whites harbor and that, in our real lives, prevent solutions from being found to the problems of inner-city poverty, black-on-black crime, joblessness among blacks, and the low number of tenured black women on leading law school faculties. Bell gives cameo accounts of how the politicians, the courts, and the general public react to this offer. In the end the offer is accepted, and on January 17, "the last Martin Luther King holiday" America would ever witness, "long lines [of] some twenty million silent black men, women, and children, including babes in arms . . . [are] directed . . . toward the yawning holds" of the aliens' ships. "Heads bowed, arms now linked by slender chains, black people [leave] the New World as their forebears had arrived."

Other tales are told in this book, equally weird and disturbing, but the point seems never to change much: Whites are racist, are determined not to see their racism, and through sometimes overt but mostly covert means, are bent on perpetuating the most profound degradation and repression of blacks in order to further their slightest economic advantage. Moreover, these whites are constantly alert for rationalizations of their racism, especially those that lay blame on the black victims, so as to ameliorate any sign of guilt that might threaten to arise.

This is the kind of book one is likely either to love or hate; it simply doesn't leave room for an indifferent response. I confess that I hated it. It either has the ring of truth for the reader, because the reader shares Professor Bell's values and beliefs, or it seems ridiculous, manipulative, and dishonest, because the reader disagrees profoundly, as I do, with Bell's world view. I learned next to nothing about American society from reading this book, though I think I learned much about Professor Derrick Bell and something about the upside-down world of liberal legal "scholarship." For the life of me, I cannot fathom how such an elaborate rendering of opinion in the guise of morality tale can be regarded by any serious person as scholarship. I do not see how anyone could be persuaded by this work. There are no facts here, just wild assertions about the world: "the inner city is . . . the American equivalent of the South African homeland" or "racial discrimination in the workplace is as vicious . . . [as] it was when employers posted signs 'no negras need apply.'" One cannot take such statements literally; they are obviously meant to evoke an emotional response or to signal an ideological posture. There is no argument here, legal or otherwise, to support the claims Bell is making, almost no reference to the relevant literatures to buttress his claims, no consideration of the alternative explanations of the problems he rightly decries.

Imagine that a white legal scholar were to offer a similarly thin and self-serving account of, say, white reaction against affirmative action, that rather than arguing the case by conventional means, invited the reader into a make-believe world which highlighted the undeserving and intransigent demands of middle-class black law professors for yet further unearned appointments to prestigious positions for which the professors offered no conventional qualifications. I venture that such a parody would not make the best seller list; it would be widely denounced for the nonsense it would so obviously be. I suppose the difference in treatment between my imagined white charlatan and the real-life Professor Bell has something to do with the three hundred years of slavery and oppression that blacks have endured and the presumption of virtue that attends any denunciation of this crime. Nevertheless, I am more than a little weary of black social critics like Bell who think that wearing their alienation on their sleeves is a substitute for carefully reasoned defenses of their positions.

The Epic Career of W. E. B. Du Bois

W. E. B. Du Bois: Writings

edited by Nathan I. Huggins (Library of America, 1986)

In the wake of the black studies movement of the 1960s, which transformed teaching and research on Afro-American life at colleges and universities around the country, Harvard undertook to establish an institute for inquiry into the history, art, and social life of black Americans. It is significant, though not surprising, that those involved in the enterprise chose to name this institute after Harvard's first black American Ph.D. and black alumnus of greatest intellectual distinction—W. E. B. Du Bois. For the generation of black intellectuals coming to maturity in the late 1960s—my generation—Du Bois's life and work offered an inspiring ideal of intellectual brilliance, iconoclasm, political commitment, and racial leadership.

His life of more than ninety years (1868–1963) had spanned the period from the adoption of the reconstruction amendments to the height of the civil rights movement. He had been a participant, and often a leader, in every significant debate on racial affairs that took place among American intellectuals during his adult lifetime. From the turn of the century until his death (in self-imposed exile, in Kwame Nkrumah's Ghana), he had also been a major figure in the worldwide Pan-African movement among intellectuals of African descent seeking to define their common cultural and political interests. His prodigious output—including major historical and sociological treatises; lyrical, powerful, and sardonic essays; biting pieces of social criticism; fiction; drama; and three autobiographies—loomed as a foreboding reminder to all embarking on the scholarly pursuits of just what could, with persistent self-application, be accomplished in a single lifetime.

A representative sampling of that life's work is provided in the volume *W. E. B. Du Bois: Writings*, edited by Nathan Huggins. This book is one in an important series of volumes that, taken together, constitute The Library of America, the "collected works of America's foremost authors in uniform hard-cover editions" according to the publisher. Du Bois's inclusion in this series places him in the company of Thoreau, James, Melville, Hawthorne, and Emerson as a foremost figure in American letters. In view of the radical politics characteristic of his last years, this inclusion has the symbolic effect of the embrace of a prodigal son. Huggins has collected from a vast body of material some 1,200 pages of text that convey the brilliance, energy, and scope of Du Bois's writings.

The volume contains in their entirety *The Souls of Black Folk* (1903), Du Bois's classic early collection of essays on Afro-American culture and politics; his pioneering history of American slavery, *The Suppression of the African Slave-Trade to the United States* (1896); and *Dusk of Dawn: An Essay Toward an Autobiography of a Race Concept* (1940). Also presented are numerous essays on topics such as racial antagonism, lynchings, racial pride among blacks, European colonialism, women's suffrage, and the Negro cultural renaissance. Many of these first appeared in the NAACP organ *The Crisis,* which in its first quarter century under Du Bois's leadership became the nation's leading black intellectual forum, with a depth and breadth of critical social and cultural analysis unmatched by any comparable publication then or now. In less than a decade under Du Bois's editorship, the circulation of this newly founded journal of Negro affairs had risen to an astounding 106,000.

One cannot approach the body of work that issued from this great man without a sense of awe at the range and scope of it. Here we have, in one and the same person, one of the nation's earliest and best empirical sociologists, an accomplished historian, an essayist and social critic of the highest order, an activist and moralist whose interests and influence spanned continents and generations. To give but one example, his very fine work of urban sociology *The Philadelphia Negro* (1899) (not included here), one of the first inquiries of its kind, still provides a model of sympathetic yet objective empirical social science. The research and writing of this treatise, done largely before his thirtieth birthday, was based on more than 5,000 interviews of people in the Philadelphia ghetto as well as months of investigation in the rural Virginia counties from which many black Philadelphians had emigrated. Du Bois extended this model of careful factual inquiry into the condition of black Americans with his series of monographs published from Atlanta University, mainly during the first decade of this century, covering such subjects as black businesses, public education for blacks, black artisans, black farmers, black family life, and black self-help organizations. Two decades would pass before work of this quality on Afro-American social life would be undertaken by others.

But for the limitations attendant on being black in turn-of-the-century America, this work would have earned Du Bois a leading place in the nation's academic establishment and a reputation as a father of the discipline of applied sociology. Yet this was not to be. Indeed, because of his increasingly bitter controversy with Booker T. Washington in the years after the 1903 publication of his celebrated critical essay "Of Mr. Booker T. Washington and Others," Du Bois found his employment options restricted and his ability to raise funds for his pioneering sociological work at Atlanta University much reduced. Moreover, he came to be drawn into a more active role as racial leader during this period, foreshadowing his ultimate decision to leave the ivory tower in Atlanta and move to the world of affairs in New York City. In 1905 he organized a meeting of blacks dissatisfied with the leadership of Booker Washington which called itself the Niagra Movement, and which was the first in a series of events leading to the founding of the National Association for the Advancement of Colored People in 1910. That same year he accepted the position of Director of Publications and Research of the NAACP and began a new stage in his career as the fiercely independent and increasingly radical editor of *The Crisis*.

It was during the twenty-four years of association with the NAACP, at the height of his intellectual powers, that Du Bois embraced and gave voice to some of his most important and controversial ideas of race relations in the United States and throughout the world. He came increasingly to see a deep connection between the racial oppression of blacks in the United States, on the one hand, and the colonial domination of Africa and Asia by the European powers, on the other. At the base of both these evils, he ultimately concluded, lay the dynamics of capitalist expansion. Accordingly he became skeptical that America's democratic capitalism could ever accommodate an equal citizenship for the descendants of the slaves. He also inveighed fiercely against the evils of colonialism, to the point of becoming a virtual apologist for the Liberian government when it was accused by the League of Nations in the early 1930s of encouraging forced labor practices against indigenous Liberian peasants. Fearing that condemnation of blacks "enslaving" other blacks would lend credibility to European colonialists' assertions that Africans were not ready for self-government, the great majority of black American intellectuals, including W. E. B. Du Bois, found themselves in the position of being either silent about or apologists for this indefensible practice. (Conservative journalist George Schuyler, whose ideology apparently left him unconcerned that he might be seen as an apologist for colonialism, was a notable exception.)

The emergent radicalism of Du Bois's vision can be clearly seen in the characterization of the slaves and freedmen as an industrial proletariat undergirding global capitalism, put forward in his historical treatise *Black Reconstruction in America* (1935). He describes capitalist industry in *Dusk of Dawn,* published five years later, as a "beast" that "kills men to make cloth, prostitutes women to rear buildings, and eats little children." By 1953 the elderly Du Bois had even become willing to eulogize Stalin. One finds among the notes for this collection a remarkable "Apologia" added to the 1954 reprint of *The Suppression of the African Slave-Trade,* in which Du Bois in effect asks the reader's forgiveness for the fact that deficiencies of his education at Harvard and Berlin had left him relatively ignorant of Marx's teachings and had led him to place too great an emphasis on moral factors and too little on economic motives when accounting for the failure of America's founding generation to eradicate slavery.

In addition to this leftward drift in political philosophy, not uncommon among intellectuals of this era, Du Bois's developing thought came to embrace a kind of racial nationalism that ultimately led to his break with the NAACP in 1934. By this time Du Bois was deeply pessimistic about the political possibilities for integration. (When the *Brown* decision was handed down in 1954 he said, "I have seen the impossible happen.") He was animated by a romantic conception of the peoplehood of blacks in the African diaspora, a conception encouraged by ideas he encountered as a student in late-nineteenth-century Germany and expressed as early as 1897 in his essay "The Conservation of the Races," in which he called for the development of a "Pan-Negro" racial solidarity among Southern blacks. Moreover, he was clearly weary of that burden of divided identity peculiar to the American Negro and brilliantly characterized in this most famous passage from *The Souls of Black Folks:* "One ever feels his two-ness—an American, a Negro; two souls, two thoughts, two unreconciled strivings; two warring ideals in one dark body, whose dogged strength alone keeps it from being torn asunder."

Du Bois thus came to advocate reliance by blacks on separate social and economic institutions and to urge greater attention by blacks to self-help measures that could be undertaken with or without white cooperation. Fearing that the fight against segregation (which he often led) had become a crusade to mix with whites for its own sake, Du Bois wrote: "Never in the world should our fight be against association with ourselves because by that very token we give up the whole argument that we are worth associating with." Among his arguments in support of the virtues of voluntary segregation and self-help was the observation that relative to the position of "begging" the white man for integration, such a posture enhanced black dignity and self-respect. In this his thinking was profoundly prescient, though far more disconsonant with the spirit of his times than was his political radicalism.

One cannot contemplate the life and work of W. E. B. Du Bois without experiencing a profound sense of the tragedy, in personal and national terms, that is the bitter legacy of African slavery in our republic. It would be foolhardy to attempt here a critical assessment of Du Bois's political beliefs, as they evolved over the course of his long life. Yet one cannot avoid the fact that by the end of his life, Du Bois was a bitter antagonist of American interests in the international arena, an unabashed apologist for global Communism, and an ardent exponent of that anti-Western animus so prominent a part of the ideology of today's "progressives." That this came to be so, notwithstanding the fact that America was finally coming to grips with its race problem in these years, seems nothing short of tragic to me. Nor can one fail to notice that in the early efforts of this sensitive and committed intellectual to come to grips with the social dilemmas of his time, there were many signs that his nearly century-long odyssey need not have ended in the embrace of totalitarianism. This is not to absolve Du Bois of responsibility for having come to adopt an ideological posture that, in view of the events of the last several decades, is impossible to credit. Rather it is to note that among the costs of our tragic racial past should be counted the estrangement of this great mind from those whom one must see as his natural allies—the defenders of freedom for all persons.

Black Crime: Answering Conservatives

"America's Black Crime Gap—and How to Close It"

by John DiIulio (*The Public Interest,* Fall 1994)

John DiIulio's essay "America's Black Crime Gap," in *The Public Interest,* Fall 1994, provides a useful summary of the appalling disparity between black and white Americans in the rates at which they are victimized by violent criminals. The statistics are staggering; the moral and political problems raised by them are profound. While this situation is not new, DiIulio shows that it has grown worse in the last decade, noting, for example, that the homicide victimization rate for black youth, already three times the rate for white youth in 1986, doubled in the five years between 1986 and 1991 while the white rate remained unchanged.

DiIulio offers two principal explanations for the racial crime gap. First, poor people cannot afford to purchase safe environments for themselves and their families, and they cannot rely on the police to keep them safe where they live. Second, inner-city black communities are exposed at a vastly disproportionate rate to the predation of violent, repeat offenders who are not kept in jail. Accordingly, he recommends a two-pronged remedy: Public policy should aim at securing the streets, schools, and housing projects of inner-city communities; and the bad guys should be kept behind bars for longer periods of time. He also offers the radical suggestion that young children in "criminogenic communities" at risk of growing up to become career criminals because of their pathological home environments, be removed from these circumstances by the state so as to prevent the intergenerational transmission of social deviance. I will comment on this briefly at the end of my discussion.

DiIulio's suggestion that we invest public resources to "harden the target" in inner-city communities, providing residents there with the kind of security the middle class takes for granted, is justified on the basis of fairness alone, in my view. Just how effective this would be is another matter, though. He speculates that significant benefits would follow a dramatic increase of police presence in high-crime areas, but has no real evidence to support this claim. Thus, the heart of his policy argument is the case for longer incarceration of violent and career criminals. Much in this argument is compelling to me: Repeat offenders commit a large number of violent crimes while awaiting trial and when out on parole. Since these offenders are much more likely to be residents of poor inner-city communities, their law-abiding neighbors bear the brunt of this burden. Keeping known bad guys in prison for a longer period of time would repay society far more than it would cost, with the poorest among us benefiting the most.

Why then do advocates for poor blacks so strenuously resist this policy proposal? Answering this question is, I believe, critical to reducing the racial crime gap. Indeed, DiIulio actually identifies two black crime gaps in his essay: Blacks are much more frequently the victims of violent crimes—call this Gap #1. But blacks are also much more often the perpetrators of violent crimes—call this Gap #2. Debate about crime policy in this country is substantially shaped, implicitly and explicitly, by Gap #2. But Gap #1 seems virtually invisible. Why is it so salient in the American political imagination that building prisons means incarcerating ever more young black men—an image associated by many with racial oppression—and yet it requires a genuine act of will to see that building prisons also means fewer rapes, robberies, and killings of innocent black men, women, and children? Why is the killing of a young black man national news when the perpetrator is white, but a barely discernible blip on the media horizon when the perpetrator is black? Why does the racial justice issue in debate on a crime bill get defined in terms of discrimination in the application of the death penalty, but not in terms of the differential extent to which police resources are allocated to the protection of black and white communities in the nation's most violent cities? Why is crime such a powerful political issue in suburban districts where crime rates are low and falling, while ultra-liberal incumbents feel no pressure to modify their positions in inner-city districts where crime rates are high and rising?

The reason it is important to take up these questions is that significant movement toward what DiIulio terms "incapacitating the criminally deviant" is unwise to undertake and unlikely to occur absent some greater measure of black authorization than seems now to be available. Longer sentences, less plea bargaining, and tougher parole standards mean substantially increased incarceration rates for black perpetrators. This will certainly be fought by black and liberal politicians in Congress and the state legislatures, and it could ultimately be resisted by rank-and-file blacks, in the jury box or even on the streets. DiIulio seems to seek black authorization for his prescription by citing Harvard law professor Randall Kennedy's interesting observation[1] that controversial issues in criminal justice policy involve not only *inter*racial conflict, but *intra*racial conflict as well, since the interests of law-abiding blacks are quite different from the interests of blacks involved in criminal activities. He fails, however, fully to appreciate Kennedy's point: Law-abiding black Americans are deeply ambivalent about these issues.[2]

This ambivalence is rooted in the obvious fact that the young black men wreaking havoc in the ghetto are still "our youngsters" in the eyes of many of the decent poor and working-class black people who are occasionally their victims. For many of these people the hard edge of judgment and retribution is tempered by sympathy for and empathy with the perpetrators. This social fact has deep political significance. It is not enough to argue (as I once did) that the black liberal representatives of these crime-ridden areas are placing ideology above the safety of their constituents when calling for prevention programs instead of prison cells. I cannot believe that these politicians are blind or indifferent to the tragic reality unfolding in their communities. And while it may be that they are making the wrong policy judgment, reaching this conclusion involves more than doing a cost-benefit analysis of the social return to expanded prison capacity. It also, and more importantly, involves a willingness to view with contempt and disdain the urban black cultural milieu from which violent predators too often arise. It requires a willingness to write off many of the perpetrators (some at a quite early age) as beyond redemption. While this may be a necessary stance in the face of the carnage DiIulio has described, it is nevertheless one that many law-abiding black people will understandably find difficult to take.

When the young white girl Polly Klaas was abducted from her home in a small town north of San Francisco, and then murdered by a violent offender out on parole, there was a national uproar. Yet the more numerous atrocities perpetrated daily by known violent criminals against ghetto children draw scant political attention. What does this tell us? Certainly not that racist America cares about murdered children when they are white but not when they are black. For were the residents of the ghetto, through their political, civic, and religious leaders, to demand in the name of justice and civil rights that their communities be protected from the predation of these vicious criminals, this demand would surely not fall on deaf ears. If the degree of energy and organizational skill invested in campaigns against racially motivated violence, or against police brutality, or against the death penalty were instead to be expended in insisting that bad men be kept behind bars, these demands would become irresistible. It is the muted response of the residents and political representatives of inner-city communities to their own victimization that accounts for the difference between the celebrity of Polly Klaas, on the one hand, and the anonymity of countless young black victims, on the other. This muted response is a direct reflection of the ambivalence toward the identification with the perpetrators of these crimes.

What is too often missing in the heated partisan discussion of crime policy in inner cities is a sense of the tragedy of this situation. If we are to move in the direction John DiIulio advises, then inner-city residents must either be persuaded to endorse or forced to endure an intensified effort to warehouse for longer periods of time a larger number of their own neighbors, cousins, and sons.

They will have to accept the social judgment that the behavior of many of their children is contemptible, irremediable, and unexcused by any exigency. They will have to cooperate in the painful lancing of this boil, not just for one time only, but year-in and year-out for as long into the future as anyone can foresee. Is it any wonder, then, that the vast majority of reflective people in these communities seek to avoid this course? What has John DiIulio to say to these conflicted people that will persuade them of the necessity to follow such a difficult path? Or does he intend that the courts force them to endure such interventions as his analysis suggests will better their children's lives? Where have we heard that before?

I do not put the matter this way out of a lack of appreciation for the important information contained in DiIulio's paper. Nor do I intend to impugn his motives. But I do think his discussion is politically naive and morally incomplete. He talks about the poor black urban communities as if there were "no there there." They have no voices, no capacities to fathom their circumstance and how to respond to it, no political clout, no resources that can be mobilized for reconstruction and redemption. But this is patently not true. In particular, as I have stated, these communities and those who represent them have the capacity to alter the political discussion in our country about the very issues of criminal justice policy with which DiIulio is concerned. Beyond that, there are elements in these communities—religious and civic volunteers working with young unwed mothers, in housing projects, in schools and hospitals, and with gang members—who are positive forces for change. It seems obvious to me that, if anything is to be done to reverse the situation in these decimated communities, it will require the mobilization of forces such as these, in addition to whatever activities government may undertake. Mobilizing the forces of decency and commitment in the inner city for the battle against violent crime requires that we treat with sensitivity and respect the reticence of such people to consign their young men in ever larger numbers to oblivion.

Finally, let me discuss briefly DiIulio's radical prescription to remove children from "criminogenic" homes and communities, and place them in boarding schools so that they might be properly socialized and develop their moral sensibilities. I will put aside the legal and administrative difficulties with this policy. Suffice it to say that I am not at all confident that we know how to create nurturing institutions on a large scale through government agency. But beyond such questions of administrative feasibility, there are the fundamental moral questions concerning how the power to remove children from their parents will be exercised, by whom, and for what cause. No answers to these questions are offered in the article; we are simply told that these are matters that serious people ought now to be prepared to take up.

One can be confident that, in our current legal culture, any effort at the expanded removal of at-risk children from "parents who have done them severe and certain harm" will trigger protracted battles and raise basic constitutional questions. It is certainly fair to ask whether the failure of parents to adequately care for their children is limited to high-crime-generating communities or extends more broadly through the society. Will the enormous power to intervene in the family affairs of citizens with which DiIulio seems willing to endow state agencies be utilized only in inner-city precincts? Perhaps, in the spirit of my earlier comments, it would be worthwhile for "serious people" to have some discussion with the residents and representatives of what DiIulio has called "criminogenic communities," before undertaking to remove their children to state-run homes in the interest of saving them from the pathological influences of their parents and neighbors.

It's a Spiritual Thing, You Wouldn't Understand

The Bell Curve

by Richard J. Herrnstein and Charles Murray
(The Free Press, 1994)

Reading Herrnstein and Murray's treatise *The Bell Curve* causes me once again to reflect on the limited utility in the management of human affairs of that academic endeavor generously termed social science. Analyses of this kind are inherently incapable of addressing in a satisfactory manner the most fundamental social problems. The authors undertake to pronounce upon what is possible in human affairs while failing to consider that which most makes us human. They begin by seeking the causes of behavior and end by reducing the human subject to a mechanism whose horizon is fixed by some combination of genetic endowment and social law. Yet we, even the dullest of us, are so much more than that.

As an economist, I am a card-carrying member of the social scientists' cabal, so these doubts now creeping over me have far-reaching, personal implications. But entertain them I must, for the stakes in the discussion this book has engendered are too high for me to eschew reflection merely because it creates discomfort. The question on the table, central to our nation's future and, I might add, to the future success of a conservative politics in America, is this: Can we sensibly aspire to a more complete social integration than has yet been achieved, of those who now languish at the bottom of American society? A political movement that answers no to this question must fail and, in my view, richly deserves to do so.

Herrnstein and Murray are not entirely direct on this point. They stress, plausibly enough, that we must be realistic in formulating policy, taking due account of the unequal distribution of intellectual aptitudes in the population, recognizing that limitations of mental ability constrain which policies are likely to make a difference and how much of a difference they can make. But implicit in their argument is the judgment that we shall have to get used to there being a substantial minority of our fellows who, because of low intelligence, may fail to perform adequately as workers, parents, or citizens. I think this judgment is quite wrong. Social science ultimately has led Herrnstein and Murray astray on the political and moral fundamentals.

In chapters on parenting, crime, and citizenship, for example, they document that performance in these areas is correlated with cognitive ability. Though they stress that IQ is not destiny, they also stress that it is often a more important cause of personal achievement than factors that liberal social scientists typically invoke, such as family background and economic opportunity. Liberal analysts have offered false hope by suggesting that, with improved economic opportunity, one can induce underclass youths to live within the law. Some citizens simply lack the wits to manage their affairs so as to avoid criminal violence, be responsive to their children, and exercise the franchise, Herrnstein and Murray argue. If we want our duller citizens to obey our laws, we must change the laws (by, e.g., restoring simple rules and certain, severe punishments), not the citizens. Thus: "People of limited intelligence can lead moral lives in a society that is run on the basis of 'Thou shalt not steal.' They find it much harder to lead moral lives in a society that is run on the basis of 'Thou shalt not steal unless there is a really good reason to'" (p. 544).

Now, a conservative case can be made for simplifying the laws, for making criminals anticipate certain and swift punishment of their crimes, and for adhering to traditional notions about right and wrong as exemplified in the commandment "Thou shalt not steal." Indeed, a case can be made for much of the policy advice given in this book—for limiting affirmative action, for seeking a less centralized and more citizen-friendly administration of government, for halting the encouragement now given to out-of-wedlock childbearing, and so on. But I can see no reason to rest such a case on the presumed mental limitations of a sizable number of citizens. In every instance there are more compelling and convincing arguments for these policy prescriptions than the generalizations about human capacities that Herrnstein and Murray claim to have established with their data.

Observing a correlation between a noisy measure of parenting skills, say, and some score on an ability test is a far cry from having discovered an immutable law of nature. Social scientists are far from producing a definitive account of the causes of human performance in educational attainment and economic success, the areas that have been most intensively studied by economists and sociologists over the last half century. The claim, implicitly advanced in this book, to have achieved a scientific understanding of the *moral* performance of the citizenry adequate to provide a foundation for social policy is, to say the very least, breathtakingly audacious.

The political stakes in this discussion are large. Republicans and conservatives may want to think through the consequences before incanting this IQ mantra in public political discourse. Try telling the newly energized Christian Right that access to morality is contingent on mental ability. Their response is likely to be, "God is not finished with us when he deals us our genetic hand."

This is exactly right. Human beings are spiritual creatures; we have souls; we have free will. We are, of course, constrained in various ways by biological and environmental realities. But with effort we can certainly make ourselves morally fit members of our political communities. We can become decent citizens and loving parents by exploiting fully our material and spiritual inheritance, despite the constraints. And we deserve from our political leaders an expansive vision that recognizes and celebrates this human potentiality. Our best political leaders have instinctively known this, but such spiritual considerations are something social scientists find hard to understand.

Nevertheless, human beings' possession of spiritual resources is key to the maintenance of social stability and progress. It is the ultimate foundation on which rests any hope that the social malaise of the underclass will be overcome. This is why I insist that the mechanistic determinism of science is, in the end, inadequate to the task of social prescription. Political science has no account of why people vote; psychology has yet to identify the material basis of religious exhilaration; economics can say only that people give to charities because it makes them feel good to do so. No analyst predicted that the people of Eastern Europe would, in Vaclav Havel's memorable phrase, rise to achieve "a sense of transcendence over the world of existences." With the understanding of causality in social science so limited, and the importance of matters of the spirit so palpable, one might expect a bit more humble circumspection from these analysts, as they presume to pronounce upon what human beings can and cannot accomplish.

Whatever the merit of their science, Herrnstein and Murray are in a moral and political cul-de-sac. I see no reason for serious people to join them there. The difficulty is most clearly illustrated by the fierce debate over racial differences in intelligence which *The Bell Curve* has spawned. The authors will surely get more grief than they deserve for having stated the facts of this matter: that on the average blacks lag significantly behind whites in cognitive functioning. I am not objecting to their data. While it is possible to argue with some of their interpretations, it is difficult to dispute their central contentions: Measurable differences exist, on the average, in the cognitive functioning of the members of various population subgroups; in the case of black and white Americans this difference is substantial; and group differences in cognitive functioning of this extent must be part of the explanation for racial differences in educational and economic achievements.

What I find problematic is their suggestion that we accommodate ourselves to the inevitability of this difference in mental performance between the races in America. This posture of resignation is an unacceptable response to today's tragic reality. We can be prudent and hardheaded about what government can and cannot accomplish through its various instruments of policy without abandoning the hope of achieving racial reconciliation within our national community. Herrnstein and Murray argue that to achieve such reconciliation, it is essential for people to begin to talk openly of racial differences in intelligence, a matter already being discussed behind closed doors. But why? The fact is that one cannot engage in such a discourse without simultaneously signaling other moral and political messages. Open talk, even if rooted in scientifically demonstrable fact, can be terribly destructive when not coupled with useful action. By concluding that no useful policy interventions exist for narrowing cognitive differences between racial groups, Herrnstein and Murray defeat their own justification for the urgency of the discussion they intend to provoke. What, exactly, are we to talk about? Just how necessary is it that we engage in a public discourse of regret concerning the unfortunate but recalcitrant disabilities of an identifiable set of our fellows?

Declaring a stark and intractable gap between the intellectual abilities of black and white Americans is a political act. It inevitably says something about the intrinsic value of persons in the respective groups, and about the fundamental obligations we have to one another, as fellow citizens of a common republic, to redress the stark inequalities evident all about us. The record of black American economic and educational achievement in the post–civil rights era has been ambiguous: great success mixed with shocking failure. Though many explanations for the failure have been advanced, the account that attributes it to limited mental abilities among blacks is singular in its suggestion that we must learn to live with current racial disparities.

It is true that, for too long, the loudest voices of African American authenticity bluffed their way past this ambiguous record by cajoling and chastising those who expressed disappointment or dismay. For decades, racial activists have offered discrimination by whites as the excuse for every black disability, treating evidence of limited black achievement as an automatic indictment of the American social order. These racialists are hoist on their own petard by the arguments and data in *The Bell Curve*. Having taught us to examine each individual life first through a racial lens, the racialists must now confront the specter of a racial intelligence accountancy that suggests a rather different explanation for the ambiguous achievements of blacks in the last generation.

So the question now on the floor, in the minds of blacks as well as whites, is whether blacks are capable of gaining equal status, given equality of opportunity. It is a peculiar mind that fails to fathom how poisonous a question this is for our democracy. Let me state unequivocally my belief that blacks are indeed so capable. Still, any assertion of equal black capacity is a hypothesis, not a fact. The fact is that blacks have something to prove, to ourselves and to what W. E. B. Du Bois once characterized as "a world that looks on in amused contempt and pity."

As one who has been urging black Americans to recognize, accept, and rise to this challenge, I find it spectacularly unhelpful to be told, "Success is unlikely given your average mental equipment, but never mind, because cognitive ability is not the only currency for measuring human worth." This is precisely what, in so many words, Herrnstein and Murray say. In an expository magazine article published on the release of *The Bell Curve*, they even celebrate a vision of humanity divided into "clans"—various nationality or racial groups that impute to themselves superiority over other clans by virtue of possessing some desirable trait to a greater degree. Thus, the Irish are poets, the Russians have soul, black Americans are great athletes, and so on. Each group, they say, draws its sense of self-esteem from the success it enjoys within its own sphere. Intelligence isn't everything, after all!

But this vision is errant nonsense; one can make no sense of it in rigorous anthropological terms. At a point when the authors should be stressing individualism as the antidote to the racist sentiments their objective analyses might feed, we find them instead engaging in the crudest of racial generalization. Let me speak plainly. Blacks are in no need of a defense of our humanity in the face of Herrnstein and Murray's evidence that there is an average difference between racial groups in performance on intelligence tests. Least of all do we need to invoke "It's a black thing; you wouldn't understand"—declaring ourselves separate in some essential way, members of a different sphere in which even blacks can be superior to all other "clans." I would have thought, and have always supposed, that the inherent equality of human beings was an ethical axiom, not contingent on psychological fact. Indeed, it has always seemed to me that learning to see ourselves as individuals first and foremost is the surest way to guarantee against the pernicious chauvinism that leads a black to feel himself superior in view of the demographic composition of the NBA, or a Jew to sneer at the goyim in light of the religious affiliations of recent Nobel physicists.

One cannot help but wonder what would lead Herrnstein and Murray to this condescending apologia. I shudder at the prospect that theirs could be the animating vision of a governing conservative coalition in this country. But I take comfort in the hope that, should conservatives be unwise enough to embrace such a vision, then the American people will be decent enough to reject it.

Epilogue
New Life: A Professor and Veritas

I want to describe my spiritual journey, not analytically as a theologian might, but rather simply as an observer of what has happened in my own life. I offer this report as evidence of what Christ has done for me and therefore of what I know he can do for others. I once heard a sermon in which the preacher addressed the question of why should anyone believe in the resurrection of Jesus Christ. This is, after all, an extraordinary thing to accept as literal truth. After discussing the biblical text, and after reviewing other historical evidence consistent with the biblical accounts, the preacher added that we have our own personal experience with this risen Savior. Perhaps the most compelling evidence that one can offer that Jesus Christ is Lord is that derived from an account of what has happened in one's life. It is such evidence that I offer here.

For the fact is that I have been born again. I was dead and now I am alive, not because of my own recuperative powers, but due to the power of Christ to mend a broken life, to "restore the years the locusts have eaten." Let me explain.

Although a wonderful and beautiful woman loved me and had agreed to become my wife, I was unable and unwilling to consummate with her the relationship that our marriage made possible. I was unable to be faithful to that relationship. I am not speaking now only of adultery. I was unable to be present emotionally. I was unwilling to set aside enough of my selfishness to build a life with someone else. Marriage involves give and take, but I gave little. My pride and a self-centered outlook eliminated any chance for a fruitful union.

I was dead in spirit, despite that fact that I had professional success as a tenured professor at Harvard—what more could one ask for? I had reached the pinnacle of my profession. When I went to Washington, people in the halls of power knew my name. I had research grants. I had prestige. Nevertheless, I often found myself in the depths of depression, saying, "Life has no meaning." I would say this out loud with such regularity that my wife came to expect it of me. This is not to say that I was suicidal or psychotic; I was not. But for me there was no real joy. My achievements gave me no sense of fulfillment. Nothing I could identify in my life had any sense of depth and meaning. I thought of myself as living on the surface of things. Life seemed to be one chore or contest after another in which I hoped to score high, to win accolades, and to achieve financial gains. But there was no continuity, no coherence, no thread of meaning that gave these various achievements an ultimate significance.

I was dead because of my slavery to drugs and alcohol. I do not want to be overly dramatic here; this "enslavement" had been going on for many years without apparently impairing my ability to function. There was no sudden degradation of my condition. I did not go off to shoot heroin between seminars, or anything quite so sordid as that. I do not want you to envision some terribly ugly or desperate and sad existence, though it became, in due course, quite sad enough. Rather there was an ordinariness about this dependency. The fact is, I thought I needed to intoxicate myself in order to enjoy an evening's entertainment, to enliven a visit with my family, to have fun at a party or a sporting event, and so on. This pattern of mild inebriation as a boon to sociability had become part of my life. It progressed eventually to the point of threatening my health and my name. Yet I did not think there was a problem; it seemed to me that there was nothing wrong at all.

These developments in my life eventually came to a point where, without some intervention, my marriage probably would not have survived. I have to wonder whether or not, without some intervention, my honors and prestige would have been sufficient to forestall the increasing depression. I have to wonder indeed whether or not my involvement with drugs and alcohol would have ruined me physically, professionally, and mentally.

What happened for me was that some people came forward to offer words about the Gospel—(in Greek, literally the "great news" of Jesus Christ). People proclaimed to me the availability of salvation and the fact that there was a way out. People asked me to consider the words of Jesus, words like the following:

> *I have come to save that which is lost;*
> *I came that you would have life, and have it more abundantly;*
> *I am the way, the truth and the life; no one comes to the Father*
>   *but through me.*
> *She loves much because she has been forgiven much.*
> *When the Son sets you free, you shall be free indeed.*

One person, whose name I do not know, is especially memorable. I was a patient in a substance abuse program in a psychiatric hospital. Each Friday the program invited a representative of some religious order to speak with the patients about spiritual issues. On this particular day a young woman came from a local church. After the formal session, during which I had voiced much skepticism about "organized religion" because of my disgust at corruption among church leaders I knew while growing up in Chicago, she approached me for further discussion. She was gentle but persistent when asking about my plans for the future. She suggested that we read the Twenty-Third Psalm together, which we did. Though I knew the psalm by heart, I had never considered its promises, nor thought of them as having been made specifically to me. This minister suggested to me that though I was quite literally walking "through the valley of the shadow of death," I need "fear no evil," for I did not walk alone. I can only say that I was startled by the implication of these words.

I was due to leave the hospital the next day. She urged that I come to church that weekend, which was Easter of 1988. Despite the fact that I had not been inside a church more than a half dozen times in the preceding decade, I accepted the invitation. The service was beautiful, especially the music. It recalled to my mind the many Sunday morning services I had attended as a child. My family was involved in an African Methodist Episcopal church, a two-hundred-year-old Christian denomination found mainly among black Americans in the United States. As a child I loved going to church services, but when I reached my teens I fell away and stopped going; there was really not much that I had retained in my life from those church experiences.

The sermon was about redemption. I wept quietly for two hours, thinking of all that I had done for which I needed to be forgiven. At the time I did not acknowledge to anyone, not even myself, that I was being touched by the Spirit of God. I did not go to the altar for prayer; I did not join the church or confess Christ as my personal Savior. I fled from that sanctuary as quickly as possible when the service had ended, not even thanking the young woman who had invited me.

But the truth is that something happened, deep inside my heart, on that Easter Sunday morning. Nothing was quite the same again after that. In the months that followed, others asked me to come to church and to read the Bible. I followed some of this advice, though not especially enthusiastically. Nothing dramatic happened.

There was, however, a minister and friend I came to know through my work as an economist at Harvard who continued to visit me. He seemed to be genuinely and deeply concerned about me; he would politely but insistently ask me questions about my life. Ray Hammond eventually persuaded me to come to a Bible study. I began to go regularly. After that I began to go to church services regularly as well.

There was not one moment when the skies opened up and something dramatic happened. There was not a particular instant when I can definitely say that I was reborn. Rather, over the months—as

I began to study the Bible, as I went to church, as I learned to pray, as I began to reflect honestly on my life, and as I began to open myself up to the Spirit of God to minister to me and to move me—I came to realize that there was something dramatic missing in my life. I realized that there was an explanation for the low condition of my life. The many things that seemed out of line were all connected to the spiritual vacancy that I became aware of.

Moreover, I began to feel myself growing and changing. I began to be aware that there was something real to this Christian business. Perhaps my greatest step forward in spiritual growth occurred when I began to think about Christianity not simply as a collection of propositions to be examined, not just as a set of truth claims that I was considering, but rather as the actual means by which a transcendent God has chosen to reach out to and establish a relationship with humanity. In other words, I began to realize that this "Jesus business" is not just an intellectual argument that people are making. It is not just a ritualistic set of conventions that people are engaging in, as I had imagined before. As a prideful intellectual, I was unwilling to accept these statements people were making on faith where I could not see the evidence. I was unwilling to have faith without evidence, when I now understand that faith *is* the evidence of things not seen. As my resistance to acknowledging the reality of the spiritual began to erode, I became more willing to entertain the possibility and indeed the truth of the spiritual things proclaimed to me. I began to make more room within my heart for the message of the Gospel. Things in my life began to change.

A relationship that I thought was dead came to life. My sense of the absence of purpose gradually lifted. As I began to study the Bible, the depth and richness and profundity of life began to open up to me. I began to see that the possibilities for joy and fulfillment are much greater than I ever imagined. I found myself seeing below the surface and finding a richness of meaning that I always dreamed of, but never believed to actually exist.

For example, I discovered what for me was a profound and life-changing truth: Freedom is not the highest value. I learned that my pursuit of personal freedom—my constant quest to be free of constraint, to be unfettered—had been the source of much of my unhappiness. Since childhood I had always thought I wanted to "do my own thing." Marriage seemed suffocating because it meant being "tied down" to and obliged to consider the concerns of another. I did not want to have children because of the responsibilities such a course would entail. I resented the claims of family and friends if they inconvenienced me in any way.

Yet, after becoming a Christian, I learned that the deepest satisfactions and most powerful sense of fulfillment can be achieved only when one is bound up with and faithfully accountable to others in relationships of mutual obligation. Holding my infant sons in my arms, and experiencing the deep satisfaction of being, on a daily basis, the kind of father and husband that I know the Lord has called me to be, I realized that the whimsical passions and fanciful pursuits of my earlier life could never have produced true happiness. Oh, I was free, all right: free to reap the bitter harvest of loneliness, aimlessness, and hopelessness that my reckless pursuit of personal, sensual gratification had produced. But now, even though my time is often not my own and I have since lost the taste for certain hedonistic delicacies that I used to savor, nevertheless I know joy beyond my wildest expectation. Life has such a sweetness. Instead of "Life has no meaning," my wife now can sometimes overhear me muttering under my breath, "Thank you, Lord."

With my spiritual growth has come an appreciation of the joy of worship and praise, and an ability to share the Gospel, that would have seemed impossible for me a few short years ago. I remember when I asked for and received into my life the baptism of the Holy Spirit—the power that the Lord has made available to all of us who believe to be able to proclaim His Gospel, to worship, to witness, to minister. I thought those things were for "churchy" people, not for me. These spiritual gifts at first seemed embarrassing and irrational to me. Emotionalism in worship grated against my intellectual style; it seemed archaic, characteristic of something primitive. Yet in due course there I was, full of joy and prepared to worship not just passively but openly. For I had witnessed what the Lord had done for me; I could not remain silent or studiously passive when my church fellowship would celebrate His glory. Through prayer, praise and worship, joyful song, and tearful testimony, my relationship with the Lord has deepened and matured. What could be irrational about wanting to proclaim His greatness, or to tell the truth about His power in my life?

I began to see the impact of this transformation on people around me. At Harvard's Kennedy School of Government I and other faculty taught an ethics course. Our students were ambitious, earnest, and ready to claim their corner on public policy truth—or to get their man or woman (or themselves) elected to public office. Our job in this course was to raise philosophical questions, to ask students about justice and right and wrong behavior in difficult situations. I began to consider how my personal spiritual experience and knowledge might inform this task of preparing people to confront the world of politics and public policy constructively.

I began to ask my colleagues among the faculty for this course about the links between personal spiritual commitment and the ethics of public service. I even circulated an excerpt of the book *Born Again* by Charles Colson, the Christian apologist who is an infamous figure from the Watergate era. He was convicted of crimes committed while working in the White House and served time in prison. After his fall from power he was converted to Christianity, and when released from prison he dedicated his life to ministry, especially among inmates. He explains this transformation in *Born Again.*

I found Colson quite interesting on the question of hubris, or pride. This was an issue of great significance to me, because pride was a part of the sin in which I was entrapped. I suffered from a vastly inflated sense of my own self-importance. I thought of myself as the center of the universe; my professional successes served only to reinforce this egocentric focus. Nothing seemed beyond my grasp; the rules (whether moral or legal) were for others, not for me. I was an exception. "Everything be damned" was my view, as long as I got what I wanted, whether it be achieving tenure at the best university, having my name mentioned in the *New York Times,* or enjoying the favors of some beautiful young woman.

Colson does a fine job of describing his own entrapment in the sin of pride in his memoir. When I read it, I thought I saw myself; I was quite taken by the account. I also thought I recognized in his story, though of course not to the same degree, aspects of the ambition and self-righteousness so characteristic of young people pursuing power and influence at the Kennedy School. We were training very bright students for careers in government service—people who combined a burning desire to make a mark on the world with strongly held convictions about what was wrong with the status quo, and a powerful sense of self-confidence. Looking at and listening to my students, I thought I could see evidence of this same problem of hubris. So I asked my colleagues, "Can we learn anything from this fellow [Colson] that we might want to try to convey to our students?"

Of course I knew that Colson, having been Nixon's henchman, would be a politically unsavory character at the Kennedy School. And I knew that few, if any, of my colleagues were themselves Christians. But my goal was not to evangelize my colleagues or our students. Nor did I intend that we hold up Colson as an ideal type. Rather I sought to communicate the insights that, ultimately, personal morality must be the bedrock of professional ethics, and religious conviction can play a central role in empowering a person to adhere to such a personal moral code. The testimony of someone like Colson about his life before and after acquiring belief in God can lead others to the kind of honest self-examination and critical reflection out of which comes genuine spiritual growth. That, anyway, had been my own experience.

So I did not expect that in a professional ethics course at Harvard we would begin to teach Christian doctrine. But I hoped my colleagues might recognize the limitations of our purely academic approach to the subject, given that in the end our aim was to shape the values and character of some future leaders of our country. Academic knowledge in ethics may influence our thinking about what we *should* do, but this is impotent without a transformation of our inner lives so that what we should do becomes what we *want* to do, and then what we in fact do. As Paul notes in his letter to the Romans:

For the good that I would, I do not; but the evil which I would not, that I do. . . . For I delight in the law of God after the inward man, but I see another law in my members, warring against the law of my mind, and bringing me into captivity to the law of sin which is in my members. Oh wretched man that I am! Who shall deliver me from the body of this death? I thank God through Jesus Christ our Lord. (Romans 7:19, 22–25)

It has been rightly said that the longest distance in the world is from the head to the heart. I wanted to inspire our students to think seriously about how they might bridge that gap.

As it turned out, my observations initiated some interesting discussions. One faculty member was deeply moved by my mentioning explicitly the role of religion, after we had gone nearly three months into the course without any reference to God or godliness. I had long talks with many others, not all positive. One distinguished older colleague, a veteran of many partisan battles, took it upon himself to come to my office, close the door carefully, and declare, "Glenn, you don't need to worry about this stuff. You're a better man than Charles Colson will ever be." He clearly had missed the point entirely! For him Colson would always be a villain, because of his political role. Yet as history has clearly shown, failures of the sort that Colson and I had experienced can befall anyone—liberal or conservative, Democrat or Republican. It was not Colson's qualities I was extolling, but rather God's qualities of mercy and grace as manifest in Colson's life. Fortunately, many of my colleagues and students were able to grasp this distinction.

This experience taught me a lesson. I am convinced that my restoration has occurred in part so that I might help others who, like me, make their professional lives in the academy to gain some appreciation for the importance of establishing a relationship with almighty God. Ours can be a spiritually barren landscape. Declarations of faith are rare in public on campus, and those who make them are often marginalized. Yet as college teachers we have the awesome responsibility of shaping the minds of young people who are at a critical phase in their development. A way must be found to challenge these young people patiently and respectfully on spiritual as well as conventional academic grounds. The simple, unadorned declaration of one's own experience with the Lord is one means to convey such a challenge.

———

The quality of my family relationships improved greatly after my conversion. I began to have honest exchanges with a number of relatives. I saw a healing of my breaches with my sister and my mother. A new and more fruitful bond developed with my two adult children from an earlier marriage, with whom I had a very attenuated relationship after their mother and I divorced nearly twenty years ago. This healing happened in part because I became willing, as a servant, to look at those relationships in a new way.

The Lord began to bless my wife and me with a family. We had our first son, Glenn Jr., in 1989. Three years later our second boy, Nehemiah Matthew, was born. Both are healthy and wonderful. Our marriage was miraculously healed—that which was dead is now raised.

What I am trying to say is that over a period of time, because of this encounter with Jesus Christ, the death and vacancy, the emptiness of my life, has been relieved. There is life now. There is hope. There is joy. There is a sense of peace. Things fit into place now in a way that they had not before.

There is nothing unique or special about me to attribute any of this to. I had done nothing to have earned the opportunity that this new change represents. But what I read in the Scripture tells us that this is why Jesus came and lived, and died, and was raised from the dead . . . that *all* of us could have this new life.

How do I know that the resurrection and the whole Gospel is real? I know not only because of an acquaintance with the primary sources from the first century A.D., or even because of the words of the Bible. I know primarily, and I affirm this truth to you, on the basis of what I have witnessed in my own life. This knowledge of God's unconditional love for humankind provides moral grounding for my work in cultural and racial reconciliation, economics, and social justice. Jesus Christ provides a basis for hope and for the most profound personal satisfaction. To paraphrase slightly a currently popular rallying cry: no Jesus, no peace.

Notes

Chapter 1. Black Dignity and the Common Good

1. John Edgar Wideman, *Brothers and Keepers* (New York: Holt, Rinehart and Winston, 1984).
2. James Baldwin, "Everybody's Protest Novel," *Partisan Review,* June 1949, emphasis added.

Chapter 2. The Moral Quandary of the Black Community

1. *A Policy Framework for Racial Justice,* Joint Center for Political Studies, Washington, D.C., 1984, emphasis added.
2. Daniel P. Moynihan, "The Schism in Black America," *The Public Interest,* Spring 1972.

Chapter 4. Two Paths to Black Progress

1. Orlando Patterson, *Slavery and Social Death* (Cambridge, Mass.: Harvard University Press, 1982).
2. Booker T. Washington, *The Story of the Negro: The Rise of the Race from Slavery* (London: T. Fisher Unwin, 1909), vol. II, 47–48.
3. Herbert J. Storing, "The School of Slavery: A Reconsideration of Booker T. Washington," in Robert Goodwin (ed.), *100 Years After Emancipation* (Chicago: Rand McNally, 1964), 47–49.

Chapter 5. The End of an Illusion

1. Cornel West, *Race Matters* (Boston: Beacon Press, 1993), p. 73.
2. Hillel Levine and Lawrence Harmon, *The Death of an American Jewish Community* (New York: Free Press, 1992).

Chapter 6. Economic Discrimination

1. Charles Moskos, "Success Story: Blacks in the Army," *Atlantic Monthly*, May 1986.

Chapter 8. Self-Censorship in Public Discourse

1. This ground has been covered by D'Souza (1991).
2. See Goffman (1959) and (1963).
3. A simplified version of this game is formally analyzed by Crawford and Sobel (1982). Also noteworthy are Austen-Smith's 1992 article and Bernheim's 1992 draft.
4. Goffman's general approach is reflected in the following passage from *The Presentation of Self*: "[Consider] the point of view of the individual who presents himself before [others]. He may wish them to think highly of him, or to think that he thinks highly of them, or to perceive how in fact he feels toward them, or to obtain no clear-cut impression. . . . Regardless of the particular objective which the individual has in mind and of his motive for having this objective, it will be in his interest to control the conduct of the others, especially their responsive treatment of him. This control is achieved largely by influencing the definition of the situation which the others come to formulate, and he can influence this definition by expressing himself in such a way as to give them the kind of impression that will lead them to act voluntarily in accordance with his own plan" (p. 3).
5. An excellent analysis of the speech and its reception may be found in "Die Opfer wissen, was der November 1938 für sie zu bedeuten hatte," *Frankfurter Allgemeine Zeitung*, November 11, 1988.
6. This is the conclusion of Benjamin Frankel, conveyed to the author in personal correspondence. It is consistent with views of the linguist Ernst Leisi as stated in the *Frankfurter Allgemeine Zeitung*, January 12, 1989.
7. The following quotations are taken from an English translation of the speech entitled "Remembrance speech by Phillipp Jenninger, MP, in connection with the pogroms carried out by the Nazi regime against the Jews in Germany 50 years ago," provided by the German consulate in Boston.
8. Numerous examples of the potential for harm are provided by Janis in his classic study (1982).
9. Revel (1983).
10. That the desire to avoid offending communal norms has shaped the work of science is a basic theme in the sociology of knowledge, as developed, for example, in Kuhn (1962).

11. Coleman (1989).
12. Havel and others (1985).

References for Chapter 8

Austen-Smith, David, 1992. "Strategic Models of Talk in Political Decision Making." *International Political Science Review*, 45–58.

Bernheim, D. B. 1992. *A Theory of Conformity*. Princeton University, draft.

Carter, Stephen. 1991. *Reflections of an Affirmative Action Baby*. New York: Basic Books.

Coleman, James S. 1989. "Response to the Sociology of Education Award." *Academic Questions* (Autumn), 76–78.

Crawford, Vincent, and Joel Sobel. 1982. "Strategic Information Transmission." *Econometrica* (November), 1431–51.

D'Souza, Dinesh. 1991. *Illiberal Education*. New York: Free Press.

Farrell, J., and R. Gibbons. 1989. "Cheap Talk with Multiple Audiences." *American Economic Review* (December), 1214–23.

Goffman, E. 1959. *The Presentation of Self in Everyday Life*. New York: Anchor Books.

———. 1963. *Stigma: The Management of a Spoiled Identity*. New York: Simon & Schuster.

Havel, Vaclav, and others. 1985. *The Power of the Powerless*. Armonk, N.Y.: M. E. Sharpe, 23–96.

Herrnstein, Richard, and James Q. Wilson. 1985. *Crime and Human Nature*. New York: Simon & Schuster.

Hirschman, Albert. 1970. *Exit, Voice and Loyalty*. Cambridge: Harvard University Press.

Howe, Irving. 1982. *A Margin of Hope: An Intellectual Autobiography*. New York: Harcourt Brace Jovanovich.

Janis, Irving. 1982. *Groupthink: Psychological Studies of Policy Decisions and Fiascoes*. 2nd ed. Boston: Houghton-Mifflin.

Kuhn, Thomas. 1962. *The Structure of Scientific Revolutions*. Chicago: University of Chicago Press.

Kurtz, Lester. 1983. "The Politics of Heresy." *American Journal of Sociology* 88 (6), 1085–1115.

Leisi, Ernst. 1989. "Die Opfer wissen, was der November 1938 für sie zu bedeuten hatte," *Frankfurter Allgemeine Zeitung*, January 12.

Miller, John. 1992. "The Violent Gene." *Diversity and Division* (Winter), 9–13.

Navasky, Victor. 1980. *Naming Names*. New York: Viking.

Revel, Jean-François. 1983. *How Democracies Perish*. New York: Harper and Row.

Sagarin, E. (ed.). 1980. *Taboos in Criminology.* Beverly Hills: Sage Publications.

Strauss, Leo. 1952. *Persecution and the Art of Writing.* Glencoe, Ill: Free Press.

Takagi, Dana. 1992. *Retreat from Race.* New Brunswick, N.J.: Rutgers University Press.

Walzer, Michael. 1988. *The Company of Critics.* New York: Basic Books.

Chapter 9. Leadership Failure and the Loyalty Trap

1. Martin Luther King, Jr., *Where Do We Go From Here: Chaos or Community* (Boston: Beacon Press, 1967), emphasis added.

Chapter 10. Second Thoughts and First Principles

1. See my review of Derrick Bell's *Faces at the Bottom of the Well* on pp. 289–292 of this book.

Chapter 16. The Family, the Nation, and Senator Moynihan

1. Daniel Patrick Moynihan, *Family and Nation* (New York: Harcourt Brace Jovanovich, 1986).
2. See Alvia Branch, James Riccio, and Janet Quint, *Building Self-Sufficiency in Pregnant and Parenting Teens* (New York: Manpower Demonstration Research Corporation, 1984).
3. Ibid., p. 39.

Chapter 17. A Crisis Grows in Brooklyn

1. Jonathan Rieder, *Canarsie: The Jews and Italians of Brooklyn Against Liberalism* (Cambridge, Mass.: Harvard University Press, 1985).
2. Thomas Edsall and Mary Edsall, *Chain Reaction: The Impact of Race, Rights and Taxes on American Politics* (New York: W. W. Norton, 1991).

Chapter 18. Other Reviews, 1992–1994

Black Crime: Answering Conservatives

1. See Kennedy's article, "The State, Criminal Law and Racial Discrimination," *Harvard Law Review,* April 1994.
2. On this point see also Regina Austin, "'The Black Community,' Its Lawbreakers and a Politics of Identification," *University of Southern California Law Review,* 1992.

Index

325